NIETZSCHE AND B

Nietzsche and Buddhism

A Study in Nihilism and Ironic Affinities

ROBERT G. MORRISON

OXFORD UNIVERSITY PRESS

OXFORD
UNIVERSITY PRESS
Great Clarendon Street, Oxford OX2 6DP

Oxford University Press is a department of the University of Oxford.
It furthers the University's objective of excellence in research, scholarship,
and education by publishing worldwide in

Oxford New York

Athens Auckland Bangkok Bogotá Buenos Aires Calcutta
Cape Town Chennai Dar es Salaam Delhi Florence Hong Kong Istanbul
Karachi Kuala Lumpur Madrid Melbourne Mexico City Mumbai
Nairobi Paris São Paulo Shanghai Singapore Taipei Tokyo Toronto Warsaw

and associated companies in Berlin Ibadan

Oxford is a registered trade mark of Oxford University Press
in the UK and in certain other countries

Published in the United States
by Oxford University Press Inc., New York

Reprinted 2000

ISBN 0–19–823556–9
ISBN 0–19–823865–7 (Pbk.)

Printed in Great Britain
on acid-free paper by
Bookcraft (Bath) Short Run Books
Midsomer Norton

PREFACE

In this work all quotes from Nietzsche are taken from the translations of Hollingdale and Kaufmann, and, for some lesser known works, Breazeale and Arrowsmith. For the Buddhist texts I have relied on the translations of the Pali Text Society, with reference to the more recent translations of Walshe (*Dīgha-Nikāya*) and Bodhi (*Majjhima-Nikāya*). Here, however, to determine key terms and to clarify certain important but obscure passages, I have consulted the relevant Pāli editions. This has resulted in my imposing my own translations of certain key terms and altering some passages which I felt were either misleading or needed clarifying. The final responsibility for all passages quoted therefore rests with me. In the use of Pāli terms, for the sake of simplicity and consistency I have followed the accepted Sanskrit model and used the stem forms, e.g. *attan* rather than *attā* for 'self', rather than the more usual nominative forms. Plurals are indicated by the addition of an *-s*. I have consistently used the Sanskrit term *nirvāṇa* throughout (apart from quotes from the Pāli) in preference to Pāli *nibbāna*, as the former is the common term in the West. For the sake of easy reference, I have included a glossary of Buddhist terms.

As the Buddhist doctrine of *paṭicca-samuppāda* or 'dependent co-arising' has it, all things come to be in dependence upon other things. In the case of the arising of this book, however, I shall restrict the 'other things' to those who have had direct contact with the work at some stage of its development, and whose helpful comments and criticisms have helped produce a better book than it would otherwise have been. I would like to thank the following in particular: Howard Robinson of Liverpool University, the internal examiner for my Ph.D. thesis on *Nietzsche and Buddhism*, who suggested that my thesis was worth writing up for publication; Dr Michael McGhee, my old supervisor at Liverpool, who read the manuscript at various stages of completion, and whose encouragement and helpful criticisms helped rejuvenate my frequently flagging spirits. Professor David Cooper of Durham University, OUP's first reader, whose comments and criticisms I found both helpful and encouraging, and caused me to seriously reflect on the structure of the work; OUP's second reader, who remained anonymous, but whose spelling allowed me an informed guess that he was an American, a guess that was later confirmed by the editor. The Venerable Sangharakshita and Alex Kennedy, who both read through the text at its thesis stage, and who both offered valuable criticisms. And, finally, Andrew Skilton of Wolfson College, Oxford, for his help with some 'Pāli teasers', and Rolf-Michael Peterssen, for his assistance with some German.

I would like to thank the following publishers for permission to quote from their translations of Nietzsche's works: Cambridge University Press for *Daybreak* (1982), *Untimely Meditations* (1983), and *Human All Too Human* (1986), translated by R. J. Hollingdale; Penguin Books for *Thus Spoke Zarathustra* (1961), *Twilight of the Idols and the Anti-Christ* (1968), *Beyond Good and Evil* (1973), and *Ecce Homo* (1979), translated by R. J. Hollingdale; Random House for *Basic Writings of Nietzsche* (1968) and *The Gay Science* (1974), translated by Walter Kaufmann, and *The Will to Power* (1969), translated by Walter Kaufmann and R. J. Hollingdale. In addition, I would also like to thank Oxford University Press for Patrick Olivelle's translation of *Upaniṣads* (1996); and Walter De Gruyter & Co. for G. J. Stack's *Lange and Nietzsche* (1983).

R.M.

CONTENTS

ABBREVIATIONS

NIETZSCHE

A	*The Antichrist*
AOM	'Assorted Opinions and Maxims' in *Human All Too Human*
BGE	*Beyond Good and Evil*
BT	*The Birth of Tragedy*
CW	*The Case of Wagner*
D	*Daybreak*
DS	'David Strauss, the Confessor and Writer', in *Untimely Meditations*
EH	*Ecce Homo*
GM	*On Genealogy of Morals*
GKS	*The Greek State*
GS	*The Gay Science*
HAH	'Human, All Too Human' in *Human, All Too Human*
HC	*Homer's Contest*
NCW	*Nietzsche Contra Wagner*
P	*The Philosopher*
PT	*On the Pathos of Truth*
PTG	*Philosophy in the Tragic Age of the Greeks*
RW	'Richard Wagner in Bayreuth', in *Untimely Meditations*
SE	'Schopenhauer as Educator', in *Untimely Meditations*
SW	*The Struggle between Science and Wisdom*
TI	*Twilight of the Idols*
TL	*On Truth and Lies in the Nonmoral Sense*
UH	'On the Use and Disadvantages of History for Life', in *Untimely Meditations*
VPN	*The Portable Nietzsche*
WC	*We Classicists*
WP	*The Will to Power*
WS	'The Wanderer and his Shadow', in *Human, All Too Human*
Z	*Thus Spoke Zarathustra*

BUDDHISM

A-N	*Aṅguttara-Nikāya*
Akbh	*Abhidharmakośabhāṣyam*
As	*Abhidhammattha-Saṅgaha*
Asl.	*Aṭṭhasālinī*
Bca	*Bodhicaryāvatāra*
D-N	*Dīgha-Nikāya*
Dhp	*Dhammapada*
Dhs	*Dhammasaṅgaṇī*
Itv.	*Itivuttaka*
Kv	*Kathāvatthu*
M-N	*Majjhima-Nikāya*
Mp	*Milindapañha*
Netti.	*Nettippakaraṇa*
PED	*Pali–English Dictionary*
PTS	Pali Text Society
S-N	*Saṃyutta-Nikāya*
Sn	*Suttanipāta*
Therī.	*Therīgāthā*
Ud.	*Udāna*
Vin.	*Vinayapiṭaka*
Vsm	*Visuddhimagga*

PART I

Nietzsche's Buddhism

I

Introduction

On an autumn day in Leipzig in the year 1864, the young Nietzsche—'a directionless and despairing 21-year-old'[1]—was browsing in a second-hand bookshop owned by his landlord and happened to come across a book entitled *The World as Will and Representation*. Despite being hesitant about purchasing a book by an author he had never heard of, a demon whispered in his ear: 'take this book home'.[2] He obeyed the demon and consequently discovered the direction that his life had lacked. This book was to make such an impression on him that in one of his early works, 'Schopenhauer as Educator', he refers back to that day as one when he found his true self:

> Certainly there may be other means of finding oneself, of coming to oneself out of the bewilderment in which one usually wanders as in a dark cloud, but I know of none better than to think on one's true educators. And so today I shall remember one of the teachers and taskmasters of whom I can boast, *Arthur Schopenhauer*. (SE 1)

In addition to finding his true vocation in life through reading Schopenhauer, it was undoubtedly Schopenhauer who first introduced him to Buddhism and Indian thought in general.[3] Schopenhauer saw in the Buddhist view of existence an early Indian parallel to his own: life was unconditionally unsatisfactory; it could never offer man true lasting happiness or fulfilment but only endless disappointment and sorrow. The only path out of this predicament was through the denial of life's fundamental impulse: the 'will to live'.

[1] According to his own description: quoted in Janaway (1989), 342.

[2] Copleston (1980), 216.

[3] The first recorded reference to anything Buddhist in Nietzsche's correspondence is from 1865, when he and his friend Rohde called their holiday retreat *nirvāṇa* (see Welbon (1968), 185). But to say as Dumoulin does that Nietzsche 'owes his understanding of Buddhism entirely to Schopenhauer' (1981: 469) is, as we shall see, simply incorrect.

At first Nietzsche was greatly influenced by this view but by the time of his first published work, *The Birth of Tragedy*,[4] he was beginning to move away from such a pessimistic *Weltanschauung* and, in his later writings, arrived at a position diametrically opposed to it—life is not to be denied but unconditionally affirmed. Schopenhauer's philosophy was seen as a preliminary symptom of an existential disease to which Europe was on the verge of succumbing: *nihilism* (i.e. a state of despair consequent upon the complete loss of belief in the accepted world-view and its inherent values). Schopenhauer had arrived at the penultimate phase of 'pessimism'.[5] The advent of nihilism was seen as a logical outcome within the history of Western culture of an original premiss of the framework of Platonism which, according to Nietzsche, became the ground of all subsequent metaphysical and religious views on man and his place in the universe. Broadly, that original premiss was that existence is bifurcated into two separate asymmetrical realms, one transitory, mundane, and of the nature of an 'appearance', the other the eternally divine and true 'reality'. It was the latter that gave life its meaning and value and man his orientation within it, as well as the capacity, through reason, to discern it. The former, the natural world, was, in contrast, relatively valueless and without meaning except, perhaps, as a means of weakly reflecting that true reality. The only truly human life was one lived in pursuit of that eternal reality. But Nietzsche now saw that, as an ironic consequence of that pursuit, modern man was approaching a more honest understanding of himself and his origins as well as the cultural institutions that reflect his past history: they all had natural origins and any talk of non-natural or divine origins was no more than the illusory creation of human vanity. When such an understanding eventually took root throughout Western culture it would thoroughly undermine its very structure, and Nietzsche foresaw the

[4] As Kaufmann says in his introduction to his translation, '*The Birth* constitutes a declaration of independence from Schopenhauer: while Nietzsche admires him for honestly facing up to the terrors of existence, Nietzsche himself celebrates Greek tragedy as a superior alternative to Schopenhauer's "Buddhistic negation of the will". From tragedy Nietzsche learns that one can affirm life as sublime, beautiful, and joyous in spite of all suffering and cruelty' [3]. In EC iv, Nietzsche comments that the book 'smells offensively Hegelian, it is in only a few formulas infected with the cadaverous perfume of Schopenhauer'.

[5] WP 9.

looming possibility that as a reaction to this loss nihilistic chaos could overrun Europe. But he also thought it possible, at least among the more educated and cultured who, it must be remembered, Nietzsche saw as his only audience, that a more civilized response to this portending disaster might be the growth of a 'European Buddhism'—a cheerful and orderly response to the apparent meaninglessness of human existence. But to Nietzsche such a response would still be a form of nihilism, what he calls 'passive nihilism', which is 'a sign of weakness',[6] a '*doing* No after all existence has lost its "meaning"'.[7] Such a response would be tantamount to accepting nihilism as the ultimate statement and judgement upon life: a European form of Buddhism which merely helps man cheerfully adjust to the seeming meaninglessness of existence. For Nietzsche such a response, although preferable to nihilistic chaos, would be a mistaken one: it would be no more than a psychological reaction within that same Platonic framework which was seen to be false. If the whole two-world framework is no more than a human invention then it follows that the question as to the value of life and man's place in it is once again an open one. As he poetically puts it in *The Gay Science*:

> At long last the horizon appears free to us again, even if it should not be bright; at long last our ships may venture out again, venture out to face any danger; all the daring of the lover of knowledge is permitted again; the sea, *our* sea, lies open again; perhaps there has never yet been such an 'open sea'. (GS 343)

Somewhere on the open sea Nietzsche eventually concluded that the only acceptable response to nihilism was not the founding of a European Buddhism, but the creation of a new vision of man and existence with values not founded on some fictitious transcendental world or being, but in life as it is in the natural world, which is man's only world. Thus the possible advent of a European form of Buddhism was a danger that would obscure the sight of that open sea, and was something he therefore wished to avoid. Nevertheless, Buddhism might have a purpose: 'a European Buddhism might perhaps be indispensable' as one of the 'many types of philosophy which need to be taught . . . as a hammer'.[8] The metaphor of the

[6] WP 23. [7] WP 55. [8] WP 132.

hammer, however, does not imply destruction but the hammer's use as a means of 'sounding out', as when one strikes a bell to examine whether it rings true or is flawed. The implication here is that the flawed would be those who were attracted to Buddhism.[9]

[9] See the TI, Foreword, for the source of this explanation.

2

Nietzsche on Buddhism

2.1. THE HISTORICAL PARALLEL

Although there were various works on Buddhism available in Europe prior to Nietzsche's time, they were mainly concerned with the late form of Buddhism as found in Tibet.[1] However, in the nineteenth century Buddhist texts, in Pāli and Sanskrit,[2] originating in the land of the Buddha's birth began to be studied and translated into the three main European languages: English, French, and German.[3] The Sanskrit texts were from what was then known as the Northern School of Buddhism—now known as the Mahāyāna form of Buddhism—and the Pāli texts from the then Southern School—now known as the Theravāda form of Buddhism. Generally speaking, the Mahāyāna texts are later and reflect a mainly literary, mythological, and philosophical development of Buddhism, whilst the Theravāda texts reflect the earlier oral tradition and are, therefore, of more historical interest regarding the character and personality of the Buddha, as well as the India of his time. Given the considerable amount of information available to Nietzsche on the Mahāyāna, and that his references to Buddhism reflect no knowledge of or interest in the Mahāyāna,[4] I can only conclude that Nietzsche's main interest in Buddhism was focused on its emergence as a historical phenomenon and was, therefore, limited to its

[1] These were mainly written by Jesuit missionaries. See De Jong (1987), 8–12.

[2] The Sanskrit texts were actually discovered in Nepal in 1830 (along with some Brāhmanical texts).

[3] See De Jong (1987), 13; Sedlar (1982), 39; and Müller (1881), 168. (NB Nietzsche was literate in both English and French.)

[4] The only mention of anything Mahāyāna-like in Nietzsche's writings is in GS (128) where, as a form of prayer, he sees the Mahāyāna Buddhist mantra 'om mane padme hum' (properly: *oṃ maṇi padme hūṃ*) as a kind of 'cud' for the Tibetan masses to chew so as to keep them happy and occupied.

Theravāda form.[5] The reason for this is that his interest was centred upon what he considered to be a direct historical parallel between India at the time of the Buddha and the Europe of his own milieu:

> The same evolutionary course in India, completely independent of ours, should prove something: the same ideal leads to the same conclusion; the decisive point is reached five centuries before the beginning of the European calendar, with [the] Buddha; more exactly, with the Sankhya philosophy, subsequently popularized by [the] Buddha and made into a religion. (GM iii. 27)

The idea that the Buddha popularized the Sāṅkhya philosophy and made it into a religion, is probably taken from Koeppen's *Die Religion des Buddha*.[6] Yet it is odd that Nietzsche should state this as if it were, at that time, an accepted fact. By then he had read both Müller's *Essays*, vol. ii and Oldenberg's *Buddha*, both of which agree that 'we look in vain for any definite similarities between the system of Kapila . . . and . . . the metaphysics of the Buddhists'.[7] Müller goes on to say 'that it is difficult to understand how, almost by common consent, [the] Buddha is supposed to have either followed in the footsteps of Kapila, or to have *changed Kapila's philosophy into a religion*'.[8]

Beginning with Vico (1668–1744), various philosophers before Nietzsche had sought in the bowels of history for intelligible signs so as to make sense of their own times in terms of the past and, like augurs of old, discern how the future might unfold. All, however, despite their differing views, concluded that the course of human

[5] He would have read in Oldenberg: 'It is to the Pâli traditions we must go in preference to all other sources, if we desire to know whether any information is obtainable regarding [the] Buddha and his life' (1882: 74).

[6] See Mistry (1981), 37–8.

[7] Müller (1881), 213–14, who is endorsed by Oldenberg (1882), 215. Kapila is said to be the founder of the Sāṅkhya system. See Frauwallner (1973), i. 222.

[8] (1881), 215, italics mine. As Frauwallner states: 'The relation between the Sāṅkhya to Buddhism is a long disputed and much debated question' (1973: i. 384 n. 147). In his view the 'Sāṅkhya originated not long after the Buddha's death' (ibid. 223). Mistry refers to the Buddha's two teachers—presumably Aḷāra Kālāma and Uddaka Rāmaputta—as being Sāṅkhya philosophers (1981: 37 n. 36). However, apart from a reference in Aśvaghoṣa's *Buddhacarita* (a poetic biography of the Buddha written sometime in the 2nd cent. CE) to Aḷāra Kālāma being a Sāṅkhya teacher, there is no other source that I can trace that connects the Buddha's two teachers with the Sāṅkhya. Müller (1881: 200) refers to them both as *brāhmaṇas*. Given that the *Buddhacarita* is the only source for one of the Buddha's two teachers being a follower of Sāṅkhya, it would be a questionable practice to base historical fact upon a single source that is a late piece of poetic literature.

history, at least in the West, revealed an intelligible purpose: human history was characterized by a gradual progress towards some end, and this end was, in some manner, the fulfilment of human striving and potential. Man and his actions were cosmologically central within a universe that was purposeful and inherently structured to fulfil that end. But to Nietzsche such a philosophy of history was no more than gross conceit and wish-fulfilment. There was simply no evidence in the study of history to premiss such a conclusion and, since the appearance of Darwin's *On the Origin of Species*, the scientific data available tended to point to an opposite conclusion: man was the centre of nothing other than his own existence; there was no extraterrestrial providential force or being looking after his destiny, nor was the natural world structured for his welfare any more than for any other animal. In an unpublished essay, Nietzsche pens a sceptical portrait of human vanity within such an ateleological cosmos:

> Once upon a time, in some out of the way corner of that universe which is dispersed into numberless twinkling solar systems, there was a star upon which clever beasts invented knowing. That was the most arrogant and mendacious minute of 'world history', but nevertheless, it was only a minute. After nature had drawn a few breaths, the star cooled and congealed, and the clever beasts had to die. (TL, p. 1)

When Nietzsche looks into the bowels of human history he does, like Hegel, discern an inner logic at work, and, also, as in Hegel's view of history, this inner logic involves the positing of an idea which is the object of knowledge. But, unlike Hegel's system, there is no dialectical unfolding and manifestation of that idea as found in Hegel's assumed hierarchical stages of the world historical process. Instead there is, at a certain point in a culture's history, Indian and Western, a realization that the root idea posited was in fact in error. For Nietzsche this root idea is always a moral idea as it involves the judgement that the highest human values, the 'good'—those which give life meaning and purpose—have their source in some other realm or being which transcends this world. In comparison with that eternal transcendent realm or being, this transitory world is relatively valueless and meaningless, even 'evil'. Consequently, all passions and attachments whose objects and ends are in this mundane world are also 'evil', and are to be resisted and conquered by the 'good' man. But, in truth, this idea of a transcendent ideal world or being has no other source than the minds of 'clever beasts [who] invented knowing'. The clever beast *par excellence* is Socrates:

> a profound *illusion* that first saw the light of the world in the person of Socrates: the unshakeable faith that thought, using the thread of causality, can penetrate the deepest abysses of being, and that thought is capable not only of knowing being but even of *correcting* it. (BT 15)

The root idea posited by Socrates involves the ideal that the ultimate goal of human striving is to attain knowledge of that reality which transcends this mundane world: the realm of the 'Forms' which are eternal, unchangeable, immaterial, and intelligible and at whose summit stands the Form of 'Absolute Beauty' (*Symposium* and *Phaedrus*) or 'the Good' (*Republic*) which are 'responsible for whatever is right and valuable in anything'.[9] And, further, that this highest human attainment is 'apprehensible only by the intellect [*nous*] which is the pilot of the soul'.[10] Nietzsche's Socrates is a 'theoretical optimist who . . . ascribes to knowledge and insight the power of a panacea'[11] because it can 'heal the eternal wound of existence'.[12] The wise man is therefore the happiest of men,[13] because 'knowledge and reason have liberated [him] from the fear of death':[14] death only occurs to the body, not the soul. Thus knowledge not only leads to happiness in this life, but to immortality. The outcome of this is a turning-away from life in this world: the 'true philosophers make dying their profession'.[15] Thus bodily appetites with their associated pleasures and the most natural human passions are seen to be a hindrance to this pursuit of knowledge, even the root of all evil.[16] Nietzsche's Socrates is even said to be 'the one turning point and vortex of so-called world history' because ever since Socrates this pursuit of knowledge 'became the real task for every person of higher gifts', the 'only truly human vocation'.[17] And, according to Nietzsche, this highest of vocations has been pursued by the 'gifted' through the whole course of Western history. In *Twilight of the Idols* he gives a rather succinct outline of this history, called 'History of an Error' or 'How the "Real World" at last Became a Myth'.[18]

[9] *Republic*, 517c.
[10] *Phaedrus*, 247c.
[11] BT 15; see also 17.
[12] BT 18.
[13] *Republic*, 576c–592b.
[14] BT 15.
[15] *Phaedo*, 68b.
[16] Ibid. 66b–d.
[17] BT 15.
[18] TI iv.

1. The real world, attainable to the wise, the pious, the virtuous man—he dwells in it, *he is it.*
(Oldest form of the idea, relatively sensible, simple, convincing. Transcription of the proposition 'I Plato *am* the truth'.)

This corresponds to Socrates who, for Nietzsche, through the works of Plato, is the effective source of this idea.

2. The real world, unattainable for the moment, but promised to the wise, the pious, the virtuous man ('to the sinner who repents').
(progress of the idea: it grows more refined, more enticing, more incomprehensible—*it becomes a woman*, it becomes Christian . . .)

Here the idea is passed on through the imbibing of Platonism by Christian theology—'for Christianity is Platonism for the "people" '.[19] The goal now becomes more distant, it is eschatologized. Plato's Forms are now 'thoughts in the mind of God'.[20] Plato's 'true world' is now the Kingdom of God.

3. The real world, unattainable, undemonstrable, cannot be promised, but even when merely thought of a consolation, a duty, an imperative.
(Fundamentally the same old sun, but shining through mist and scepticism; the idea grown sublime, pale, northerly, Königsbergian.)

For Nietzsche Kant represents the beginning of the end. Kant's 'real world', the noumenon or *Ding-an-sich* ('thing-in-itself'), is no longer a proper object of knowledge. As Kant himself says: 'I have found it necessary to deny *knowledge* in order to make room for *faith*'.[21] In other words belief in the two-world framework persists, but 'knowledge' is now knowledge of the limitations of 'knowledge', and those limitations restrict its sphere to the world of 'appearance', the phenomenal world. This, for Nietzsche, is the end of transcendental metaphysics. The pursuit of 'truth' finally leads to the truth that there is no 'truth'.

4. The real world—unattainable? Unattained, at any rate. And if unattained also *unknown*. Consequently also no consolation, no redemption, no duty; how could we have a duty to something unknown?
(The grey of dawn. First yawnings of reason. Cockcrow of positivism.)

5. The 'real world'—an idea no longer of any use, not even a duty any longer—an idea grown useless, superfluous, *consequently* a refuted idea: let us abolish it!

[19] BGE, Preface. This is taken from Augustine who referred to Christianity as 'Platonism for the multitude'. (Quoted in Chadwick (1986), 25, but without source.)

[20] Chadwick (1986), 44.

[21] Kant (1933), 29.

(Broad daylight; breakfast; return of cheerfulness and *bon sens*; Plato blushes for shame; all free spirits run riot.)

6. We have abolished the real world: what world is left? The apparent world perhaps? . . . But no! *with the real world we have abolished the apparent world!*

(Mid-day; the moment of the shortest shadow; end of the longest error; zenith of mankind; INCIPIT ZARATHUSTRA.)

I agree with Clark[22] that these final three stages represent stages in Nietzsche's own thinking. And, to me, Nietzsche is thereby claiming (as did Schopenhauer) to be the inheritor of the true implications of Kant's philosophy, implications which Kant, himself, because of his Christian beliefs, would not face. In *Human all too Human* he admits 'there could be a metaphysical world; the absolute possibility of it is hardly to be disputed. We behold all things through the human head and cannot cut off this head'.[23] However, he considers that such knowledge would be 'the most useless of all knowledge'. Nevertheless, previous religious and metaphysical views are of value to a psychologist like Nietzsche as they possess value as 'symptoms' which reveal their true source.[24] What 'has hitherto made metaphysical assumptions *valuable*, . . . is passion, error and self-deception'.[25] Like Hume before him, Nietzsche sees reason as the slave of the passions. Therefore, when one has discerned the 'human all too human' 'foundation of all extant religions and metaphysical systems, one has refuted them!'[26] Kant's 'faith' would be such an 'error and self-deception', a 'symptom', and his *Ding-an-sich*, even if it did exist, would be valueless and useless in determining how we should live as we can have no access to it or knowledge of it. Thus Nietzsche accepts Kant's view of the empirical limitations of knowledge, but rejects his 'faith' since this only tells us what we desire, not what is. Nietzsche therefore claims to see the implications of Kant's philosophy, even though Kant could not.[27]

I would suggest that stage 5 represents Nietzsche's notion of 'active nihilism',[28] where one actively frees oneself from the values, goals, convictions, articles of faith, and unconscious assumptions

[22] (1990), 112. [23] HAH 9. [24] TI ii. 2. [25] HAH 9.
[26] HAH 9.
[27] Nietzsche's views on Kant are probably derived from his reading of Lange. See Stack (1983*a*), ch. viii.
[28] WP 22, 23.

founded upon the two-world framework; in other words until 'the horizon appears free to us again'. Stage 6 would then be the 'open sea', where the creators of new and critically honest values venture out and transcend nihilism. Nihilism as a 'transitional stage'[29] would then be completed. Therefore, when Nietzsche refers to himself as a nihilist,[30] he is only a nihilist in the sense here of active nihilism, i.e. the nihilism that destroys the old 'lies' as a means to creating something new. Nihilism persists only as long as the 'error' persists. Once the error has been completely eradicated, nihilism ends. Thus Nietzsche would no longer be a nihilist but a creator of new values.

After Kant comes the realization that 'God is dead'[31] and the rise of science (by 'science' Nietzsche means science in the broad sense connoted by the German *Wissenschaft*). Science displaces religion[32] and continues with a secularized form of the Socratic ideal in the pursuit of scientific knowledge: 'Hence the image of the *dying Socrates*, as the human being whom knowledge and reasons have liberated from the fear of death, is the emblem that, above the entrance gate of science, reminds all of its mission—namely, to make existence appear comprehensible and thus justified'.[33] Thus science still works within the two-world framework and although it no longer accepts that the 'true world' is in any sense that which is sought by religion, it is still conditioned by the Socratic notion that knowledge of 'reality' is the true goal of all human striving, and that realizing that goal will somehow bring mankind happiness and human fulfilment—at least in this world. For Nietzsche this is now a baseless assumption: why should a deeper knowledge of the phenomenal world be, a priori, connected with our happiness and fulfilment? Thus 'science also rests on a faith; there simply is no science "without presuppositions"'.[34] However, it is through scientific pursuits that these presuppositions are eventually brought to light. For example, in Nietzsche's stage 4 he mentions 'positivism' which sees science, and philosophy based upon scientific method, as the only means to knowledge. Yet Comte, the founder of positivism, assumes that progress is a necessary law of human history.[35] But to Nietzsche this is a baseless assumption. This comes to light, later, with Darwin, where man becomes just another animal without any necessary laws to guarantee his future progress. 'God is

[29] WP 7. [30] WP 25. [31] See GS 125 and 343.
[32] This is also Freud's view in his *The Future of an Illusion*.
[33] BT 15. [34] GS 344. [35] See Edwards (1967), vi. 415.

dead', but the cultural and philosophical implications of this event will take time to be seen.[36] When they are we shall have reached Nietzsche's 'conclusion' of the original Socratic premiss: the pursuit of 'truth' finally reveals the truth that what we saw as true was in fact an error, a product of self-delusion and wish-fulfilment. But stage 6 in Nietzsche's 'History of an Error' will not come to pass through any historical necessity: there is the danger of nihilistic anarchy breaking out or of a European Buddhism establishing itself as a consequence of 'passive nihilism'. Stage 6 only comes to be if a path of 'active nihilism' is followed.

Obviously, in India, this 'conclusion' was not the outcome of science; but it too, without science, arrived at the same conclusion, or at least one similar to that of stage 5: loss of belief in any transcendental world or being. But not having an Indian Nietzsche, India went along the erroneous path of passive nihilism, which rather than seeing nihilism as a transitional stage, and surpassing it, sees it as the ultimate statement upon life: life actually is without any possible meaning or value. This is a path Nietzsche now fears may appeal to many in the West, as when the source of their esteemed values—the 'real world'—can no longer be believed in, there will be, in response, a deep sense of loss, even the feeling of an oncoming 'awe-inspiring *catastrophe*'.[37] Life then appears to lack any truly human aim or purpose, and mankind's hitherto deepest questions are felt to be pointless. For those not strong enough to respond to this challenge of the open sea, the appeal of a cheerful and refined nihilistic and non-theistic religion like Buddhism might be irresistible. Indeed, Nietzsche is no doubt basing this judgement upon his own experience. In a letter to his friend Carl von Gersdorff,[38] he relates that after reading an 'English translation of the Sutta Nipáta . . . The conviction that life is valueless and that all goals are illusory impresses itself on me so strongly, especially when I am sick in bed, that I need to hear more about it, but not mixed with Judeo-Christian phraseology'.[39] He goes on to say: 'In my opinion, the *will to knowledge* may remain as the ultimate region of the will to live, as a region between willing and ceasing to

[36] See GS 108, 109, 125, 343, and TI ix. 5.
[37] GM iii. 27.
[38] Quoted in Middleton (1969), 139.
[39] This must have been Coomaraswamy (1874), as it was the only English translation available at that time.

will . . . a bit of Nirvana, as long as the soul thereby approaches a state of pure contemplation'. It seems, therefore, that when Nietzsche judges Buddhism to be a dangerous enticement to his *Angst*-ridden contemporaries, he is no doubt speaking from personal experience: it was a dangerous allure to him. But what led Nietzsche to find a similar historical process in India?

As I said earlier, Nietzsche's interest in Buddhism was mainly historical. He conjectured that a similar evolutionary course to the one just sketched had already occurred in India, and that it reached its conclusion at the time of the Buddha. Somewhere in the distant past of Āryan-cum-Brāhmanical culture, that 'same ideal' as the one posited by Socrates must have been posited by some 'clever beast' of an Āryan. However, Nietzsche doesn't tell us who that Āryan Socrates might have been or when this same ideal was posited. Nevertheless, from the various books he read on India and Buddhism, and perhaps from the unrecorded discussions he no doubt had with fellow philologists who were specialists in Sanskrit and Indian studies,[40] he would have received the impression that that same ideal also permeated Indian religio-philosophical thinking prior to the Buddha. For example, he would have read in Müller's essay 'Buddhist Pilgrims' that in the first book of the *Ṛg-Veda*: 'rebellious reason' sought for 'the idea which had yearned for utterance . . . the idea of a supreme and absolute Power' behind all the many gods.[41] This may, in Nietzsche's mind, have corresponded to his notion of Socrates searching, by means of the intellect, for the reality underlying all appearance. However, it has more affinity with the pre-Socratics and Nietzsche would have been all too aware of that. Müller then goes on to relate how out of the Veda(s) two antagonistic strands developed, one of reason—the

[40] Welbon (1968: 185) reckons that Nietzsche did in fact learn some Sanskrit at Leipzig from Max Müller's first teacher, Herrmann Brockhaus. But he gives no source for this. However, if as I've suggested, Nietzsche's interest in Buddhism was historical, it would not have been Sanskrit that would have interested him so much as Pāli.

[41] Müller (1881), 239–40, from *Ṛg-Veda*, I. 164. 46. Müller, however, does not bring out the important point that this move towards monism was not initially theistic. *Brahman*, at first conceived of as the magical force or power inherent in the recitation of the 'hymns' of the Veda(s) during sacrifice, eventually came to be looked upon as a kind of impersonal power underlying the whole universe. Later, this *brahman* came to be seen by many in theistic terms as the supreme god Brahmā. Nevertheless, *brahman*, as an impersonal absolute, has remained an integral part of the more philosophic schools of Hinduism down to the present day (see Basham (1989), 29). Oldenberg (1882) does not bring this point out either.

Brāhmanical philosophy—and one of faith—the Brāhmanical ceremonial—in which the former 'threatened to become the destruction of all religious faith'.[42] The philosophical strand, developed in the early Upaniṣads, eventually blossomed into a variety of philosophical schools, which 'were allowed to indulge in the most unrestrained freedom of thought', and in whose philosophies 'the very names of the gods were never mentioned'.[43] Here, however, we do find a form of thinking that might fit part of the same ideal, at least for Nietzsche's purpose: the idea that 'there existed but one Being, without second; that everything else was but a dream and illusion, and that this illusion might be removed by a true knowledge of the one Being'.[44] Without this true knowledge, what we accept as reality is likened to a dream or an illusion. Such an image may have appeared to Nietzsche to have affinities with the image of the Divided Line from Plato's *Republic*, where the state of illusion would loosely correspond to *Eikasia* or 'illusion', and true knowledge to *Noesis* or 'knowledge of the Good itself'.[45] However, in Müller's outline, this idea only appears just before the birth of the Buddha.[46] Thus if Nietzsche were to base his historical theory on Müller the time-scale between the idea and the conclusion would be no more than 100 years at most, whereas its Western counterpart extends over some 2,300 years. However, I will show later how such a difference in time-scale may be explained.

Oldenberg, in his book *The Buddha*, states that:

> Invariably, whenever a nation has been in a position to develop its intellectual life in purity and tranquillity through a long period of time, there recurs that phenomenon, specially observable in the domain of the spiritual life . . . : an old faith, which promised to men somehow or other by an offensive and defensive alliance with the Godhead, power, prosperity, victory and subjection of all their enemies, will, sometimes by imperceptible degrees, . . . be supplanted by a new phase of thought, whose watchwords are no longer welfare, victory, dominion, but rest, peace, happiness, deliverance.[47]

He then proceeds 'to trace step by step the process of that self-destruction of the Vedic religious thought, which has produced Buddhism as its positive outcome'.[48] The first step is found in the final book of the *Ṛg-Veda*, where we have what a modern Indian

[42] (1881), 243. [43] Ibid. 244. [44] Ibid.
[45] See Melling (1987), 106–8.
[46] (1881), 245. [47] (1882), 3. [48] Ibid. 18.

scholar sees as 'possibly the oldest expression of philosophic doubt in the literature of the world' and 'a landmark in the history of Indian thought'.[49] I quote the two most important verses from Oldenberg's book:

> Who knows the secret? Who proclaimed it here,
> Whence, whence this manifold creation sprang?
> The gods themselves came later into being—
> Who knows from whence this great creation sprang?
>
> He from whom all this great creation came,
> Whether His will created or was mute,
> The Most High Seer that is in highest heaven,
> He knows it—or perchance even He knows not.[50]

After this initial burst of agnosticism which, incidentally, occurred at about the same time as the search for some underlying power behind all phenomena, the *ātman/brahman*,[51] Oldenberg sketches the various views found in the literature that succeeded the Veda(s) and which, aside from that spurious burst of scepticism, he describes as 'That imbecile wisdom which knows all things', but in reality is without any depth of understanding.[52] However, by the time of the early Upaniṣads, thought acquires depth as man now 'looks for the essence of the essence, for the reality, the truth of phenomena, and the truth of the true'.[53] What eventually emerges is the notion of the *ātman/brahman* seen as the true reality behind all diverse phenomena. Gaining knowledge of this deeper reality led to what Oldenberg calls 'the origin of monastic life in India', as consequent upon gaining such knowledge one renounced the world: 'Knowing him, the *Ātman*, Brāhmans relinquish the desire for posterity, the desire for possessions, the desire for worldly prosperity, and go forth as mendicants'.[54] But, according to Oldenberg, there still 'remained for Indian speculation the task of finding its way back from this ultimate ground of all being to the empirical state of being, to define the relation which subsists between the *Ātman* and the external world'.[55] The outcome of

[49] Basham (1989), 24. [50] (1882), 16–17.

[51] Ibid. 24 ff. *Brahman*, which in the sacrificial Vedic tradition was the 'sacred' power that made the sacrifice efficacious, became in the Upaniṣads an immanent absolute which was the unchanging essence of all things. Within the individual, this essence is called the *ātman* or 'Self'.

[52] Ibid. 22.

[53] Ibid, 23–4.

[54] Ibid. 31, quoting from 'The Brāhman of the Hundred Paths'. [55] Ibid. 36.

this speculation was that many 'may have felt that thought had reached a chasm, over which to throw a bridge was not in their power'.[56] And as knowledge of the *ātman/brahman* was the ultimate goal of all human striving and such knowledge led to renouncing the world, combined with the seemingly impassable chasm between *ātman* and the phenomenal world, there arose 'an ever increasingly bitter criticism of this world' and 'the birthplace of Indian pessimism'.[57] The world is a world of sorrow, but 'the *ātman* . . . dwells afar and untouched by the sorrows of the world'.[58] Thus 'Man must separate himself from all that is earthly, . . . must live as though he lived not'.[59] What then follows is the extension of the mendicant life outside the preserve of the Brāhmanical tradition with various teachers 'who profess to have discovered independently of the Vedic tradition a new, and the only true path of deliverance'.[60] Oldenberg then describes a rather gloomy picture of a people who are fast becoming disaffected with life, where even 'the young, wearied of life before life had well begun . . . [were] eager for renunciation'.[61] Eventually the 'earnest thinkers of the masculine, classical period of Brāhmanical speculation' gave way to the 'heterodox' thinkers, the *samaṇas*,

> a younger generation of dialecticians, professed controversialists with an over-weening materialist or sceptical air, who were not deficient in either the readiness or the ability to show up all sides of the ideas of their predecessors, to modify them, and to turn them into their opposites. System after system was constructed, it seems, with tolerably light building material. We know little more than a series of war-cries: discussions were raised about the eternity or transitoriness of the world and the ego, or a reconciliation of these opposites, eternity in the one direction or transitoriness in the other, or about the assertion of infiniteness and finiteness of the world, or about infiniteness and finiteness at the same time, or about the negation of infiniteness as well as finiteness. Then sprung up the beginnings of a logical scepticism, and the two doctrines, of which the fundamental propositions run, 'everything appears to me true,' and 'everything appears to me untrue,' and here obviously the dialectician, who declares everything to be untrue, is met forthwith by the question whether he looks upon this theory of his own also, that everything is untrue, as likewise untrue. Men wrangle over the existence of a world beyond, over

56 (1882), 41. 57 Ibid. 58 Ibid. 42.
59 Ibid. 60. 60 Ibid. 65. 61 Ibid.

the continuance after death, over the freedom of the human will, over the existence of moral retribution.[62]

If one had to fit the 'same ideal' of Nietzsche's Socrates into this exposition of Oldenberg, it would be within certain aspects of the early Upaniṣadic tradition. Here there is the search for some underlying reality beyond the plurality of phenomena combined with the idea that knowledge of this reality represents the highest human attainment and is, therefore, the ultimate goal of human endeavour. The chasm which emerged in trying to reconcile the *brahman* with the world of phenomena does have a general affinity with the irresolvable problems Socrates had in trying to reconcile the Forms with their phenomenal counterparts—the problem of 'participation'. And there is also the underlying pessimism (in relation to the world) of this ideal which leads the philosopher to renounce the world and the ordinary pleasures of life as they now become a hindrance to the achievement of the goal. Oldenberg's statement that 'Man must separate himself from all that is earthly, . . . must live as though he lived not',[63] must have reminded Nietzsche of the passage in the *Phaedo* where Socrates says that the philosopher must train 'himself throughout his life to live in a state as close as possible to death', and 'that true philosophers make dying their profession'.[64] In both cases the pleasures of the body have to be renounced.[65] And, according to Müller, all this was the outcome of 'rebellious reason'. Thus there are, in both Müller and especially Oldenberg, affinities between certain aspects of the philosophy of the early Upaniṣads and that of Socrates which Nietzsche would have easily discerned, and which could be construed as having some affinity with his same ideal. However, in temporal terms, the parallel diverges. As Oldenberg has it: 'Wherever a Socrates appears, Sophists cannot fail to follow'.[66] But whereas the Sophists of Greece made no lasting impression upon Western culture, and Socrates' same ideal lived on through the ages in the garb of Christian

[62] Ibid. 67–8. [63] Ibid. 60. [64] *Phaedo*, 67a–b.

[65] In the case of the *Symposium*, however, one could say they are, using a modern term, 'sublimated'—a notion that, as I shall later show, is central to Nietzsche's own philosophy.

[66] (1882), 67. Some leading Sophists, however, were contemporary with Socrates. Two Socratic dialogues, *The Gorgias* and *The Protagoras*, are named after two prominent Sophists.

theology, into modern times, the 'Sophists' of ancient India—the *samaṇas*—were much more effective: they made a lasting impression upon Indian culture and, in the case of one particular *samaṇa*, the Buddha, upon the whole of the East.[67]

Although their philosophies were diverse and in some cases completely opposed to one another, all the *samaṇas* were united in rejecting the authority of the *brāhmaṇas* and the Veda(s). As Oldenberg mentioned, '[w]e know little more [of what they taught] than a series of war-cries' and for what we do know we are almost entirely dependent on the Buddhist texts, especially the *Sāmaññaphala Sutta*. Oldenberg mentions the views of two, Makkhali Gosāla and Pūrana Kassapa, of whom the former is said by the Buddha to be 'the worst of all erroneous teachers'.[68] Gosāla was a strict determinist claiming that man had no power in determining his own life and denied the existence of any moral law. However, after thousands of lives in various forms, all of which are strictly determined, every person eventually puts an end to suffering. Pūrana Kassapa also denied that there are any moral actions: 'If a man makes a raid on the south bank of the Ganges, kills and lets kill, lays waste . . . burns . . . he imputes no guilt to himself; there is no punishment of guilt'. And so too with what many regarded as moral actions such as performing good works: 'there is no reward for good works'.[69] Oldenberg also gives the views of Ajita Kesakambalin, without mentioning him by name: 'the wise and the fool, when the body is dissolved, are subject to destruction and to annihilation; they are not beyond death'.[70] Thus, as Oldenberg has it, the *samaṇas* 'wrangle[d] over the existence of a world beyond, over the continuance after death, over the freedom of the will, over the existence of moral retribution', whether the universe was infinite or finite, eternal or transitory, or even whether such a thing as truth or knowledge was possible or not. To Nietzsche, much of this would have had a modern ring to it: the growth of scepticism and materialism; the denial of any form of life after death in some other world; the denial of any reality other than the natural world; the denial of a moral order independent of man; the growth of atheism

[67] In the Buddhist Pāli texts, one often finds the compound term *samaṇa-brāhmaṇa*, which refers to all the *religieux* at the time of the Buddha. The general difference between them is that whereas the *samaṇas* rejected the authority of the Veda(s) and had their own doctrines, the *brāhmaṇas* or Brāhmans accepted the Veda(s) as 'revealed truth' (*śruti*).

[68] Ibid. 68. This statement is found at A-N i. 286. [69] Ibid. 69. [70] Ibid.

and agnosticism and the deterministic elements of scientific positivism. Even the questions as to whether the universe was infinite or finite, eternal or transitory,[71] would have reminded him of Kant's antinomies. All in all, in a general sense, this would have appeared to Nietzsche to have affinities with what he saw around him: the undermining of the values that formed the foundation of Western culture through the unbridled pursuit of knowledge, and the subsequent feeling of uncertainty and moral despair as an effect of that pursuit felt among those whom Nietzsche would have seen as his audience.[72] And he would have noted that, in India,

> At this time of deep and many-sided intellectual movements, which had extended from the circles of the Brahmanical thinkers far into the people at large, . . . when dialectical scepticism began to attack moral ideals—at this time, when a painful longing deliverance from the burden of being was met by the first signs of moral decay, Gotama [the] Buddha appears upon the scene.[73]

And because 'Our age is in a certain sense ripe (that is to say, decadent) as the age of the Buddha was',[74] 'Buddhism is silently gaining ground everywhere in Europe'[75] as an answer to that growing insecurity and moral decay. But as Nietzsche saw Buddhism as thoroughly nihilistic, he wanted to counter any influence it might have.

2.2. HOW NIETZSCHE SAW BUDDHISM

The essence of what Nietzsche means by nihilism is most clearly stated in the *Will to Power*:

[71] These were questions raised by some *samaṇas* when they met the Buddha. The Buddha saw them as irrelevant to the religious life.

[72] In a letter by H. von Kleist to Wilhelmine von Zenge, quoted by Nietzsche in *Schopenhauer as Educator*, 3, we can get an idea of the kind of effect Kant had on some: '"Not long ago", he writes in his moving way, "I became acquainted with the Kantian philosophy—and I now have to tell you a thought I derived from it, which I feel free to do because I have no reason to fear it will shatter you so profoundly and painfully as it has me.—We are unable to decide whether that which we call truth really is truth, or whether it only appears to us to be. If the latter, then the truth we assemble here is nothing after our death, and all endeavour to acquire a possession which will follow us to the grave is in vain.—If the point of this thought does not penetrate your heart, do not smile at one who feels wounded by it in the deepest and most sacred part of his being. My one great aim has failed me and I have no other"'.

[73] Oldenberg (1882), 69–70. [74] WP 239. [75] WP 240.

Extreme positions are not succeeded by moderate ones but by extreme positions of the opposite kind. Thus the belief in the absolute immorality of nature, in aim- and meaninglessness, is the psychologically necessary effect once the belief in God and an essentially moral order becomes untenable. Nihilism appears at this point . . . because one has come to mistrust any 'meaning' in suffering, indeed in existence. One interpretation has collapsed; but because it was considered *the* interpretation it now seems as if there were no meaning at all in existence, as if everything were in vain. (WP 55)

The root of nihilism is an act of self-deception: man 'project[s] . . . value [and meaning] into the world'[76] such as 'God', 'soul', 'moral law', 'aim', 'being', 'unity', and thereby invents a '*true* world' which is '*a purely fictitious world*' to create for himself a sense of security and purpose: they make his life meaningful '*in order to be able to believe in his own value*'. But eventually this fictitious world is seen by some for what it is: an act of self-deception. And so when these values and categories are '*pull[ed] out* again . . . the world looks *valueless*'. The effect of all this upon those who see it and are affected by it is a psychological state of depression and despair, the 'recognition of the long *waste* of strength, the agony of the "in vain", insecurity, the lack of any opportunity to recover and regain composure . . . as if one had *deceived* oneself all too long'.[77] To be overcome by all this creates the ground for passive nihilism, a *Weltanschauung* expressive of the psychological condition of the 'decline and recession of the power of the spirit'.[78] Life and the world now appear as if they were worthless and meaningless because they are seen through the dull eyes of spiritual weariness. Thus, in a sense, passive nihilism is just another projection on to the world, the world judged and interpreted through the eyes of a psychological malaise which prevents the world being understood and interpreted from a healthier and less blinkered perspective. As Nietzsche remarks, 'the world might be far more valuable than we used to believe'.[79] Thus passive nihilism must be understood for what it is: an expression of 'weariness of spirit', and be resisted and overcome. This requires *active* nihilism, 'a sign of increased power of the spirit'.[80] Active nihilism,

[76] Nietzsche is no doubt borrowing from Feuerbach's idea that God is the projection of the highest human qualities which are, as yet, only potential in man. For man to retrieve his own power he must withdraw these projections. See GS 285.
[77] WP 12. [78] WP 22. [79] WP 32. [80] WP 22.

which understands the roots of nihilism, sees nihilism as 'only a *transitional stage*'.[81] It is 'an active force of destruction'[82] with regard to our previous religious goals and values and their modern secular expressions which, to Nietzsche, were, for example, John Stuart Mill's Utilitarianism, Kant's categorical imperative (conscience substituted for God), faith in science, and egalitarianism and socialism with their blind faith in the 'eventual triumph of truth, love, and justice' and 'equality of the person',[83] all of which are secularized Christian ideals—the equality of the person being the secularized form of 'we are all equal before God'. But, as Nietzsche remarks in *Zarathustra*, now that God is dead, 'let us not be equal before the mob'.[84] Such secular expressions are rooted in the same nihilistic assumptions. The result of active nihilism is 'complete nihilism',[85] where nihilism itself is negated and man can begin to look at the world and himself with fresh eyes and a deeper understanding, having put the old self-deceptions behind him. But Buddhism, being a form of passive nihilism,[86] was a threat to this negation of nihilism.

Buddhism was such an 'extreme position of the opposite kind', a 'rebound from "God is truth" to the fanatical faith "All is false"; Buddhism of *action*'.[87] The Buddha's response to the possible 'awe-inspiring *catastrophe*' of his own time was to found a religion which rather than help people overcome the newly felt meaninglessness of existence, which would have been active nihilism, simply helped them adjust to it with a certain degree of cheerful acceptance: 'the supreme goal is cheerfulness, stillness, absence of desire, and this goal is *achieved*'.[88] Although the Buddha helped avoid, in his own time, what Nietzsche considered one very real social danger resulting from loss of belief—destructive anarchy, a *bellum omnium*

[81] WP 7. [82] WP 23. [83] WP 30. [84] Z iv. 1. [85] WP 28.
[86] WP 23.
[87] WP 1. The source of 'All is false' is probably the *Uraga Sutta* (Discourse on the Snake) from the *Suttanipāta*. Verses 10–13 from Coomaraswamy (1874) state: 'The priest, who does not look back to the past or look forward to the future, being freed from covetousness . . . lust . . . hatred . . . ignorance, (and believing) that *all is false*, gives up Orapára, as a snake (casts off its) decayed, old skin' (italics mine). Nietzsche himself makes use of the simile of the snake sloughing its old skin: see GS, Prelude in Rhymes, 8; GS 26 and 307. He also uses another refrain from the *Khaggavisāṇa Sutta* (Discourse on the Rhinoceros Horn) of the *Suttanipāta*: 'walks lonely like the rhinoceros', at D 469.
[88] A 21. Oldenberg refers to 'that internal cheerfulness, infinitely surpassing all mere resignation, with which the Buddhist pursues' his goal (1882: 222).

contra omnes—he nevertheless failed to understand nihilism for what it is—a *Weltanschauung* expressive of a psychological reaction of despair that comes from seeing through the illusion man was living under, that 'the world does not have the value we thought it had',[89] and concluding that the world, therefore, must be worthless and meaningless. The Buddha, not seeing the root of nihilism, accepts nihilism as the ultimate statement upon existence: life is without any inherent value or meaning or purpose. Indeed it is quite the opposite: it 'is now considered *worthless as such*' and the only enlightened response to it is a 'nihilistic withdrawal from it, a desire for nothingness'.[90] Consequently, if human existence has to be given an aim it must reflect this ultimate judgement and present a goal appropriate to it. The Buddha gives us *nirvāṇa*, the ultimate panacea, a state of complete desirelessness wherein all terrestrial troubles and existential *Angst* will be extinguished, and even death will be met with nothing more than a sigh of ultimate relief. Thus Nietzsche sees Buddhism as 'a religion for the end and fatigue of civilization', where the cultured yet fatigued, who have 'grown kindly, gentle, over-intellectual [and] who feel pain too easily',[91] can escape from this worthless existence and 'withdraw from pain into that Oriental Nothing—called Nirvana'.[92] Nietzsche therefore fears that Buddhism will appeal to the 'Ultimate Man' of *Zarathustra*,[93] who represents his enfeebled cultured contemporaries, who, although they see themselves as beyond the rabble, will find the seemingly bovine happiness offered by Buddhism as irresistible. For Nietzsche, this represents a more deceptive and alluring danger than destructive anarchy, and he fears that this Ultimate Man may very well become a preferred goal to his *Übermensch*.[94]

To attain *nirvāṇa* is to attain a state of 'cheerfulness' and 'absence of desire', a goal which is actually attainable.[95] Thus the Buddhist path does lead 'to an actual and *not* merely promised *happiness on earth*'.[96] And, although Nietzsche does not directly mention it, this discovery of a method which leads from a state of despair and depression to one of happiness on earth must correspond to what the Buddhist tradition sees as Gotama's attaining

[89] WP 32. [90] GM ii. 21. [91] A 22. [92] GS, Preface.
[93] Z, Prologue, 5.
[94] As the crowd shout out to Zarathustra, 'Give us this Ultimate Man, O Zarathustra . . . You can have the *Übermensch*!' (ibid.)
[95] A 21. [96] A 42.

the state of *bodhi* or 'Enlightenment', i.e. that which makes him a Buddha or 'Enlightened One'. The Buddha then reveals the Dhamma or 'Teaching' of the way to achieve what he had achieved. The essence of this, according to Nietzsche, is to refrain from action motivated by desire: '"One must *not* act"—said . . . the Buddhists, and conceived a rule of conduct to liberate one from actions'.[97] One is to be liberated from this sorrowful web of existence by denying to the desires their outlet in action: 'action binds one to existence'[98] and thereby ensnares one in the tangled net which is unenlightened existence. The only desire permitted in this scheme is the 'yearning for the nothing'.[99] However, this is not morality speaking, but 'hygiene': Buddhism no longer speaks of the 'struggle against *sin*', but, quite in accordance with actuality, the 'struggle against *suffering*' which is simply a physiological fact. It therefore has the 'self-deception of moral concepts behind it—it stands in my language, *beyond* good and evil'.[100] The Buddha's teaching is a cure for the 'state of *depression*', which Nietzsche sees as a physiological state arisen among the more gentle and civilized, and which rests upon '*two* physiological facts . . . *firstly* an excessive excitability of sensibility which expresses itself as a refined capacity for pain, *then* an over-intellectuality, a too great preoccupation with concepts and logical procedures under which the personal instinct has sustained harm to the advantage of the "impersonal"'.[101] To counteract this the 'Buddha takes hygienic measures', such as:

> life in the open air, the wandering life; with moderation and fastidiousness as regards food; with caution towards all alcoholic spirits; likewise with

[97] WP 458. [98] WP 155. [99] BT 21.

[100] A 20. Nietzsche also says, 'Good and evil', says the Buddhist—'both are fetters: the Perfect One became master over both' (GM iii. 17); and: 'Emancipation even from good and evil appears to be the essence of the Buddhist ideal' (WP 155). These statements, written in and after 1887, represent a shift in Nietzsche's view of Buddhism. In his previous work, *Beyond Good and Evil* (1886), 56 he says that the Buddha, like Schopenhauer, was still 'under the spell and illusion of morality', and not beyond good and evil. He also says something similar at WP 1. This change may have come from his reading of Oldenberg (1882), who states that Buddhist morality was only 'a means to an end' (p. 289), and that 'in the struggle against sorrow and death', all the Buddhist has at his disposal is 'a skilful knowledge of the law of nature', as within the whole of existence there is no prescribed moral order as such but 'only the natural law of the necessary concatenation of causes and effects' (p. 324).

[101] Oldenberg refers to the condition of 'spiritual over-excitement [and] exhaustion of the nervous system' being a common condition among many of the Buddha's contemporary *religieux* (1882: 316).

caution towards all emotions which produce gall, which heat the blood; *no* anxiety, either for oneself or for others. He demands ideas which produce repose or cheerfulness—he devises means for disaccustoming oneself to others. He understands benevolence, being kind, as health-promoting. *Prayer* is excluded, as is *asceticism*; no categorical imperative, no *compulsion* at all, not even within the monastic community (—one can leave it—). All these would have the effect of increasing that excessive excitability. For this reason too he demands no struggle with those who think differently; his teaching resists nothing *more* than it resists the feeling of revengefulness, of antipathy, of *ressentiment* (—'enmity is not ended by enmity': the moving refrain of the whole of Buddhism . . .). And quite rightly: it is precisely these emotions which would be thoroughly *unhealthy* with regard to the main dietetic objective. The spiritual weariness he discovered and which expressed itself as an excessive 'objectivity' (that is to say weakening of individual interest, loss of centre of gravity, of 'egoism'), he combated by directing even the spiritual interests back to the individual *person*. In the teaching of [the] Buddha egoism becomes a duty: the 'one thing needful', the 'how can *you* get rid of suffering' regulates and circumscribes the entire spiritual diet. (A 20)[102]

Nietzsche obviously takes the notion of the Buddha as the 'supreme physician' quite literally,[103] rather in the manner of a Victorian doctor who sends his out-of-sorts patients to the seaside for the sea-air, and warns them off too much alcohol and rich food as well as any activity that might stimulate and over-excite their sensibilities, such as getting into heated discussions about philosophy and religion!

Nirvāṇa is therefore the outcome of a life of enlightened self-interest. The Buddhist practitioner simply avoids all actions that have a disturbing or 'unhealthy' effect upon himself and develops attitudes whose effects are calming and health-promoting and conduce to cheerfulness: 'when evil is hated, [it] is not for its own sake, but because it opens the way to states that are harmful to us (unrest, work, care, entanglements, dependence)'. It is an extremely simple life, living 'entirely in *positive* feelings . . . peace-

[102] Elsewhere, Nietzsche calls the 'victory over *ressentiment*' the 'first step to recovery. "Not by enmity is enmity ended, by friendship is enmity ended": this stands at the beginning of [the] Buddha's teaching—it is *not* morality that speaks thus, it is physiology that speaks thus' (EH i. 6). No doubt he took this quote from Oldenberg (1882: 292–3), who quotes *Dhammapada*, verses 222–3 and *Vinaya*, 347–8 on this theme.

[103] Nietzsche would have come across this in Coomaraswamy's (1874) translation of the *Suttanipāta* (p. 119). Oldenberg (1882: 191), also mentions the notion of the Buddha as a physician.

able, good-natured, conciliatory and helpful', reflecting the absence of the usual worldly desires, because 'one impoverishes the soil in which [such] . . . states grow'.[104] Only the bare necessities of life are accepted. In this state the Buddhist can happily accept the fact that the world is without inherent meaning or value, without feeling depressed or anxious. To attain *nirvāṇa* is to overcome the sense of loss and depression felt when life was seen to be without the value and meaning we thought it had, by following the Buddha's prescription of living a healthy life. As a consequence one learns cheerfully to adjust to the world's nihilistic reality, and becomes 'the Buddhist type or perfect cow'.[105]

It is hardly surprising then that the Buddha's ideal recruit was one who was 'good and good natured from inertia (and above all inoffensive); also from inertia, this type lived abstinently, almost without needs'.[106] The Buddha's genius was to understand 'how such a [late] human type must inevitably roll, . . . into a faith that promises to *prevent* the recurrence of terrestrial troubles (meaning work and action in general)'.[107] Buddhism may even have owed its origin and sudden spread throughout India to a 'tremendous collapse and *disease of the will*'.[108] And Nietzsche, who liked to suggest physiological origins to replace transcendental ones, puts forward, with a certain irony, the notion that 'the spread of Buddhism (not its origin) depended heavily on the excessive and almost exclusive reliance of the Indians on rice which led to a general loss of vigour'.[109]

Despite the fact that Nietzsche understood Buddhism to be nihilistic and thus to be avoided, he does find some worthy aspects to it when contrasted with that other nihilistic religion, Christianity. For

[104] WP 342.

[105] WP 342. It may well be that the *Voluntary Beggar* in *Zarathustra* is the Buddha. He announces to Zarathustra that the way to attain 'happiness on earth' is to 'become as cows'. 'If we do not alter and become as cows, we shall not enter the kingdom of heaven. For there is one thing we should learn from them: rumination' (Z iv. 8). 'Rumination' is probably Nietzsche's interpretation of Oldenberg's references to the practice of *jhāna* or 'meditative absorption' being 'exercises of spiritual abstraction' (*Übungen innerer Versenkung*), which are 'to Buddhism as prayer is to other religions' (Olderberg 1882: 313–14). However, becoming like a cow is not necessarily a pejorative development. In GM, Preface, 8, Nietzsche comments that if some readers find his 'aphoristic form' incomprehensible, then 'one thing is necessary above all else if one is to practice reading as an *art*', which is that 'one has almost to be a cow' and learn '*rumination*'. In other words, one has to 'meditate' upon them.

[106] GS 353. [107] GS 353. [108] GS 347. [109] GS 134.

example, whereas Buddhist nihilism appears after a long spell of refined cultural activity which culminates in lofty philosophic reflection—reflection which unearths the 'truth' of its moral and religious structures—Christianity owes its origins to the crude and ill-constituted who, full of resentment and vengefulness, attack life itself.

Buddha against the 'Crucified'. Among the nihilistic religions, one must always clearly distinguish the Christian from the Buddhist. The Buddhist religion is the expression of a fine evening, a perfect sweetness and mildness—it is gratitude toward all that lies behind, and also for what is lacking: bitterness, disillusionment, rancour; finally, a lofty spiritual love; the subtleties of philosophic contradiction are behind it, even from these it is resting: but from these it still derives its spiritual glory and sunset glow.

The Christian movement is a degeneracy movement composed of reject and refuse elements of every kind: it is not the expression of the decline of a race, it is from the first an agglomeration of forms of morbidity crowding together and seeking one another out. . . . it is founded on a rancour against everything well-constituted and dominant: . . . It also stands in opposition to every spiritual movement, to all philosophy: it takes the side of idiots and utters a curse on the spirit. Rancour against the gifted, learned, spiritually independent: it detects in them the well-constituted, the masterful. (WP 154)[110]

This is the main distinction Nietzsche makes between the two nihilistic religions: Buddhism has no ground in *ressentiment* against life whereas Christianity—or, as we might say, Christendom—is a product of it. Both are 'anti-life', but whereas the former is coolly and rationally led to this view, the latter forms it reactively as an expression of *ressentiment—ressentiment* against 'everything well-constituted and dominant'. The Buddha understands that 'nothing burns one up quicker than the affects of *ressentiment*',[111] and therefore forbids it. Christianity, however, is fuelled by it, and takes 'the side of everything weak, base, ill-constituted'.[112] The villain of the piece, however, is not Jesus, but Paul. For Nietzsche, 'Christendom' was Paul's creation. In the *Antichrist* he says: 'The word "Christianity" is already a misunderstanding—in reality there has been only one Christian, and he died on the cross'.[113] Then along came Paul, 'the antithetical type to the "bringer of glad tiding", the genius of hatred, of the vision of hatred, of the inexorable logic of

[110] See also A 21. [111] EH i. 6. [112] A 5. [113] A 39.

hate'.[114] Through Paul, Christianity, which Nietzsche saw as a 'beginning to a Buddhistic peace movement',[115] became 'mankind's greatest misfortune'.[116]

Buddhism is also 'a hundred times colder, more veracious, more objective' than Christianity,[117] and is 'the only really *positivistic* religion history has shown us'. '[I]t has the heritage of cool and objective posing of problems in its composition', and 'arrives *after* a philosophical movement lasting hundreds of years'.[118] Christianity, on the other hand, has nothing but 'contempt for intellect and culture',[119] and teaches 'men to feel the supreme values of intellectuality as sinful, as misleading, as *temptations*'.[120] Nor does Buddhism deceive as does Christianity by promising fictitious goals and fearful fables such as a God on the cross,[121] but goals that are real and can be actually achieved.[122]

Thus, although Buddhism, along with Schopenhauer and Christianity, adheres to the view that it is 'better *not* to be than to be',[123] it offers a healthier or more 'hygienic' response to life. Unlike Christianity, 'it no longer speaks of "the struggle against *sin*" but, quite in accordance with actuality, "the struggle against *suffering*". It already has—and this distinguishes it profoundly from Christianity—the self-deception of moral concepts behind it'.[124] And it is because Buddhism is more health-promoting, and is not an affront to the cultured and intelligent, that it is slowly gaining ground in Europe as a cure for 'diseased nerves'.[125]

As it is not my task to evaluate the contrast Nietzsche gives between Buddhism and Christianity, nor to offer a critique of his views concerning Christianity, I shall simply address the obvious question: are Nietzsche's views on Buddhism correct?

[114] A 42. [115] A 42. [116] A 51. [117] A 23. [118] A 20.
[119] A 22. [120] A 5. [121] WP 240. [122] A 21. [123] WP 685.
[124] A 20. [125] WP 240.

3

Is Buddhism a Form of 'Passive Nihilism'?

To ask whether Buddhism is or is not a form of passive nihilism is to ask whether the *summum bonum* of Buddhism, *nirvāṇa*, can be understood in this sense. In other words, is the seeking after the goal of *nirvāṇa* 'a sign of weakness',[1] a consequence of the 'decline and recession of the power of the spirit'[2] and a pervading 'state of *depression*'[3] that comes from seeing that the world does not have the value we thought it had? Is the attainment of *nirvāṇa* the fulfilment of 'the instinct of self-destruction, the will for nothingness',[4] a kind of pre-Freudian 'death-instinct', 'the striving for peace and extinction'[5] finding its consummation? Although Nietzsche does not refer directly to any specific Buddhist doctrine, the doctrine he most likely has in mind in this context, and which I shall use as the framework within which to approach this question, is the doctrine of the 'Four Noble Truths' (*catur-ariya-sacca*). For example, Nietzsche's whole judgement upon Buddhism turns on what he sees as its response to 'the struggle against *suffering*'.[6] Its final goal and answer is to 'withdraw from pain into that Oriental Nothing—called Nirvana'.[7] Here we have the first and third of the Noble Truths: *dukkha* or 'suffering and unsatisfactoriness' and the 'cessation of *dukkha*' (*dukkha-nirodha*) which is synonymous with *nirvāṇa*. The second Noble Truth, 'the origin of *dukkha*' (*dukkha-samudaya*) which is 'thirst' (*taṇhā*), Nietzsche no doubt linked with Schopenhauer's *Wille* as, like Schopenhauer's *Wille*, 'thirst' is understood to be the cause of all suffering, and the goal of both Schopenhauer and Buddhism is seen in terms of the extinction of

[1] WP 23. [2] WP 22. [3] A 21. [4] WP 55.
[5] Edwards (1967), vii. 109. [6] A 20. [7] GS, Preface, 3.

Wille and thirst respectively.[8] However, as I will be examining the notion of *taṇhā* fully in Part II, and Nietzsche has nothing directly to say on *taṇhā*, as *taṇhā* can be understood as the ground from which all action springs, here I will look at Nietzsche's view that in Buddhism 'action . . . binds one to existence'. The fourth Noble Truth is the 'Noble Eightfold Way' (*ariya-aṭṭaṅgika-magga*) or the various practices and doctrines that lead to *nirvāṇa*. Following these practices, which Nietzsche thinks of as physiological remedies such as 'caution towards all emotions which produce gall',[9] allows the Buddhist, who previously found life too painful and depressing, stoically and cheerfully to await the day when he assumes he will be consumed in the great nothingness called *nirvāṇa*. As I will be comparing the Buddhist 'way' with Nietzsche's notion of 'self-overcoming' (*Selbstüberwindung*) in Part II, I will not deal directly with the Four Noble Truths here.

3.1. 'SUFFERING' OR *DUKKHA*

In *Zarathustra*, obviously drawing upon the Buddhist tradition of the 'Four Sights' without mentioning it,[10] Nietzsche says of the first three sights:

> They encounter an invalid or an old man or a corpse and straight away say 'Life is refuted!' But only they are refuted, they and their eye that sees only one aspect of existence. (Z ii. 9)

Although Nietzsche sees Buddhism as 'the only really *positivistic* religion history has shown us . . . as it no longer speaks of "the struggle against *sin*", but, quite in accordance with actuality, "the

[8] e.g. Schopenhauer says: 'We have already seen in nature-without-knowledge her inner being as a constant striving without aim and without rest, and this stands out much more distinctly when we consider the animal or man. Willing and striving are its whole essence, and can be fully compared to an unquenchable thirst' (Schopenhauer 1969: i. 311–12). Elsewhere he refers to 'the thirst of will' (ibid. 327), and 'the fiery thirst of . . . wilfulness' (ibid. 389).

[9] A 20.

[10] His source is probably Oldenberg (1882), 102–3. Oldenberg mentions 'a helpless old man, a sick person, and a dead body', the first three 'sights', but also adds the 'fourth sight' not mentioned by Nietzsche, 'a religious mendicant with shaven head . . . a picture of peace and of deliverance from all pain of impermanence'. The first three sights represent *dukkha*, whereas the religious mendicant represents the spiritual path. The four sights are found at D-N ii. 21–30.

struggle against *suffering*" ',[11] the Buddha, because of his supposed refined weariness, can only see 'one aspect of existence', that life is only suffering. He does not see as Nietzsche does that suffering can also be seen as 'the ultimate liberator of the spirit',[12] a liberation that requires 'active nihilism', which is 'a sign of strength'.[13] That life is suffering or *dukkha* is, indeed, an aspect of the first of the Buddha's Four Noble Truths:

> And this, monks, is the Noble Truth of *dukkha*: birth is *dukkha*, and old age is *dukkha*, and disease is *dukkha*, and dying is *dukkha*, association with what is not dear is *dukkha*, separation from what is dear is *dukkha*, not getting what you want is *dukkha*—in short the five aggregates of grasping [*upādāna-khandhas*] are *dukkha*. (Vin. i. 9)

However, the full meaning of the term *dukkha* has connotations quite beyond what the term 'suffering' can signify,[14] as it can also include what the majority of mankind would regard as the opposite of suffering, i.e. pleasure and happiness. This apparent contradiction is resolved when the full connotation of the term is examined. According to the *suttas*, there are three kinds of *dukkha*: 'suffering *qua* suffering' (*dukkha-dukkhatā*), 'suffering by way of transformation' (*vipariṇāma-dukkhatā*), and 'the unsatisfactoriness of unenlightened existence' (*saṅkhāra-dukkhatā*).[15] 'Suffering *qua* suffering' is traditionally interpreted as simply painful physical and mental experiences (*dukkha-vedanā*). 'Suffering by way of transformation' means that although our present state may be one of happiness, if we are aware that our happiness is inextricably linked and dependent upon factors that are outside our control, or which are liable to change, then this awareness itself is a form of *dukkha* as 'unsatisfactoriness'. However, the most important form of *dukkha*, because of its all-inclusiveness, is *saṅkhāra-dukkhatā* or, what we might call 'existential unsatisfactoriness'. *Saṅkhāra* is an extremely difficult technical term to translate as it depends very much upon context. Here, however, it is used in the sense of any volition or conation informed by 'spiritual ignorance' (*avijjā*) as

[11] A 20. [12] GS, Preface, 3.

[13] WP 22–3. See also WP 382, 585, 686, 852–3, 910, 1004, and 1052 for nihilism as sign of strength.

[14] See PED.

[15] D-N iii. 216; S-N iv. 259; S-N v. 56.

well as that which is determined or conditioned by, or is a consequence of such activity.[16] In other words, all unenlightened activity as well as the consequences of such activity, are regarded as *dukkha*. However, this is a Noble Truth, an *ariya-sacca*, it is how an Āryan sees the world, how the enlightened see the world. The full implications of this Noble Truth of *dukkha* are not therefore easily available to the unenlightened.

The fullness of what Buddhism means by *dukkha* can be seen in the *Mahāvibhāṣāśāstra*,[17] where it is said that compared to the *dukkha* of the beings in various 'hell realms' (*nārakas*), the *dukkha* of the animals seems pleasant; and compared to the *dukkha* of the human world, the *dukkha* of the various *devas* or 'divine beings' seems pleasant. And, as Vasubandhu comments:

> The Āryans make of existence in the most sublime heaven (Bhavāgra) an idea more painful than do fools make of existence in the most dreadful hell (Avīci).[18]

Obviously, *dukkha* is not some quality inherent in objects themselves, but is also part of a subject's perspective on things. From the perspective of an Āryan or someone who has gained some 'transformative insight' (*paññā*) and who therefore is said to 'see and know things as they really are' (*yathā-bhūta-ñāṇa-dassana*), even the prospect of unrelenting bliss in the highest reaches of the Buddhist cosmos, the *bhavāgra*, where the life-span is said to be 80,000 *kalpas* (the equivalent of billions of earth years), is seen as *dukkha*.[19] Even if one ignores such cosmologies as being too fantastic, they have their experiential subjective counterparts as mental states systematized in the various Abhidhammas. These form the substance of Buddhist psychology. And, according to Buddhism as well as the other Indian traditions for whom the practice of 'meditation' *(bhāvanā)* is an essential part of the religious life, states of overwhelming bliss and rapturous happiness can be attained here and now. Yet, at least from the Buddhist point of view, such experiences taken as ends in themselves are a form of *dukkha*, even though they are necessary aspects of the process which culminates in *nirvāṇa*. They are *dukkha* in that one can experience them whilst still being a 'non-Āryan', i.e. a *puthujjana* or 'worldling'. In other

[16] See PED, and Aung (1910), 273 ff.
[17] Pruden (1988–90), iii. 1044 n. 29.
[18] Ibid. 900.
[19] Ibid. 471.

words, although such states of blissful meditative experience are understood in Buddhism as necessary conditions for the arising of 'transformative insight' (*paññā*),[20] wherein one 'sees and knows things as they really are' and thereby sets up a process that necessarily culminates in 'the cessation of *dukkha*' (*dukkha-nirodha*), the third Noble Truth, nevertheless, from the perspective of an Āryan, such states are deemed 'unsatisfactory' (*dukkha*). Without transformative insight, even though one may attain such blissful states, being ignorant of the true nature of things one will eventually lose one's way and fall away from the spiritual path into lower states. Another danger is that one can fall victim to grand self-delusion: rather ironically, the Buddhist texts state that through attaining such states one may be reborn as the 'Great God', the Mahā-brahmā, who erroneously thinks he is 'the Maker and Creator, the ... Father of All That Have Been and Shall Be', but who, when questioned by a Buddhist monk, turns out to be a bit of a self-deluded old charlatan.[21]

From what has been said so far, Nietzsche's charge that Buddhism is pessimistic as it sees life as suffering is obviously wrong if it is taken in the sense that it sees life as only suffering *qua* suffering (*dukkha-dukkhatā*). When Buddhism refers to the goal as being 'the cessation of *dukkha*' (*dukkha-nirodha*) it is a misunderstanding on Nietzsche's part to interpret that solely as a 'withdraw[al] from pain' or as being no more than the ending of a 'state of *depression*'. As Govinda has pointed out, 'out of the 121 classes of consciousness which are discussed in Buddhist psychology, sixty-three are accompanied by joy and only three are painful, while the remaining fifty-five classes are indifferent. A stronger refutation of pessimism than this statement is hardly possible'.[22] In other words, from the Buddhist perspective the potential for happiness far outweighs the potential for suffering, even for unenlightened beings. What *saṅkhāra-dukkhatā*, or the 'unsatisfactoriness of unenlightened existence', seems to indicate is that as long as the potential that all beings are said to have for attaining the goal of *nirvāṇa* is not actualized, whether they are aware of it or not, whether they are blissfully happy or not, from the Āryan perspective they can be said to be in a state of *dukkha* in that they are

[20] It is by attaining 'transformative insight' that one becomes an *ariya*, or 'Noble One'.

[21] D-N i. 221.

[22] (1969), 63.

existentially incomplete. This is the Noble Truth of *dukkha* as distinct from the fact of *dukkha*.

3.1.1. *The Buddha as the Bovine* Décadent

With regard to how the Buddha himself appears in the texts, he hardly conforms to some Nietzschean 'gentle Gotama, meek and mild'. The Buddha, shortly after his 'Awakening' (*bodhi*), encountered the naked ascetic Upaka, who, being impressed by the Buddha's appearance, asked him: 'whose Dhamma do you profess?' The Buddha then addressed Upaka in verse:

> Victorious over all, omniscient am I,
> Among all things undefiled,
> Leaving all, through death of craving freed,
> By knowing for myself, whom should I follow?
> For me there is no teacher,
> One like me does not exist,
> In the world with its devas
> No one equals me.
> For I am perfected in the world,
> The teacher supreme am I,
> I alone am all-awakened,
> Become cool am I, *nirvāṇa*-attained.
> To turn the dhamma-wheel
> I go to Kasi's city,
> Beating the drum of deathlessness
> In a world that's become blind. (Vin. i. 7)

Upaka, however, was not that impressed. He replied: 'It may be (so), your reverence,' shook his head, and went off on his own way. It is certainly ironic that the Buddha, who was capable of having such an effect upon young worldly people, had no effect upon this particular fellow *religieux* (*samaṇa*) who was, nevertheless, initially impressed by the Buddha's appearance.[23] Whether the Buddha was or was not what he claimed to be, the figure that comes across in the Pāli texts (which is our only source) is not one of a man weary of life who has discovered nothing more than a universal cure for

[23] As Schumann (1989: 63) remarks regarding this encounter with Upaka, 'It would have been easy for the compilers of the Pāli Canon to have cut out this episode, which is somewhat detrimental to the Buddha's image. That they did not do so speaks for their respect for historical truth'.

depression. The common epithets of the Buddha are the bull (*usabha*), the elephant (*nāga*), and the lion (*sīha*). He is compared to a bull bursting free of his bonds or an elephant tearing down creepers.[24] Like a lion he is fearless[25] and 'roars his lion's roar' (*sīhanāda*) to quell the other teachers.[26] He is 'a bull among men, a noble hero (*paravaṃvīra*) . . . a conqueror (*vijitāvin*)'.[27] In the *Bhayabherava Sutta* (Discourse on Fear and Terror) the Buddha relates how, before his Awakening, he sought out 'frightening and horrifying' places in forests at night so as to conquer his fear and terror. At his birth, 'Brahmans skilled in signs' are said to have predicted that as he was 'endowed with the thirty-two marks of a Great Man (*mahāpurisa*) . . . only two courses are open. If he lives the household life he will become a ruler, a wheel-turning righteous monarch (*rājā cakkavattin*) . . . But if he goes forth from the household life into homelessness, then he will become an Arahant, a fully enlightened Buddha'.[28] The idea is that the heroic qualities required to become a righteous monarch are also those required to become a Buddha. *Nirvāṇa* is not a goal for the meek: 'No slacker nor man of puny strength may win *nibbāna*'.[29] Indeed, as I shall attempt to show later on, the qualities required to become a Buddha seem to be similar to those required to become a Nietzschean *Übermensch*. The impression one derives from the Pāli texts is of a very vigorous, energetic, and supremely confident man of attractive appearance—quite the antithesis of someone who was weary with life.

From a recently published work by Mohan Wijayaratna,[30] which relies entirely upon the Theravāda Canon, despite the fact that some of the Buddha's disciples did, indeed, enter the Buddhist monastic life because of some painful experience, 'many of the Buddha's disciples were young people. To join him, most of them had abandoned wealth, a life of luxury, and even a young wife [*sic*]'.[31] And from the impression the texts give us, it does not appear that these young people were weary of life, that they might have thought it 'better *not* to be than to be',[32] that they were forms of 'degenerating life',[33] decadents whose instincts were in decay resulting in a state of depression and a pervading sense of life's

[24] Sn 29. [25] Sn 213. [26] M-N i. 68. [27] Sn 646.
[28] D-N ii. 17 ff.
[29] S-N i. 278.
[30] (1990). [31] Ibid. 4. [32] WP 685. [33] TI ix. 36.

utter meaninglessness. They seemed relatively happy and fun-loving young men who were deeply impressed not only by what the Buddha said but by his very appearance, his vitality and energy.[34] If the Buddha had been a peaceful yet rather cowed and world-weary sort, it is highly unlikely that he would have made such an impression upon so many young people. It is difficult to believe that they renounced their previous way of life simply because they found it too burdensome and depressing. It is more likely that they renounced it because of something they were attracted to, which perhaps appealed to their sense of adventure and the promise of a more fulfilling and meaningful way of life. In comparison to the latter, their old lives were *dukkha*. In the case of the thirty or so young 'friends of high standing', who were on a picnic with their wives, and who encountered the Buddha in some woods whilst searching for a courtesan (one of them had no wife) who had made off with their belongings, what the Buddha actually communicated to them is in all probability not exactly what the texts tell us—we are given a stock passage frequently connected with 'conversions'—it is, nevertheless, basic Buddhist doctrine. He arrests their attention by asking them: 'Which is better for you, that you should seek for a woman or that you should seek for yourself?' The stock passage then continues:

> the Lord talked a progressive talk . . . on giving, . . . on virtuous conduct [*sīla*], . . . on heaven, he explained the peril, the vanity, the depravity of pleasures of the senses, the advantage in renouncing them.
>
> When the lord knew that [their minds] were ready, malleable, receptive, unbiased, uplifted, gladdened, then he explained to them the teaching on Dhamma which the awakened ones have themselves discovered: *dukkha*, the arising [of *dukkha*], the cessation [of *dukkha*], and the way [to the cessation of *dukkha*]. And just as a clean cloth without black specks will take a dye easily, even so . . . Dhamma-vision, dustless, stainless, arose [in them] . . . that 'whatever is of the nature to arise, all that is of a nature to cease'. (Vin. i. 23)

At least according to the Buddhist texts it is quite clear that these young men (and many others) were inspired by the Buddha, and it was this fact that led them to give up their worldly pursuits and become monks (*bhikkhus*). Others may have been enticed by the Buddhist view of the religious life as expressed in the

[34] Wijayaratna (1990), 5 ff.

Dhammapada, where the image of the Buddhist life does not correspond with Nietzsche's talk of gloom and despondency, and whose terms are stronger than his own references to cheerfulness:

> Happy, indeed, we live,
> we who possess nothing.
> Feeders on rapture we shall be
> as the Radiant *devas*. (Dhp. 200)

Given such a view of the religious life, it is understandable how some young men of high standing might forfeit the prospect of a successful and relatively happy worldly life in order to become feeders on rapture, even though, before their encounter with the Buddha, such a prospect had never entered their minds. And it would surely have taken more than a sweet and mild[35] but wearied form of life to convince them of such a prospect.[36]

Personally, I find it difficult to see how such young men, who were in all probability enjoying life, could be inspired to give up their previous way of life so as to follow a materially austere religious path whose final aim was nothing short of complete existential suicide. How could such a prospect sit side by side with being a feeder on rapture? Even assuming that the Buddha was a cunning Pied Piper, if his teaching did not, in time, bring the promised results, then surely many of these people would have eventually deserted him—after all, what young person would be happy living the life of a monk (*bhikkhu*)—a sexually abstinent life on one begged meal a day, with no possessions other than three pieces of cloth for clothing and a begging-bowl? But, at least according to the texts, this was not the case. And, if this is the case, it would not be so surprising if many young men of high standing who, prior to encountering the Buddha were quite content with their lot, should give up the household life and take up the homeless life under his direction. It is difficult to believe that all the Buddha did was to show them the way to fulfil their 'instinct of self-destruction'[37] by becoming 'nirvāṇized'. I find it more reasonable to assume that the

[35] WP 154.

[36] One could, of course, make a comparison with Socrates, another arch-*décadent* according to Nietzsche, who had to drink the hemlock after being accused of corrupting the youth of Athens. But Socrates was not offering them complete 'extinction' as an ultimate reward for becoming a philosopher. If he had, then the likes of Alcibiades would no doubt have found him much less attractive.

[37] WP 55.

Buddha convinced them that in comparison with the prospect of the life he now opened up to them, their previous lives were 'unsatisfactory' (*dukkha*) as were, by implication, the lives the vast majority of mankind led. And it would also make sense to see that the reason their previous way of life now appeared unsatisfactory was because, relatively speaking, it was existentially less fulfilling. What the Buddha offered them was the prospect of a more meaningful ideal of what a human being can become. I will return to this interpretation of *dukkha* later, and make now one final point concerning the notion of *dukkha*.

If many were weary of life it could, in the Indian context of a vista of endless rebirths, make sense to take up a life that held out the prospect of becoming extinguished once and for all. After all, it would not make sense to commit suicide as one would simply return to face life all over again. In a depressed state the thought of such a prospect of endless becoming could appear unbearable. And even if people were not depressed and weary of life, which is the impression the Pāli texts give, it could nevertheless be argued that the prospect of endless 'again-becoming' might appear to many—perhaps the more reflective types—as a burden they would rather do without, even though they were not too dissatisfied with their present lot. And, this being the case, the notion of putting an end to all future rebirth and thereby becoming extinct, might be appealing. It is true that the Buddha does refer to the goal in terms of the end of the cycle of rebirth or, more correctly, 'again-becoming' (*puna-bhava*), which is to attain *nirvāṇa*, but the question as to what 'no-more-again-becoming' (*apuna-bhava*) or *nirvāṇa* actually means I shall again defer until later.

From the Buddhist perspective one would be giving up more than an endless series of *ordinary* lives. According to the Buddhist teaching on *kamman*, what one becomes in the future is determined both by how one acts in the present, as well as the consequences of one's past actions that have not matured as yet. This is not to say that whatever one experiences in the present is directly a consequence of previous actions. In the *Saṃyutta-Nikāya*[38] the Buddha declares that those *samaṇas* and *brāhmaṇas* who say 'That whatsoever pleasure or pain or mental state a person experiences, all that is a consequence of previous acts', are wrong. Pain, for

[38] S-N iv. 230–1. See also A-N i. 174ff.

example, can originate 'from phlegm, from wind, from the union of bodily humours, from changes of the seasons, from being attacked by adversaries,[39] from sudden attacks from without,[40] as well as from the consequences of one's previous *kamman*'. What Buddhism does say is that to the degree that one acts 'skilfully' (*kusalatā*), the consequences (*vipākas*) will be correspondingly pleasant, and vice versa. It is therefore possible, through 'skilful action' (*kusala-kamman*), to be reborn as a 'god' (*deva*) in some blissful heaven where, according to the tradition, all one's desires are instantly met. And, if one continues with skilful actions, it must, in principle, be possible to continue as a *deva* even after the effects of the actions that put one there in the first place have died away. Thus the possibility of a perpetually blissful existence in some heaven or other, which for the Buddhist would be a less satisfactory state than *nirvāṇa*, is entirely within one's own power: whatever change occurs would always occur within that state and, providing one's actions were skilful, maintain it. It does seem rather perverse, then, if *nirvāṇa* did mean total extinction, to turn one's back on the prospect of unending bliss and prefer extinction. Yet even if one could dwell for ever in such a state this would still fall under the category of *saṅkhāra-dukkhatā*, so in what sense could endless bliss be regarded as a form of *dukkha*? How is it possible to become dissatisfied with such a heavenly prospect? After all this prospect, or something akin to it, seems to be the religious goal of a large part of mankind. Again the Buddhist answer to this will depend upon what *nirvāṇa* actually is, as such a prospect is *dukkha* only in contrast to *nirvāṇa*. Nevertheless, I think that enough has been said to show that according to the teachings of Buddhism the notion that life is *dukkha* does not correspond to Nietzsche's interpretation of it, i.e. that life is simply suffering. Nor does the image the texts convey regarding the person of the Buddha give the impression that he was weary of life, that he was a Nietzschean *décadent*. And neither is it the case that the main reason people turned away from ordinary life to follow the Buddhist path was that they were simply weary of life and depressed. Nietzsche, nevertheless, does think that the Buddhist way of life, unlike what is claimed by other

[39] e.g. 'as when one goes out hastily at night and is bitten by a snake' (from commentary, n. 4 of PTS trans.).

[40] e.g. when one is 'arrested as a robber or adulterer' (from the commentary, n. 5, ibid.). I presume one is supposed to be innocent!

religions, actually fulfils its promises. Its followers do overcome their supposed weariness and depression and become relatively happy,[41] overcoming their suffering through achieving a state of bovine-like contentment in which they can contemplate their eventual extinction at death in the knowledge that this is the only way of life that accords with reality and truth. It will appear as the perfect answer to those for whom life has become meaningless and who suffer as a consequence.

3.2. ACTION BINDS ONE TO EXISTENCE

According to Nietzsche, 'In Buddhism this thought predominates: "All desires, all that produces affects and blood, draw one toward actions"—only to this extent is one warned against evil. For action . . . binds one to existence'.[42] This, indeed, is what Buddhism does say about *kamman* or 'action': it is our desires that move us to action,[43] and, depending on the ethical quality of our actions, we will, as a consequence, be reborn somewhere within *saṃsāra*,[44] either within the 'lower realms' (*hīna dhātu*), 'middle realms' (*majjhima dhātu*), or 'exalted realms' (*paṇīta dhātu*).[45] Nietzsche goes on to add that because for Buddhism 'all existence has no meaning', it follows that such drives and desires that affirm existence must also be meaningless: Buddhists 'see in evil a drive towards something illogical: to the affirmation of means to an end one denies'.[46] The idea here is that since in Buddhism the goal is to put an end to continued existence and all *dukkha*, and it is through our past and present actions that we are born into and suffer in this life and will continue to exist and live unsatisfied beyond it, it would be illogical for the Buddhist to act on these drives as this would affirm the antithesis of his goal, i.e. continued existence and *dukkha*, or simply *saṃsāra*. As existence is now seen to be pointless and meaningless, any actions which affirmed existence would themselves be pointless and meaningless. Hence, because the Buddhists 'seek a way of non-existence . . . they regard with horror all

[41] A 20. [42] WP 155. [43] A-N i. 134, 262; v. 262.

[44] Literally, 'going or wandering through', *saṃsāra* refers to the continual round of rebecoming, lifetime after lifetime, of unenlightened existence in various realms, a process that is said to have no calculable beginning (S-N ii. 178ff.) and which can only cease through attaining *nirvāṇa*.

[45] A-N i. 223. [46] WP 155.

affective drives'[47] and 'conceived a rule of conduct to liberate one from action',[48] that rule being 'One must *not* act'.[49] Some 'good' actions, however, are permitted, but 'only for the time being, merely as a means—namely, as a means to emancipation from *all* actions'[50]—*nirvāṇa,* being the complete 'absence of desire',[51] is a state of emancipation from all actions. The kind of drives Nietzsche has in mind are such as 'the feeling of revengefulness, of antipathy, of *ressentiment* . . . enmity', and 'all emotions which produce gall, which heat the blood' or cause anxiety. All these and similar affects are 'thoroughly *unhealthy* with regard to the main dietetic objective', which is to 'get rid of suffering', as they would have the effect of increasing that 'excessive excitability which expresses itself as a refined capacity for pain'.[52]

This appears to be Nietzsche's understanding of the Buddhist doctrine of *kamman* or action: that the goal is to achieve a state of complete emancipation from *all* actions through restraining those desires and actions which affirm existence (which are what Buddhism calls *akusala* or 'unskilful' actions), and cultivating those 'good' actions which act merely as a means to that end (which are what Buddhism calls *kusala* or 'skilful' actions).

Nietzsche is quite correct in seeing that for Buddhism all actions expressive of such affects and desires do indeed 'bind one to existence' or, in Buddhist terms, to 'continual re-becoming' (*punabhava*) within *saṃsāra*. And the affects he mentions such as *ressentiment*, enmity, and revengefulness are good examples of the kind of affects that Buddhism regards as *akusala* or unskilful, in that they are antithetical to the spiritual quest and are just the kind of affects which, if they are not restrained, will lead to continued existence, specifically within the lower realms of *saṃsāra*. Yet he sees the effects of such unskilful actions—the *dukkha*—as being almost immediate and physiological, for example they heat the blood, produce gall, and cause anxiety. But Buddhism, although not denying that there may be some immediate effects and that some of these may well have physiological symptoms, understands that the effects of our actions, whether skilful or unskilful, may in fact take years and even lifetimes to manifest, as they manifest only when conditions are appropriate. Therefore, at least as far as Buddhism is concerned, as the *kamma-vipākas* or 'effects of action' can

[47] WP 155. [48] WP 458. [49] WP 458.
[50] WP 155. [51] A 21. [52] A 20.

take lifetimes to manifest and can also 'ripen' in realms other than the human one, the effects of action cannot be reduced to the merely immediate physiological.

Nietzsche also says that the goal to be achieved, *nirvāṇa*, is a state of non-action, a state which, due to 'absence of desire', is one of 'emancipation from *all* actions', and that this goal is achieved only by: (1) not acting out 'evil' affects; (2) acting out 'good' ones, which, being merely a means to *nirvāṇa*, cease when *nirvāṇa* is attained. This leaves us with *nirvāṇa* which, being a state of non-action creates no future effects; and, since what one is at present is a product of past action, both good and evil, whatever one is will simply cease to be, without residue, at death. Since, in the following section, I will examine whether the goal of Buddhism is to become extinct at death or not, here I will only consider whether, or in what sense it can be said that, someone who has attained *nirvāṇa*, being without any desires, is emancipated from *all* actions.

Whilst it is true that Buddhism does refer to the goal in terms of the 'cessation of action' (*kamma-nirodha*) and says that the way leading to the cessation of action is the Noble Eightfold Path[53] or, we could say, by means of skilful action (i.e. Nietzsche's good action), it would be a mistake to conclude that one who has realized *nirvāṇa* no longer acts. For example, after attaining *nirvāṇa*, the Buddha spent some forty-five or so years being very active, and his actions were very much expressive of certain affects, i.e. 'compassion' (*anukampā*) and 'concern' (*anudayā*) for the welfare of others.[54] And his message to those disciples who had also attained *nirvāṇa* was not one of non-action:

> I, monks, am freed from all snares, both those of *devas* and those of men. And you, monks, are freed from all snares, both those of *devas* and those of men. Go, monks, and wander for the blessing of the manyfolk, for the happiness of the manyfolk out of compassion for the world, for the welfare, the blessing, the happiness of *devas* and men. Let not two (of you) go by one (way). Monks, teach the Dhamma which is lovely at the beginning, lovely in the middle, and lovely at the end. (Vin. i. 19)[55]

So is there a contradiction here? On the one hand *nirvāṇa* is referred to as the cessation of action, and, on the other, when someone attains this goal they are exhorted to travel about bringing the message of the Buddha to the rest of mankind, motivated

[53] A-N iv. 132–3. [54] S-N i. 206. [55] See also S-N ii. 199.

by their compassion and concern for the welfare of their fellow beings.

According to the Buddhist texts, 'action' (*kamman*) is synonymous with 'will' (*cetanā*),[56] and making a somewhat concise and simplified account of what is a very complex matter,[57] what we are actually addressing here is matter of certain kinds of willing and intending. When Buddhism talks of *nirvāṇa* in terms of the cessation of action (*kamma-nirodha*), what actually ceases are certain kinds of willing and intending, i.e. willing and intending formed and conditioned by 'spiritual ignorance' (*avijjā*) and the various kinds of affects that constitute unenlightened existence, e.g. the three 'biases' (*āsavas*), which are said to be destroyed at the attainment of *nirvāṇa*:[58] the 'bias of sense desire' (*kāma-āsava*), the 'bias of desiring some future form of existence' (*bhava-āsava*), and the 'bias of spiritual ignorance' (*avijjā-āsava*). Often a fourth bias is added, that of the bias of views (*diṭṭhi-āsava*); in other words, willing and acting influenced by or dependent upon various doctrines, theories, opinions, etc., including, ultimately, as the Parable of the Raft illustrates, even Buddhist ones.[59] The cessation of action (*kamma-nirodha*) only implies the cessation of the kind of willing that creates the kind of 'consequences' (*vipākas*) and 'fruits' (*phalas*) that keep one bound to unenlightened existence, the kind of willing that can only arise in the minds of unenlightened beings. On attaining *nirvāṇa*, such willing ceases. This is what the cessation of action actually means. As the *Mahācattārīsaka Sutta* informs us, there are three kinds of 'action' (*kammanta*): 'wrong action' (*micchā-kammanta*), and two kinds of 'right action' (*sammā-kammanta*). There is right action which is 'affected by the biases' (*sa-āsava*), 'involved in [creating] merit' (*puññā-bhāgiya*), and 'ripens in future rebecoming' (*upadhi-vepakka*); and there is right action that is 'noble' (*ariya*), 'without the biases' (*anāsava*), and 'beyond the mundane world' (*lokuttara*).[60] This latter kind of action

[56] A-N iii. 415. [57] e.g. see Keown (1992). [58] S-N ii. 29 and elsewhere.

[59] M-N i. 134–5. Here, the Buddha's Dhamma or 'teaching' is compared with a raft that one uses to ferry oneself from this shore (*saṃsāra*) to the further shore (*nirvāṇa*). Having reached the further shore, one is no longer dependent upon the raft: 'Even so, monks, is the Dhamma taught by me similar to a raft, being for the purpose of crossing over, not for the purpose of acquiring. Monks, when you know that the Dhamma is like a raft, having renounced [attachment to] good states, how much more so bad states'.

[60] M-N iii. 74.

is not karmic, and will therefore not produce effects that will ripen within *saṃsāra*. This distinction between the two kinds of right action is also found in other contexts. When asked 'where do skilful moral actions (*kusala-sīlas*) cease without remainder', the Buddha replies when one 'possesses virtue (*sīlavant*), not when one is regulated by virtue (*sīlamaya*)'.[61] In other words, there is a kind of skilful action equivalent to the first kind of right action, which is regulated by and dependent upon moral guidelines as to what is skilful and what is not. But, having practised the first kind of right action, one can eventually become a virtuous person, a *sīlavant*, one who is free from all biases and whose willing and acting are naturally virtuous and skilful and not dependent upon any moral guidelines. This second kind of skilful action therefore has to be distinguished from the kind of skilful action 'regulated by virtue', i.e. that is dependent upon the conscious effort to restrain unskilful actions, and develop skilful actions. When the Buddha is said to be in full 'possession of all skilful states',[62] this can be said to mean that his actions, being no longer dependent on or regulated by any moral guidelines or rules as to what is skilful, let alone unskilful, are naturally skilful. Therefore, when Nietzsche says that *nirvāṇa* is a state of 'emancipation from *all* actions' because of the 'absence of desire', we have to add that it is a state where only certain kinds of actions cease, not all actions.

3.3. THE 'ORIENTAL NOTHING—CALLED NIRVANA'

In Buddhism, there are in fact two *nirvāṇas*, *nirvāṇa* and *parinirvāṇa*, the prefix *pari-* meaning 'complete' or 'full'. Sometimes the two are synonymous, but where a distinction is made *nirvāṇa* refers to the attainment of *bodhi* or 'Awakening', and *parinirvāṇa* to the state or non-state attained at the death of a nirvāṇized person. Therefore, the question whether the final goal of Buddhism is to become non-existent, which is how Nietzsche understands it, refers to *parinirvāṇa*. *Nirvāṇa*, in Nietzsche's terms, would then be the attainment of a '*happiness on earth*',[63] a state of 'cheerfulness, stillness, absence of desire',[64] before finally attaining the 'Oriental Nothing' of *parinirvāṇa*, or annihilation, at death.

[61] M-N ii. 27. [62] M-N ii. 116. [63] A 42. [64] A 21.

When the Buddha was questioned as to the state or non-state, after death, of one who has attained *nirvāṇa*, he answers:

'Just as a flame blown out by the force of the wind, Upasīva,' said the Blessed One, 'goes to a setting none can reckon, so a sage released from his psycho-physical embodiment [nāma-kāya] goes to a setting none can reckon'.

'He who has gone to his setting, does he not exist, or does he exist unchanging in eternity? Explain this to me well, sage, for thus is the state known to you'.

'There is no measuring of one who has gone to his setting, Upasīva', said the Blessed One. 'That no longer exists for him by which people might refer to him. When all conditions [*dhammas*][65] are removed, then all ways of telling are also removed'. (Sn 1074–6)

Just as the bourn of a blazing spark of fire
Struck from the anvil, gradually fading,
Cannot be known,— so in the case of those
Who've rightly won release and crossed the flood
Of lusts that bind, and reached the bliss unshaken,
The bourn they've won cannot be pointed to. (Ud. viii. 10)

The whereabouts or non-whereabouts after death of one who has realized *nirvāṇa*, is considered to be beyond the 'range of designations' (*adhivacana-patha*), the 'range of language' (*nirutti-patha*), the 'range of concepts' (*paññatti-patha*), the 'sphere of understanding' (*paññā-āvacana*), and the 'circling of *saṃsāra*'.[66] Elsewhere, the Buddha, probably with some irony, says that the state of a Tathāgata[67] is untraceable here and now, let alone after death, even by the gods of Indra, Brahmā, and Pajāpati.[68] The reason a 'Tathāgata is liberated from [such] reckoning' is that 'he is deep, immeasurable, unfathomable like the mighty ocean'.[69] When the wanderer Vacchagotta questions the Buddha on these matters, and is told that none of his categories fitted the case, Vacchagotta replies: 'I have fallen into bewilderment . . . I have fallen into confusion, and the measure of confidence I had gained through previ-

[65] i.e. all the conditions that constitute an unenlightened being.

[66] D-N ii. 68.

[67] Literally, the 'Thus-gone', an epithet of the Buddha, but sometimes applied to anyone who has realized *nirvāṇa*.

[68] M-N i. 140.

[69] M-N i. 487. See also the whole of S-N, pt. 10, 'Kindred Sayings about the Unrevealed' (*avyākata-saṃyuttam*) on this topic of the existence or non-existence of a Tathāgata after death.

ous conversation with Master Gotama has now disappeared'. To which the Buddha retorts:

It is enough to cause you bewilderment, Vaccha, enough to cause you confusion. For this truth, Vaccha, is deep, hard to see and hard to understand, peaceful and sublime, unattainable by mere reasoning, subtle, to be experienced by the wise. It is hard for you to understand when you hold another view, accept another teaching, approve another teaching, pursue a different training, and follow a different teacher. (M-N i. 487)

If the Buddha taught a doctrine of annihilationism, such a notion is certainly not beyond the range of concepts, etc., and it would not make sense to refer to the person who was annihilated as unfathomable like the mighty ocean. Therefore we can only assume that in the Buddha's terms, what he had in mind was something quite radical, something that was beyond the grasp of those who are still under the influence of saṃsāric affects. All that these texts tells us is that the Buddhist view on these matters points to some kind of state or mode of being that is simply beyond categorization.[70] As another text tells us, whatever an unenlightened being can imagine and conjecture, such imaginings and conjectures, being the product of an unenlightened mind, are bound to be mistaken.[71] According to the above quote, the truth of the matter is only available to 'the wise' (*paṇḍita*), i.e. those who understand 'things as they really are' (*yathā-bhūta*). This is all in accord with the most fundamental Buddhist doctrine of 'dependent co-arising' (*paṭicca-samuppāda*), which is said to form what might be called the intellectual content of the Buddha's attainment of *bodhi* or 'enlightenment'.[72] This doctrine states that all things, whether material, biological, mental, or spiritual, come to be in dependence upon conditions, and when those conditions cease what came to be also ceases. The truth of such matters as whether a Tathāgata exists or does not exist after death is a truth only available under certain conditions, those conditions being, for example, the absence of any affects and opinions rooted in either 'attachment' (*lobha*), 'ill-will' (*dosa*), or 'delusion'

[70] Sn 749. [71] S-N iv. 386f.

[72] e.g. see Ud, ch. 1. As another text tells us: 'He who sees dependent co-arising sees the Dhamma. He who sees the Dhamma sees dependent co-arising' (M i. 191–2). Dhamma here means 'truth' or 'things as they really are'. Elsewhere, the Buddha says to Vakkali: 'He who sees me, Vakkali, sees the Dhamma. He who sees the Dhamma sees me' (S iii. 120). 'Seeing the Buddha' probably means seeing *bodhi* or 'enlightenment', the 'content' of which is formulated as 'dependent co-arising', which is said to be the true nature of things, the Dhamma.

(*moha*), and the attainment of a certain state of 'meditative concentration' (*samādhi*), which is here the culmination of an augmenting series of spiritual states which forms the necessary condition for 'seeing and knowing things as they really are' (*yathā-bhūta-ñāṇa-dassana*).[73] According to Buddhism, 'Seeing and knowing things as they really are', or seeing into the truth of such matters, is only available under certain conditions. As the Buddha says to Kaccāyana, when asked what 'right-view' (*sammā-diṭṭhi*) was:

> The majority of the world, Kaccāyana, relies upon two [views]: Existence and non-existence.
>
> Now he, who with right insight [*sammappaññā*] sees the arising of the world as it really is [*yathā-bhūta*] does not hold [the view] that the world is non-existent. But he, who with right insight sees the passing away of the world as it really is, does not hold [the view] that the world is existent. . . .
>
> Everything exists: that is one extreme. Nothing exists: this is the other extreme. Not going to either extreme the Tathāgata teaches the truth [Dhamma] of the Middle [Way]: (which is 'dependent co-arising'). (S-N ii. 17)

From the Buddhist point of view, applying the categories of 'existence' (*atthitā*) or 'non-existence' (*natthitā*) to anything means departing from the truth of 'dependent co-arising': that things come to be in dependence upon conditions, and cease to be when those conditions cease. All things only have a relative existence—the terms 'existence' and 'non-existence' being understood here as implying some kind of 'absolute existence' and 'absolute non-existence'. Therefore, to try and determine whether a Tathāgata exists or not after *parinirvāṇa*, is to assume that one of these extreme views can reveal the truth of the matter. But to say that he exists would be to fall into the 'wrong-view' (*micchā-diṭṭhi*) of 'eternalism' (*sassatavāda*). To say that he does not exist would fall into the wrong-view of 'annihilationism' (*ucchedavāda*). Therefore, whatever the case may be, it would be incorrect to say that Buddhism teaches a doctrine whose final goal is annihilation.

Even in the Buddha's own day, he was accused of being a 'nihilist' (*venayika*), of teaching a 'doctrine of annihilation' (*ucchedavāda*),[74] a doctrine usually associated with the *samaṇa* Ajita Kesakambalin, a materialist and contemporary of the Bud-

[73] See S-N ii. 30; iii. 13; v. 414f. This area will be examined in detail in ch. 11.3 'Self-overcoming and Power'.

[74] M-N i. 140; A-N iv. 174.

dha. According to the *Sāmaññaphala Sutta*, Ajita taught that 'the talk of those who preach a doctrine of survival [after death] is vain and false. Fools and wise, at the breaking up of the body, are destroyed and perish, they do not exist after death'.[75] In the *Brahmajāla Sutta*, there is a list of seven varieties of *ucchedavāda*: the materialistic version associated with Ajita, and six other immaterial versions, each of which claims that there is a progressively subtler immaterial 'self' (*attan*) which survives physical death, and it is only when this self finally passes away, presumably by means of some spiritual attainment, that annihilation actually occurs. All these views are said by the Buddha to be *micchā-diṭṭhis* or 'wrong-views',[76] and as such form no part of his doctrine. The kind of view that Nietzsche has of the goal of Buddhism would, therefore, be considered a wrong view by the Buddhists themselves. Elsewhere, when General Sīha asks the Buddha whether there is any way in which it could be said: 'The recluse Gotama asserts annihilation [*uccheda*], he teaches a doctrine of annihilation [*ucchedavāda*]?', the Buddha replies that there is: 'I indeed assert the annihilation of attachment, ill-will, and delusion; I assert the annihilation of manifold evils and unskilful states of mind'.[77]

Interestingly enough, the Buddhists judge that the 'eternalist' view is to be preferred to the 'annihilationist' view. In the *Majjhima-Nikāya*,[78] in what amounts to a Buddhist version of Pascal's Wager, the 'doctrine of "there-is"' (*atthikavāda*)—which affirms that actions have karmic consequences, that there is a world beyond this one, that there are those who have realized this by themselves—is to be preferred to the 'doctrine of "there-is-not"' (*natthikavāda*), which affirms the opposite views. The advantage of being a 'there-is-ist' (*atthikavādin*) over a 'there-is-not-ist' (*natthikavādin*) is that one 'will be praised here and now by intelligent persons' for holding such a view, even if this doctrine turns out to be incorrect and there is not a world beyond, etc. But if there is,

[75] D-N i. 55. Yet, elsewhere, Ajita is listed among those who on discussing the fate of a disciple after death, say, 'So and so is *reborn* thus and thus' (S-N iv. 297; italics mine).

[76] D-N i. 34–6. Annihilationism, therefore, was certainly not simply a materialistic doctrine. In these instances where the survival after physical death of a subtle immaterial 'self' is recognized, they no doubt point to some spiritual-cum-mystical goal, perhaps of the drop of water merging with the ocean variety.

[77] Vin. i. 233. This is repeated at A-N iv. 180 and, with a Brāhman interlocutor, at Vin. iii. 2.

[78] M-N i. 401–4.

which is what the Buddhists assert, then 'after the breaking up of the body, after death, he will be reborn in a happy destiny, even a heavenly world', as well as being praised in this life.[79] The 'there-is-not-ist' has nothing to look forward to as if his doctrine is correct he will nevertheless be condemned by the wise here and now, and will have no future life to look forward to. But if his doctrine is wrong, which is what the Buddhists think, then as well as being condemned by the wise here and now, after dying he will be reborn into a nasty and painful realm. So, if one is not sure who to believe, better to put one's 'money' on the 'there-is-ist'. The Buddhists, therefore, see themselves as having more in common with those eternalists who follow, for example, the Upaniṣadic doctrine that teaches that 'a man turns into something good by good action and into something bad by bad action',[80] rather than the likes of Ajita Kesakambalin, who, as we saw, taught an annihilationist creed in that 'the talk of those who preach a doctrine of survival [after death] is vain and false. Fools and wise, at the breaking up of the body, are destroyed and perish, they do not exist after death'.[81]

Although the Buddha's answer to questions regarding the state or non-state after the death of one who has realized *nirvāṇa* clearly denies an annihilationist interpretation, and puts knowledge of such things beyond the reach of rational categorization, nevertheless there are a few *suttas* that, in quite positive terms, refer to some kind of 'beyond'. Two passages from the *Udāna* that lend themselves to such an interpretation are:

> Monks, there is that state [*āyatana*] wherein is neither earth nor water nor fire nor air; wherein is neither the sphere of infinite space nor that of infinite consciousness, nor the sphere of no-thingness or that of neither apperception nor non-apperception; where there is neither this world nor a world beyond nor both together, nor sun and moon. There, monks, I declare there is no coming [*āgati*] or going [*gati*], no duration [*ṭhiti*] or decay [*cuti*] nor coming to be [*upapatti*]; it is without support [*apatiṭṭhita*], without result [*appavatta*] and has no foundation [*anārammaṇa*]. This, indeed, is the end of *dukkha*. (Ud. 80)

> Monks, there is an unborn [*ajāta*], an unbecome [*abhūta*], an unmade [*akata*], an uncompounded [*asaṅkhata*]. Monks, if that unborn, unbecome, unmade, uncompounded were not, no escape [*nissaraṇa*] from the born, the become, the made, the compounded would be known here. But since,

[79] M-N i. 404. [80] *Bṛhadāraṇyaka Upaniṣad*, IV. 4. 5. [81] D-N i. 55.

monks, there is an unborn, unbecome, unmade, uncompounded, therefore an escape from the born, the become, the made, the compounded is known [*paññāyati*]. (Ud. 80–1; It 37)

How one interprets such *udānas* or 'inspired utterances' is no easy matter. But they do counter any annihilationist view of Buddhism. Other *suttas* refer to some form of 'consciousness' (*viññāṇa*) or 'mind' (*citta*) that could be construed as continuing in some mysterious manner after *parinirvāṇa*.[82] However, delving into such areas will take us beyond the scope of this book.

With regard to Nietzsche's view of Buddhism as a nihilistic religion, one is left wondering if Oldenberg had not mistranslated the term *vibhava-taṇhā* or 'thirst for annihilation' as *der Vergänglichkeitsdurst* or 'thirst for impermanence',[83] but translated it more correctly as *Selbstvernichtungsbegehren* or 'thirst for self-annihilation',[84] given that this thirst for annihilation is considered to be an unskilful state to be abandoned, Nietzsche might have paused to reconsider whether Buddhism actually taught a nihilistic doctrine or not. But we will never know.

[82] e.g. see S-N iii. 45; 53–4, and D-N i. 223. For an interesting view on these matters, see Harvey (1989 and 1995).

[83] See p. 224 of Helmuth von Glasenapp's edn. of Oldenberg's *Buddha* (Stuttgart, 1959). Hoey in Oldenberg (1882), 211, translates *der Vergänglichkeitsdurst* as 'the thirst for power', which is completely misleading. However, he may have looked back to the Pāli term and translated *vibhava* as 'power'. *Vibhava* can mean 'power, wealth, prosperity', but in this context means 'non-existence'. The reason for these opposing meanings is that the prefix *vi-* can denote 'expansion', function as a negative prefix, as well as being an intensifier (see PED). *Vibhava-taṇhā* is one of the three kinds of *taṇhā* listed by Oldenberg, the other two being *kāma-taṇhā* or 'thirst for sensual pleasure', and *bhava-taṇhā* or 'thirst for being'. See S-N v. 421 and elsewhere.

[84] See Nyanatiloka's *Buddhistisches Wörterbuch*.

4

How Did Nietzsche Reach his Understanding of Buddhism?

I think a reasonable case has been made which refutes Nietzsche's claim that Buddhism is a form of 'passive nihilism', that it teaches a goal which ends with the individual being completely annihilated at *parinirvāṇa*. But how did Nietzsche reach this conclusion? Was he misled by his sources?

The only recorded sources for Nietzsche's acquaintance with Buddhism are Oldenberg's *Buddha*, Müller's *Selected Essays* (vol. ii), Koeppen's *Die Religion des Buddha* (2 vols.), Coomaraswamy's abridged translation in English of the *Sutta-nipāta*, and what he read in the works of Schopenhauer. Mistry mentions that he 'possibly . . . drew information on Buddhism from his friend Ernst Windisch, the Buddhologist, to whose Sanskrit studies he refers to in his correspondence' to his friend Deussen, and another friend Rohde.[1] However, nothing directly relating to Buddhism or Indian thought is found in any of these letters. This is surprising as, given the attention Nietzsche gives to Buddhism in his writings, one would have expected to find some mention of his thinking in this area in his letters to his life-long friend Deussen, who was a Sanskrit scholar. Yet, as Sprung remarks, in his correspondence with Deussen, 'Nietzsche . . . never once bothered to seek information from or discuss issues [relating to Buddhism or Indian thought in general] with him'.[2] What we are left then are the above works as the only definite sources of Nietzsche's knowledge of Buddhism.

Of the works on Buddhism, Koeppen's was the first Nietzsche read.[3] For Koeppen, *nirvāṇa* 'is . . . first and foremost the total extinction of the soul, the extinction in nothingness, plain destruction . . . Nirvana is the blessed Nothingness: Buddhism is

[1] (1981), 16. [2] (1983), 174.

[3] Mistry (1981) records that Nietzsche borrowed Koeppen's work from the university library at Basle during the winter semester of 1870–1.

the gospel of annihilation'.[4] Here we have a source for Nietzsche's view that *nirvāṇa* is the 'desire for nothingness',[5] that it implies total annihilation of the individual at death. But what about the later works of Müller and Oldenberg?

Müller seems to have had a change of mind as to whether *nirvāṇa* is annihilationist or not. For example, in his essay, 'Buddhism', he says that in Buddhism . . .

> True wisdom consists in perceiving the nothingness of all things, and in a desire to become nothing, to be blown out, to enter into the state of Nirvâna. Emancipation is obtained by total extinction, not by absorption in Brahman, or by recovery of the soul's true estate.[6]

Yet Müller is bemused by the apparent contradiction between Buddhism as a philosophy and as it is found existing in the world.

> How a religion which taught the annihilation of all existence, of all thought, of all individuality and personality, as the highest object of all endeavours, could have laid hold of the minds of millions of human beings, and how at the same time, by enforcing the duties of morality, justice, kindness, and self-sacrifice, it could have exercised a decidedly beneficial influence, not only on the natives of India, but on the lowest barbarians of Central Asia, is a riddle which no one has as yet been able to solve.[7]

He attempts to resolve this apparent dilemma by distinguishing between 'Buddhism as a religion and Buddhism as a philosophy. The former addressed itself to millions, the latter to a few isolated thinkers'.[8] In another essay, 'The Meaning of Nirvāṇa', Müller begins to have doubts whether Buddhism is annihilationist or not and comes up with another distinction. He thinks that, perhaps, in relation to the Buddhist Pāli texts, only the later Abhidhamma[9]—what he calls the 'Basket of Metaphysics'—is actually nihilistic, as well as the *Prajñā-Pāramitā* or 'Perfection of Wisdom' literature of the later Mahāyāna schools of Buddhist thought which taught the doctrine of *śunyatā* or 'emptiness'. He comments:

[4] Koeppen, translated by Mistry (1981), 179.
[5] GM ii. 21.
[6] (1881), 219. The essay is dated 1862.
[7] Ibid. 246. This is from the essay 'Buddhist Pilgrims' (1857).
[8] Ibid.
[9] The Pāli canon is divided into 'three collections' (*tipiṭaka*), the *sutta-piṭaka* or 'collection of dialogues', the *vinaya-piṭaka* or 'collection of discipline', and the *abhidhamma-piṭaka* or 'collection of further teachings', with the latter being an attempt to analyse, define, and systematize what is found in the *suttas*. It is generally accepted to be the work of monks.

The only ground, therefore, on which we may stand, if we wish to defend the founder of Buddhism against the charges of Nihilism and Atheism, is this, that, as some of the Buddhists admit, the 'Basket of Metaphysics' was rather the work of his pupils, not of the Buddha himself.[10]

He then proceeds to wonder whether the *nirvāṇa* taught by the Buddha, as distinct from the annihilationist creed found in the Abhidhamma, was in fact a 'self-ness, in the metaphysical sense of the word—a relapse into that being which is nothing but itself', i.e. what is referred to above as 'the soul's true estate'. Eventually, in the next essay, he decides that 'the sayings of the Buddha [that] occur in the first and second parts of the canon . . . are in open contradiction to . . . metaphysical Nihilism',[11] as when one examines the sayings found in the *Dhammapada*, 'one recognizes in them a conception of Nirvâṇa, altogether irreconcilable with the Nihilism of the third part of the Buddhist Canon',[12] i.e. the Abhidhamma. Müller therefore comes to distinguish between the earliest teachings found in the *suttas*, teachings that he sees if not reflecting what the Buddha actually taught, are as near to the Buddha as we can determine, and the Abhidhamma and later Mahāyāna *Prajñā-Pāramitā* teachings on *śūnyatā* or emptiness, both of which he considers as thoroughly nihilistic. Therefore, only the Abhidhamma's and the *Prajñā-Pāramitā's* conception of *nirvāṇa* is nihilistic. The earlier doctrines found in the *suttas* are not, implying that whatever the Buddha taught it was not annihilationism.

Along with Koeppen, Oldenberg's description of northern India at the time of the Buddha as being in a state of spiritual malaise, no doubt influenced Nietzsche's view of India. Yet Oldenberg, when it comes to the status of *nirvāṇa*, does not think it implies complete annihilation.[13]

In the religious life, in the tone which prevailed in the ancient Buddhist order, the thought of annihilation has had no influence.[14]

If anyone describes Buddhism as a religion of annihilation, and attempts to develop it therefrom as from its specific germ, he has, in fact, succeeded in

[10] Müller (1981), 286–7, from his essay 'The Meaning of Nirvâṇa' (1857).
[11] Ibid. 303, from the essay 'Buddhist Nihilism' (1869).
[12] Ibid. 305.
[13] See Oldenberg (1882), 265–85 for his account. [14] Ibid. 265.

wholly missing the main drift of [the] Buddha and the ancient order of his disciples.[15]

After discussing the two 'inspired utterances' (*udānas*) I quoted earlier from the *Udāna*,[16] he finally concludes in a more poetic tone:

For the Buddhist the words 'there is an uncreated' [*akata*] merely signify that the created can free himself from the curse of being created—there is a path from the world of the created out into dark endlessness. Does the path lead into a new existence? Does it lead into the Nothing? The Buddhist creed rests in delicate equipoise between the two. The longing of the heart that craves the eternal has not nothing, and yet the thought has not a something, which it might firmly grasp. Farther off the idea of the endless, the eternal could not withdraw itself from belief than it has done here, where, like a gentle flutter on the point of merging in the Nothing, it threatens to evade the gaze.[17]

Given the views found in both Müller's later essays[18] and in Oldenberg's work on *nirvāṇa*, it is odd that Nietzsche gives no consideration to their conclusions about *parinirvāṇa*, in spite of the fact that he knew both Müller and Oldenberg were eminent scholars in the field of Pāli Buddhist studies, and their works were representative of the latest Pāli scholarship. Why he paid no attention to them we can only surmise. Perhaps the Sanskrit and Pāli scholars he talked with at the university of Basle convinced him that both Müller and Oldenberg were wrong. But, given our present sources, this is impossible to determine. Even Nietzsche's 'mentor', Schopenhauer, whose works were no doubt his first contact with Buddhism, does not interpret *parinirvāṇa* as nihilistic. His view is a little akin to Oldenberg's.

If *Nirvana* is defined as nothing, that means only that *Samsara* contains no single element that could serve to define or construct *Nirvana*.[19]

Nirvāṇa, for Schopenhauer, was 'denial of the will' and *saṃsāra* 'the affirmation of the will'.[20] In his later *Parerga and Paralipomena*, he says that

[15] Ibid. 266. [16] Ud. 80 and 81. [17] Oldenberg (1882), 283–4.

[18] Oldenberg (1882: 283 n.) favourably quotes Müller, from the latter's introd. to his trans. of the *Dhammapada* (1881). Referring to the notion of the 'uncreated' (*akata*) from verse 383 of the *Dhammapada*, Müller says: 'This surely shows that even for [the] Buddha a something existed which is not made, and which, therefore, is imperishable and eternal'.

[19] Schopenhauer (1969), ii. 608. [20] Ibid. 609.

the *denial of the will-to-live* does not in any way assert the annihilation of a substance, but the mere act of not-willing; that which hitherto *willed* no longer *wills*. As we know this being, this essence, the *will*, as thing-in-itself merely in and through the act of *willing*, we are incapable of saying or comprehending what it is or does after it has given up this act. And so *for us* who are the phenomenon of willing, this denial is a passing over into nothing.[21]

From what Schopenhauer says elsewhere,[22] to achieve *parinirvāṇa* would be the equivalent to a return to some state of 'primordial being', which is not too far removed from what both Müller and Oldenberg were hinting at. Therefore, given Nietzsche's known sources, it is clear that however he arrived at his view that Buddhism was a form of passive nihilism, that it succumbed to annihilationism, it was not due to his being influenced by the views of either Müller, Oldenberg, or even Schopenhauer.

To conclude this first part I will look at another influence on Nietzsche which I think may reveal the real source of his considering Buddhism to be a form of passive nihilism: the opinions and ideas about culture and religion he absorbed somewhat uncritically from his reading in the field of anthropology.

As Thatcher remarks, Nietzsche, 'like other revolutionary thinkers of his time . . . seeks a new understanding of man by revealing the hidden sources of human life, culture and civilization'.[23] Just as Darwin was revealing man's animal origins, anthropologists such as Tylor and Lubbock were revealing—or thought they were revealing—the natural origins of certain aspects of contemporary civilization, especially the natural origins of our religious beliefs. One crucial idea that Nietzsche borrowed from them, and used in his own work, was that the origin of all belief in a world other than the

[21] (1974), ii. 312. [22] Ibid. 400.

[23] (1983), 293. Thatcher's articles (1982 and 1983) on the influences of the anthropological works of Tylor, Bagehot, and Lubbock on Nietzsche's thinking are most illuminating. He clearly illustrates that many of Nietzsche's views on the origins of morality, custom, and religion were, at times, almost direct borrowings from the works of Bagehot and Lubbock. The key theme of these anthropologists is the notion of 'survivals'—groups of surviving 'savages' whose cultures have remained relatively unchanged from ancient times through to the present. From their anthropological field studies, they concluded that in recording the beliefs and habits of these survivals they were, like palaeontologists, discovering the real origins of our own more sophisticated systems of morality and religion, origins which, in the course of time, are forgotten. As Thatcher (1983: 269) remarks, quoting Lubbock, '"the earlier mental stages through which the human race has passed are illustrated by the condition of existing, or recent, savages," allowing us to recognise that many primitive ideas are still "rooted in our minds, as fossils are embedded in the soil"'.

natural world stems from the fact that in our dream life we seem to encounter another world. As Lubbock writes:

During sleep the spirit seems to desert the body; and as in dreams we visit other localities and even other worlds, living, as it were, a separate and different life, the two phenomena are not unnaturally regarded as complements of one another. Hence the savage considers the events in his dreams to be as real as those of his waking hours, and hence he naturally feels that he has a spirit which can quit the body . . . When they dream of their departed friends or relatives, savages firmly believe themselves to be visited by their spirits, and hence believe, not indeed in the immortality of the soul, but in its survival of the body.[24]

Nietzsche, obviously with this passage in mind, writes:

Misunderstanding of the dream. The man of the ages of barbarous primordial culture believed that in the dream he was getting to know a *second real world*: here is the origin of all metaphysics. Without the dream one would have had no occasion to divide the world in two. The dissection into soul and body is also connected with the oldest idea of the dream, likewise the postulation of a life of the soul, thus the origin of all belief in spirits, and probably also of the belief in gods. 'The dead live on, *for* they appear to the living in dreams': that was the conclusion one formerly drew, throughout millennia. (HAH 5)

Nietzsche, building on the ideas he found in Lubbock and others, thinks he now understands the natural origin of the two-world framework, the duality of body and soul and belief in the survival of the latter after death, as well as belief in spirits and even the origin of metaphysics—all have a genealogy whose original source is the world of dreams, in the fact that our primitive ancestors thought they encountered another world in their dreams, which Nietzsche regards as 'a failure of the intellect'.[25] He does not seem to consider any other possible source, as 'Without the dream one would have no occasion to divide the world in two'.[26] In time, this two-world schema, as it is passed on from primitive times through the generations—its origin having been forgotten—becomes so established, becomes almost an a-priori category inherent in all our

[24] Quoted in Thatcher (1983), 297, from Lubbock's *The Origin of Civilisation and the Primitive Condition of Man* (1870). According to Thatcher (1983: 295), Nietzsche acquired a German translation of the third edition in 1875.

[25] GS 151: 'But what first led to the positing of "another world" in primeval times was not some impulse or need but an *error* in the interpretation of certain natural events, a failure of the intellect'.

[26] HAH 5.

thinking, that it informs all religious and philosophical thought and speculation. Nietzsche even sees the continuance of this schema into the domain of contemporary science in the form of the pursuit of some 'true world' beyond the world of the senses. What we are therefore presented with is 'the history of an error'.[27] Yet this 'error' is not always detrimental to human development, as in the case of the Greeks whose conception of the Olympian gods was 'a mirror image of the most successful specimens of their own class . . . an idealization, not an antithesis, of their own nature'.[28] They 'made poetry out of reality, instead of yearning to escape from it'.[29] In the Greek gods, '*the animal* in man felt deified and did *not* lacerate itself, did *not* rage against itself!'[30] The Greeks even blamed their gods rather than themselves for their misfortunes. But, since Plato, through Christianity and metaphysics and on into the modern scientific world, the two-world framework has been grasped as a means of escaping from and condemning the natural world. For those for whom life is too much of a burden, who suffer from life and even want to revenge themselves upon life, the 'other world' becomes something to escape to, becomes a justification for turning one's back upon the natural world and condemning it as evil and worthless. Consequently, given this 'revealed' genealogy of the two-world schema from his anthropological reading, when Nietzsche encounters Müller's and Oldenberg's interpretations of *parinirvāṇa* as implying some 'eternal realm' that the nirvāṇized person passes into at death, and given that other scholars judged Buddhism to be annihilationist, he would be highly suspicious of any talk of some state beyond the natural world and would most likely judge that this was an interpretation of *décadents* reading their own wishes and values into Buddhist doctrine.[31]

[27] In TI iv, Nietzsche recounts this 'History of an Error' only from Plato onwards. But its genealogy obviously reaches far back into man's primitive past.

[28] WC 150.

[29] WC 63.

[30] GM ii. 23.

[31] A case could certainly be made against Müller in this regard. Müller struggled for a definition of religion that would encompass all religions and which would be grounded in the natural world. However, as his *An Introduction to the Science of Religion*—a 'science' based upon philology—and his *Natural Religion* show, he struggled to fit Buddhism into his scheme. Eventually, he came up with a definition within which Buddhism might fit: '*Religion consists in the perception of the infinite under such manifestations as are able to influence the moral character of man*'. (1889: 188). *Nirvāṇa*, to fit into this definition, would be the 'perception of the infinite' and *parinirvāṇa* the passing over into that infinite.

When we add to this the accounts, especially in Oldenberg, of the cultural changes which preceded the Buddha, depicting an age grown weary of metaphysical speculation, where agnosticism was rife among the philosophers, where the old morality and religious beliefs were being gradually undermined and within which Nietzsche saw an historical parallel to his own time, we have a reason why Nietzsche may have rejected the views of Müller and Oldenberg concerning *parinirvāṇa*. The Buddha arrives on this stage as an atheist, having rejected the established religious tradition, Brāhmanism. He teaches a religion of 'self-redemption' making no appeal to any divine being or realm. His teachings have regard only to 'natural laws' and he is therefore regarded by Nietzsche as a 'profound physiologist'. And as Nietzsche understands the Buddha as discovering 'the necessary conditions out of which alone [morality] can grow', and having discovered these conditions 'no longer wants it (Buddhism)',[32] which I would understand as implying that the Buddha rejected the two-world schema, one can understand how Nietzsche sided with those who interpreted *parinirvāṇa* as annihilationist: given that there is no other world than this natural world and *nirvāṇa* is a state one achieves in this world, as *parinirvāṇa* entails the end of *saṃsāra* and *saṃsāra* is the only world, Buddhism must therefore be annihilationist. However, as I've argued above, I think Nietzsche was wrong.

[32] WP 151.

PART II

Ironic Affinities

5

Introduction

One common and general feature shared by both Nietzsche and Buddhism is the centrality of man in a godless cosmos,[1] in the sense that both look to man, and not any external power, being, or numinous source, for their respective solutions to what they perceive as the problem(s) of existence. For Nietzsche the problem is the oncoming nihilism; for Buddhism it is the unsatisfactory nature of what the vast majority of mankind regard as a meaningful and purposeful human existence. Both see man as an ever-changing flux of forces possessing what may generally be called physical and psychological aspects. And within this flux there is no autonomous or unchanging subject corresponding to such terms as 'self', 'ego', or 'soul'. Both also emphasize the hierarchy that exists or can exist between individuals and within the individual's own nature. For Nietzsche the postulated pinnacle of his hierarchy is the *Übermensch*, a goal which no one has yet attained but which is a potential, if not for all, at least for some. In the case of Buddhism the goal is said to have been realized and attained in the person of Gautama the Buddha some 2,500 years ago, and is a goal that all beings are said have the potential to realize. Another feature shared by both, and which is the main theme of Part II, is that their respective goals are to be achieved through a process of 'self-overcoming' (*Selbstüberwindung* in Nietzsche's case, *citta-bhāvanā* in Buddhism's), and this self-overcoming is understood as the spiritual expression of a more basic and natural force (will to power in Nietzsche's case, *taṇhā* in Buddhism's).

[1] Buddhism accepts the existence of 'gods' (*devas*) and other 'spirit-like' beings found in Indian cosmology, even the God Brahmā who thinks he is 'the Lord, Maker and Creator' (*issaro kattā nimmātā*) of all beings (D-N i. 222). But they play no essential part in the Buddhist spiritual life. For a good account of this see Southwold (1978) and Smart (1981).

6

Nietzsche's View of Man

Although Nietzsche's proposed answer to the prospect of nihilism—the creation of new values—was a task he did not complete, he did leave us with his monistic alternative and replacement for God, which would have functioned as the arbitrator in his proposed creation of new values—his vision of existence characterized as *Wille zur Macht* or 'will to power'. It is only through this notion that one can make overall sense of Nietzsche. As a principle of explanation, it brings together and unites much that in isolation seems contradictory and even bizarre, and it is also the maxim which underpins his thinking on subjects such as culture, art, morality, philosophy, religion, as well as providing a continuity between his earlier and later writings, despite the fact that the will to power did not explicitly appear until *Zarathustra*.[1] It is, as we shall see, an explanatory principle gleaned from Nietzsche's understanding of human nature and the natural sciences, and it provides a new and interesting perspective on human history and culture as well as providing the new *Weltanschauung* upon which the post-nihilistic future would be built.

As I said in Chapter 2, the idea that 'God is dead' is not simply a theological—or anti-theological—statement, but is primarily a cultural one, i.e. an idea with far-reaching cultural and social implications. The bifurcation of existence into 'mundane' and 'transcendental', 'worldly' and 'divine', 'appearance' and 'reality', 'becoming' and 'Being' conjoined with the understanding that all that is good, meaningful, worthy, and real has its source and origin in that which somehow transcends this ordinary world and life, had, according to Nietzsche, been undermined through the pursuit of one of the West's highest values: truth. Truth has won but the consequence is that '*the highest values devaluate them-*

[1] In an essay entitled 'On Moods', the 18-year-old Nietzsche wrote: 'Conflict is the soul's staple diet, and it knows how to extract enough sweetness and nourishment from it.' Quoted in Hayman (1980), 54. See also Hollingdale (1973), ch. 4.

selves'.[2] The source of truth, the 'real world', has been negated by truth. What, then, is the status of that world previously judged to be an 'appearance'? Nietzsche replies:

We have abolished the real world: what world is left? The apparent world perhaps? . . . But no! *with the real world we have also abolished the apparent world!* (TI iv)

The 'apparent' world is the only one: the 'real' world has only been *lyingly added* . . . (TI iii. 2)

What we are therefore left with is simply 'the world' or, more correctly, the world and life as encountered and interpreted by its own latest prodigy, man. And when the man Nietzsche contemplates life and the world he eventually concludes that it is 'the will to power which is the will of life'.[3] And since it is life as he sees and understands it that is to be the ground upon which any new vision of existence is to be created and upon which any future values are to be built, it follows that 'power' is Nietzsche's criterion of evaluation: the greater quantum of power a thing or person manifests, the greater value it or they possess. And it also follows that any attempt to re-evaluate and reinterpret human institutions such as religion, science, philosophy, politics, and the ideologies they give rise to, as well as the individuals who create them and express themselves within them, will also be in terms of power. As Nietzsche himself puts it: 'What is the objective measure of value? Solely the quantum of enhanced and organized power'.[4] And even 'valuation itself is only this will to power'.[5] It is through this notion that the world and life once again become 'intelligible':

The world seen from within, the world described according to its 'intelligible character'—it would be 'will to power' and nothing else. (BGE 36)

Just as Nietzsche's early mentor Schopenhauer had 'filled in' Kant's noumenal 'thing-in-itself' with *Wille*, Nietzsche replaces Schopenhauer's *Wille* with his will to power and interprets Schopenhauer's goal of 'the denial of the will to live' as merely a rather decadent expression of the will to power, what Nietzsche calls the '"last will" of man, his *will to nothingness*'.[6] However, despite the assertiveness of his statements, Nietzsche, unlike Schopenhauer, never considered his notion of the world as will to

[2] WP 2. [3] GS 349. [4] WP 674. [5] WP 675.
[6] GM iii. 14. See also GM iii. 1 and 28.

power to be an absolute metaphysical truth, but a practical working hypothesis[7] derived from his study of life both in its subjective aspect, his 'psychological observations', and in its objective aspect, his readings in the realm of the natural sciences.

The most succinct expression of this hypothesis unifying both the subjective and objective aspects of existence under the single principle of will to power, is found in *Beyond Good and Evil.* Nietzsche states his premiss:

Granted that nothing is 'given' as real except our world of desires and passions, that we can rise or sink to no other 'reality' than the reality of our drives . . . is it not permitted to make the experiment and ask the question whether this which is given does not *suffice* for an understanding even of the so-called mechanical (or 'material') world? I do not mean as a deception, an 'appearance', an 'idea' (in the Berkeleyan and Schopenhaueran sense), but as possessing the same degree of reality as our emotions themselves—as a more primitive form of the world of emotions in which everything still lies locked in mighty unity and then branches out and develops in the organic process . . . as a kind of instinctual life . . . as an *antecedent form* of life? (BGE 36)[8]

What Nietzsche is saying is that our unmediated and direct reality is our 'subjective' experience, and the primary events that constitute that experience are our various drives, emotions, and passions. They are the 'given' and, as Nietzsche explains elsewhere,[9] they are also the primary forces that give form to and construct our perceptions, relations, and understanding of the world as object. On the premiss of this given, Nietzsche then makes his 'experiment' by taking a further hypothetical step: if the only world we have direct access to is this given, it follows that any attempt to understand the objective world of nature will be an act of this given. As Nietzsche puts it elsewhere, we can only understand nature in our own image[10] by 'employ[ing] man as an analogy to this end'.[11] After all,

[7] BGE 36.

[8] Nietzsche does not, on the whole, distinguish between 'affect' (Affekt), 'desire' (Begier), 'passion' (Leidenschaft), 'drive' (Trieb), 'instinct' (Instinkt), and 'emotion' (Gefühl). On the whole, I will use the term 'affect' as a synonym for them all, as is Nietzsche's tendency.

[9] e.g. see D 119.

[10] GS 112.

[11] WP 619. As Nietzsche comments in PTG 11, 'man imagines the existence of other things by analogy with his own existence, in other words anthropomorphically'.

what other 'reality' do we have such privileged access to that could function as a basis for such an understanding of nature, that could claim to be more 'real'? And, as Nietzsche's psychological observations led him to conclude that the fundamental principle governing our 'inner life' is the will to power, on the hypothesis that we can only understand the natural world in our own image, it follows that: 'The world seen from within, the world described and defined according to its "intelligible character"—it would be "will to power" and nothing else'.[12] This is Nietzsche's proffered and, we must remember, hypothetical, replacement for the now unbelievable Christian world-view.

But what were Nietzsche's reasons for wanting to extend his notion of the will to power from the exclusively human arena to one which encompasses existence in general, given that his given was the 'world of desires and passions'? My answer is that Nietzsche, as the title of Copleston's book has it, was primarily a 'Philosopher of Culture', and within the contemporary culture of his time the prestige of the natural sciences was a growing influence in any discourse on man and the world.[13] The natural sciences were beginning to present an atheological world-picture within which man's supposed divine ancestry was being relegated to mere poetic fiction—Nietzsche, in his hyperbolic style, would call it a lie. As a philologist, Nietzsche had first-hand experience of the destructive effect the sciences were having: 'the philologists, . . . are the destroyers of every faith that rests on books'.[14] However, his scientific interests and knowledge extended far beyond the confines of

[12] BGE 36. Interestingly enough, Nietzsche's 'rejected' mentor Schopenhauer says something along the same lines: 'The double knowledge which we have of the nature and action of our own body, and which is given in two completely different ways, [i.e. as the subjective and objective aspects of our bodily experience] has now been clearly brought out. Accordingly, we shall use it further as a key to the inner being of every phenomenon in nature. We shall judge all objects which are not our body . . . *according to the analogy of this body* [*italics mine*]. We shall therefore assume that as, on the one hand, they are representation, just like our body, and are in this respect homogeneous with it, so on the other hand, if we set aside their existence as the subject's representation, what remains over must be, according to its inner nature, the same as what in ourselves we call *will*. For what other kind of existence or reality could we attribute to the rest of the material world?' (1969: i. 104–5).

[13] Kant e.g. included in his philosophical writings *The Metaphysical Foundations of Natural Science*.

[14] GS 358.

philology and included physics, chemistry, physiology, and anthropology.[15] Thus any philosophy of man that Nietzsche proposed had, if it were not to be undermined by science, to be actually underpinned by it. He envisages such sciences becoming 'the foundation-stones of new ideals',[16] which 'prepare the way for the future task of the philosophers'.[17] Science in itself, however, cannot create values but actually requires 'a value creating power, in the *service* of which it could *believe* in itself'.[18] To this end scientists are to become the servants of value creating philosophers like Nietzsche himself.[19] The contrary state of affairs, in which science becomes the dominant force in creating new ideals could, in Nietzsche's view, be disastrous for man. As he puts it in an earlier work:

> Is life to dominate knowledge and science, or is knowledge to dominate life? Which of these two forces is the higher and more decisive? There can be no doubt: life is the higher, the dominating force, for knowledge which annihilated life would have annihilated itself with it. (UH 10)[20]

Since it is his understanding of human nature that is the prime analogate in his attempt to understand the natural world, any scientific theory that could act as a foundation-stone and serve his axiology would have to reflect his hypothesis of the world as will to power, or at least be susceptible to modification in serving that hypothesis. Yet in his scientific reading he could not but conclude that the dominating *Weltanschauung* was a mechanistic one, a view that was antithetical to his own view of human nature. And as it is his view that whatever we understand we do so only in our own image, it follows from it that the prevailing view of the world of nature as a mechanism must reflect, on the part of those who put forward and support such mechanistic theories, an assumed if not conscious view of human nature. To reduce human nature or, by implication, life, to a mere mechanism is, for Nietzsche, merely symptomatic of a rather sickly and decadent form of life.[21] One influential scientist who, for Nietzsche, symbolized this view and whose evolutionary theories he considered to be a danger to man-

[15] See list of scientific books read by Nietzsche in Middleton (1969), 64 n. 22.
[16] D 453.
[17] GM i. 17.
[18] GM iii. 25.
[19] BGE 211.
[20] We saw earlier how the pursuit of truth can lead to nihilism.
[21] GS, Preface, 2.

kind's future, was Charles Darwin. To counteract Darwin and what he symbolized Nietzsche had to find an antithesis to the mechanistic view of nature. This he found in the ideas of the eighteenth-century Jesuit scientist R. J. Boscovitch, whose view of nature was not mechanistic, but dynamic. In Boscovitch Nietzsche found his 'servant'; in Boscovitch's dynamic theory of nature he uncovered his 'foundation-stone'. But, before I examine Nietzsche's response to mechanistic materialism and his 'cure' for it—Boscovitch—we must return to the primary analogate, 'our world of desires and passions', and see how Nietzsche's understanding of human nature as will to power was influenced by, and probably derived from, the ancient Greeks.

6.1. THE GREEK PARADIGM

Throughout the whole history of Western culture there has only ever been a single people who, in terms of Nietzsche's view of culture, achieved a perfect form of it: the Greeks,[22] the peak of whose culture was during the sixth and fifth centuries BCE.[23] They have been 'the only people of genius in world history'[24] because they created so many great individual human beings,[25] beings who 'shine in the radiance of a higher humanity'.[26] The reason Greek culture threw up so many great individuals was, for Nietzsche, to be found in its attitude towards and creative response to the given of *Beyond Good and Evil*, 36: 'our world of desires and passions'. Succinctly stated, the Greeks Nietzsche so admired did not alienate man from nature, they did not seek to explain what is best and most worthy in man by appealing to some higher non-natural source, but saw what greatness individuals had achieved as a continuation of nature, as having its roots solely in the natural world in 'our world of desires and passions':

> the 'natural' qualities and the properly called 'human' ones have grown up inseparably together. Man in his highest and noblest capacities is Nature

[22] WC 76. Here Nietzsche means 'the younger Greece' from Homer to Socrates (PTG 2). In SW 199 he says: 'What I seek in history are not happy ages, but those which offer a favourable soil for the *production* of genius. This is what I find in the times before the Persian wars [i.e. before 449 BCE]. One cannot become too well acquainted with this period.'

[23] HAH 68. [24] WC 65. [25] WC 14. [26] WC 76.

and bears in himself her awful twofold character. His abilities generally considered dreadful and inhuman are perhaps indeed the fertile soil, out of which alone can grow forth all humanity in emotions, actions and works. (HC, p. 51)

The Greeks accepted that human nature contains some dreadful and inhuman forces, but their genius, according to Nietzsche, was in their methods of dealing with them. The paradigmatic method is found in the *Works and Days* of the eighth-century poet Hesiod:

Strife is no only child. Upon the earth
Two Strifes exist; the one is praised by those
Who come to know her, and the other blamed.
Their natures differ; for the cruel one
Makes battles thrive, and war; she wins no love
But men are forced, by the immortal's will,
To pay the grievous goddess due respect.
The other, first born-child of blackest Night
Was set by Zeus, who lives on high,
Set in the roots of earth, an aid to men.
She urges even lazy men to work;
A man grows eager, seeing another rich
From ploughing, planting, ordering his house;
So neighbour vies with neighbour in the rush
For wealth: this Strife is good for mortal men—
Potter hates potter, carpenters compete,
And beggar strives with beggar, bard with bard.[27]

Hesiod sees two *Eris*-goddesses upon the earth, or two forms of Strife, a cruel one who 'makes battles thrive, and war', and the other 'first-born child of blackest Night' who 'is good for mortal men' because, through envy, she puts 'even lazy men to work'. Thus 'potter hates potter, carpenters compete, | And beggar strives with beggar, bard with bard'. Nietzsche comments that 'this is one

[27] HC 54–5; Translation taken from Hesiod (1973) in preference to Mügge's translation of Nietzsche's translation. Kant, however, took up this theme long before Nietzsche. In his essay *Idea for a Universal History with a Cosmopolitan Purpose*, Kant says that 'Nature should . . . be thanked for fostering social incompatibility, envious competitive vanity, and insatiable desires for possession or even power. Without these desires, all man's excellent natural capacities would never be aroused to develop . . . the sources of the very unsociableness and continual resistance which cause so many evils, at the same time encourage man towards new exertions of his powers and thus towards further development of his natural capacities' (1971: 44). This is Kant's attempt at theodicy, as he goes on to say all this seems 'to indicate the design of a wise creator'.

of the most noteworthy Hellenic thoughts and worthy to be impressed on the newcomer immediately at the entrance-gate of Greek ethics'.[28] It is one of the most noteworthy because, first, it cautions those taking up Hellenic studies to leave behind them at the 'entrance-gate' their own Christian notion of ethics if they wish to comprehend the Greeks; and, secondly and more importantly, it shows that the natural passions of 'jealousy, spite, envy, [can incite] men to activity but not the action of war to the knife but to the action of *contest* ... [making of the "good" *Eris*] ... a *beneficent* deity'.[29] As Nietzsche goes on to comment: 'What a gulf of ethical judgement [lies] between us and him'.[30] The Greeks did not judge envy, love, ambition, and other human passions and desires as being either moral or immoral in themselves: they were simply non-moral and natural. But they could be used by men, as in Hesiod's example, either destructively by becoming dreadful and inhuman—the 'bad' *Eris*—or creatively by means of the 'good' *Eris*, which, through the notion of 'contest' or *agon*, becomes the pursuit of 'excellence' or *aretē*. Even in the realm of art, 'the Greek knows the artist *only as engaged in a personal fight*':[31]

Artists ambition'.—The Greek artists, the tragedians for example, poetized in order to conquer; their whole art cannot be thought of apart from contest: Hesiod's good *Eris*, ambition, gave their genius its wings. (HAH 170)

And even

Plato's dialogues [are] for the most part the result of a contest with the art of the orators, the sophists, and the dramatists of his time, invented for the purpose of enabling him to say in the end: 'Look, I too can do what my great rivals can do; indeed I can do it better than they. No Protagoras has invented myths as beautiful as mine; no dramatist such a vivid and captivating whole as my *Symposium*; no orator has written orations like those in my *Gorgias*—and now I repudiate all this entirely and condemn all imitative art. Only the contest made me a poet, a sophist, an orator'. (HC. Translation from VPN pp. 37–8)

28 HC, 54. 29 HC, 55. 30 HC, 55

31 HC. Translation from VPN, p. 37. It is important to realize that 'contest' or *agon* refers only to the 'good' *Eris*, not the 'bad' *Eris*. When Nietzsche contemplates Greek life without the contest, he comments: 'If on the other hand we remove the contest from Greek life, then we look at once into the pre-Homeric abyss of horrible savagery, hatred, and pleasure in destruction' (HC, p. 60). Given that he thinks that, as an eventual outcome of nihilism, we might head towards such an end, one can see how important this Greek model was in his search for an answer to nihilism.

Here is the primary source of Nietzsche's answer to nihilism. Nihilism unfolds as the truth dawns that humanity's esteemed values and special place in the cosmos are nothing other than human inventions. In reality there is no ontological separation between man and nature—man is *homo natura*; there is no other world than the natural one—the natural world is reality. But in the two-world system the natural world is judged to be antithetical to the 'good' and man's natural desires and passions, being of the natural order, are determined to be 'evil'. Therefore, if we negate the 'good', we will remove the very means by which the 'evil' is kept in check, our morality. When this morality breaks down, which Nietzsche thinks it inevitably will, and there is no 'new morality' to replace it, all we will be left with is the fearful prospect of the brutal world of the *bellum omnium contra omnes* completely overrunning what civilization and culture mankind has so far achieved, without any prospect of a meaningful alternative. We will simply return to a completely animal-like existence. But, following Hesiod and the Greek model, there need not be a *bellum omnium contra omnes* as the outcome of this nihilism. There is not only the bad *Eris* but also the good *Eris* which, manifesting as *agon*, reveals to Nietzsche the way out of nihilism whilst 'remaining true to the earth': the 'sublimation' (*Sublimierung*) of the drives and passions of *homo natura* towards the creation of a new type of man—the *Übermensch*.[32] For the latter to come about, however, the *agon* must shift from being between individuals to one between the vying drives and passions within the individual, what Nietzsche calls 'self-overcoming' (*Selbstüberwindung*). Just like *Eris*, the will to power has the potential for both good and bad. Uncontrolled and misdirected it can and does lead to unmitigated cruelty, barbarism, and tyranny. Yet when controlled and directed intelligently, it helped create, through certain rare individuals, the great flowering of Hellenic culture. Through 'self-overcoming', which we can say is the will to power become internalized, Nietzsche wants to unfold the as-yet-unrealized creative potential of the will to power even further, and

[32] Z, Prologue, 3. To 'remain true to the earth' means not to 'believe those who speak to you of superterrestial hopes . . . Once blasphemy against God was the greatest blasphemy, but God died, and thereupon the blasphemers died too. To blaspheme the earth is now the most dreadful offence' because the earth now has a new meaning: 'The *Übermensch* is the meaning of the earth'. One could add that to conclude that because 'God is dead' life no longer has any meaning or purpose would be, in Nietzsche's eyes, an even more 'dreadful offence'.

create a new level of humankind, the *Übermensch*. Therefore, this path of self-overcoming not only constitutes Nietzsche's answer to nihilism, but is also his replacement for the old, displaced religious and spiritual quest. Life can now have a new meaning and purpose, a new 'morality': to continually re-create oneself by way of a path of self-overcoming. And it was the ancient Greeks who supplied Nietzsche with his basic paradigm.

This paradigm, although it is complete in itself, represents the will to power only in its subjective aspect, the will to power derived from the given—'our world of desires and passions'. But, as we saw earlier, Nietzsche proposed that, as an experiment, we could extend this paradigm from its subjective domain to the whole world *per se*. The reason for this, as I have suggested, is that for any new *Weltanschauung* to be taken seriously in the post-God era, it would have to be underpinned by the new 'religion' of science. Yet the dominant scientific view was mechanistic materialism, a view that was antithetical to Nietzsche's new paradigm of the world as will to power. The individual who symbolizes, for Nietzsche, many of the inherent dangers that this scientific view has for mankind's future welfare, is Charles Darwin. Therefore, before we go on to Nietzsche's search for an alternative scientific view of the world amenable to his proposed view of the world as will to power, I will take a Darwinian 'interlude' so as to see just what it was that Nietzsche found so abhorrent in the dominant scientific *Weltanschauung*.

6.2. NIETZSCHE AND DARWIN

As Kaufmann correctly claims, Nietzsche was 'aroused from his dogmatic slumber by Darwin, much as Kant was a century earlier by Hume'.[33] Nietzsche's direct references to Darwin extend throughout both his published and unpublished writings (Mostert lists fifty-two in the as then incomplete Colli and Montinari edition of Nietzsche's complete works), from his attack on David Strauss for seeing Darwin as 'one of the greatest benefactors of mankind',[34] to his own denial that his notion of the *Übermensch* was Darwinist: 'scholarly oxen have suspected me of Darwinism'.[35] Nietzsche saw

[33] Kaufmann (1974), p. xiii. NB: Mostert (1979) disagrees.
[34] DS 7. [35] EH iii. 1.

Darwin and Darwinism, and the sciences in general, as a nihilistic threat to Western Culture, and a much more dangerous one than any system of metaphysics could ever be: they were empirically based; they had 'facts' as their premisses; and it is these facts that will gradually make us 'deaf to the siren songs of old metaphysical bird-catchers who have all too long been piping to [man] "you are more! you are higher! you are of a different origin!"'.[36] The sciences, and in particular Darwin and Darwinism, are a danger not simply because of their 'facts' which, on the whole, Nietzsche accepts,[37] but because of what he sees as their baseless optimism, an optimism that goes back to Socrates: 'Socrates is the prototype of the theoretical optimist who, with his faith that the nature of things can be fathomed, ascribes to knowledge and insight the power of a panacea'.[38] Scientists like Darwin are still unwittingly working within the Christo-Platonic framework whilst the very products of their labour actually undermine that very framework:

> It is still a *metaphysical faith* that underlies our faith in science—and we men of knowledge of today, we godless men and anti-metaphysicians, we, too, still derive *our* flame from the fire ignited by a faith millennia old, the Christian faith, which was also Plato's, that God is truth, that truth is *divine*. (GM iii. 24)

This 'baseless optimism' is, according to Nietzsche, derived from an unconscious and unquestioned assumption rooted in the 'faith millennia old': that the pursuit of truth will lead to the 'divine', that the discovery of the 'truth' is now the ultimate panacea. When science finally reveals the truth of the world, we shall then enter 'heaven', even though that 'heaven' is here on earth. Darwin, however, is still listening to the dying echoes of the 'siren songs of the old metaphysical bird-catchers' as the penultimate paragraph of his *On the Origin of Species* shows:

> As all the living forms of life are the lineal descendants of those which lived long before the Silurian epoch, we may feel certain that the ordinary succession by generation has never once been broken, and that no cataclysm has desolated the whole world. Hence we may look with some confidence to a secure future of equally inappreciable length. And as natural selection works solely by and for the good of each being, all corporeal and mental endowments *will tend to progress towards perfection.* [*Emphasis mine*][39]

[36] BGE 230. [37] See UH 9. [38] BT i. 15. [39] Darwin (1975), 489.

Perhaps this paragraph exemplifies what Nietzsche has in mind when he wonders: 'to what extent the fateful belief in divine providence . . . still exists . . . to what extent Christian presuppositions and interpretations still live on under the formulas "nature", "progress", "perfectibility", "Darwinism" '.[40] In the above passage, Darwin does seem to exhibit an 'absurd trust in the course of things',[41] which the facts of his theory cannot back up: there are no 'facts' from which one could infer any 'progress towards perfection'. Scientists like Darwin, though they may no longer believe in God, do not understand the consequences of their work and are, in Nietzsche's eyes, dangerously irresponsible. They act 'as if what happens were no responsibility of ours' because they are still under the influence, albeit unconsciously, of this 'fateful belief in divine dispensation'.[42] As Nietzsche rather dramatically puts it in the *Gay Science*: 'Whither is God? . . . I will tell you. *We have killed him*—you and I'. Thus speaks the madman to those in the market place; but they just 'stared at him in astonishment'. He concludes:

> I have come too early . . . my time is not yet. This tremendous event is still on its way, still wandering; it has not yet reached the ears of men. Lightning and thunder require time; the light of the stars requires time; deeds, though done, still require time to be seen and heard. This deed is still more distant from them than the most distant stars—*and yet they have done it themselves*. (GS 125)

When the deeds are finally seen and heard their nihilistic consequences will have dawned, and then it might be too late—so Nietzsche thinks. Darwin's theory of natural selection working upon random variations is such a deed, but Darwin, like other scientists, does not fully grasp the consequences of his own deeds.[43]

Even modern writers do not seem to grasp this point. C. U. P. Smith writes, of this passage of Darwin's: 'this [statement of

[40] WP 243. [41] WP 243. [42] WP 243.

[43] From Darwin's autobiography, it is quite clear that Darwin was not so naïve: he eventually lost his Christian faith and ended up an agnostic as a direct result of his scientific investigations. But in a sense this goes toward proof that Nietzsche was at least partly correct: Darwin's theory gives no evidence of any divine dispensation at work in nature. And when the real consequences are perceived there will be little room for blind optimism regarding man's future. Indeed, quite the opposite. Perhaps some who see the consequences will be driven to join 'the suicides' in Robert Louis Stevenson's story *The Suicide Club*, where one member, on being asked why he joined the club, said that he had been induced to believe in Mr Darwin: ' "I could not bear" said this remarkable suicide, "to be descended from an ape" ' (Harmondsworth, 1964), 22.

Darwin's] could easily be read by the unwary as a support for the idea of progression up the *scala naturae*'.[44] And Nietzsche, being one of the unwary, 'never saw that Darwin had broken free from this time-honoured philosophy,[45] [therefore . . . Nietzsche's] understanding of evolution remained pre-Darwinian'.[46] Yet Darwin himself says:

> The inhabitants of each successive period in the world's history have beaten their predecessors in the race for life, and are, in so far, *higher in the scale of nature.* [*Emphasis mine*][47]

It does seem, therefore, very easy to become one of Smith's unwary. All one has to do is take Darwin at his word. However, it seems to me that it is rather Smith, himself, who is here one of the unwary.[48] Yet the source of this ambiguity in Darwin's *Origins* is, in all probability, Darwin's own mind. Regarding the related topic of 'design', Darwin says in a letter to Asa Gray before becoming an agnostic:

> I am conscious that I am in an utterly hopeless muddle. I cannot think that the world, as we see it, is the result of chance; and yet I cannot look at each separate thing as the result of design.[49]

If there is design, then there will be a *scala naturae*. If it is all the result of chance, then there can be none.

Gillespie relates that 'Darwin's relationship to the idea of intelligent design was constantly ambivalent',[50] and that 'Design was a nagging doubt that never left Darwin's mind'.[51]

Nietzsche would see this as an excellent example: Darwin has, in his theory, effectively killed off any notion of divine providence or design; yet he cannot fully accept the conclusions of his own findings because he is still conditioned—albeit unconsciously—by what he has imbibed from his Christian background in the form of uncritically held beliefs and hopes. Take away those beliefs and

[44] (1987); 70.

[45] i.e. the Great Chain Of Being, a 'metaphor for the order, unity, and the completeness of the created world, thought of as a chain extending to include all the possibilities of existence, from God to the tiniest particle of inanimate matter' (Flew 1983: 60).

[46] Smith (1987), 71.

[47] Darwin (1975), 345.

[48] Darwin's *Origins* went through six editions in his lifetime; therefore, if he had any doubts concerning these statements he had plenty of opportunities to recant them. That he did not must say something. This can only give weight to Nietzsche's point.

[49] Quoted in Gillespie (1979), 87. [50] Ibid. 86. [51] Ibid. 88.

hopes and what we are left with from the standpoint of man's previous values is what appears to be a neutral, valueless cosmos without any inherent meaning or purpose. For Nietzsche, this will be the inevitable result of the scientific pursuit of truth: we will eventually come to understand that these 'optimistic' beliefs are no more than man-made fictions. When this understanding finally dawns, because most, if not all, will be unable to comprehend what has actually happened, they will merely acquiesce to what seems to be left once the optimistic beliefs have been removed, i.e. an apparently meaningless and mechanistic cosmos. And such a *Weltanschauung* can only lead to one end: a *bellum omnium contra omnes*.[52] Man will be swamped by nihilistic creeds. Therefore, when Darwin's doctrine

> of the lack of any cardinal distinction between man and animal—doctrines which I consider true but deadly—are thrust upon the people for another generation . . . no one should be surprised if the people perishes of petty egoism, ossification and greed, falls apart and ceases to be a people; in its place systems of individualist egoism, brotherhoods for rapacious exploitation of non-brothers . . . may perhaps appear in the arena of the future. (UH 9)

Whether Nietzsche actually read any of Darwin's books is difficult to determine. Mostert relates that, 'In the debate on Darwinism, Nietzsche actually remained an outsider. Only Darwin's essay *Biographical Sketch of an Infant* (1877) had evidently been read by him (cf. his letter to Paul Reé, 3–4 August, 1877). There seems to be no further evidence that Nietzsche ever read any of Darwin's works'.[53] However, one book that was held in much esteem by the young Nietzsche was Lange's *The History of Materialism*, which contains the chapter 'Darwin and Teleology'. Stack tells us that 'Lange saw clearly the revolutionary implications of Darwin's theory of evolution by means of natural selection and saw that it dealt a deathblow to any Platonic, Aristotelian or Christian belief in a teleology in nature'.[54] But whether Nietzsche actually read Darwin or not, or fully understood Darwin's theory of Natural Selection, or even whether he is being 'fair' to the man Darwin,[55] his overall thesis about the eventual effects that Darwinism will produce remains: Darwin and Darwinism are perhaps the main contributors to that

[52] DS 7. [53] (1979), 239. [54] (1983*a*), 156.

[55] Like Nietzsche's 'Socrates', his 'Darwin' is not so much Darwin the man, as a symbol for certain views and unconscious assumptions that Nietzsche sees are all too common among the scientific community.

'truth' which undermines the cultural values of the West for the reasons I have outlined.

6.2.1. *Nietzsche's Response to Darwin*

Nietzsche accepts the general conclusion of Darwin's theory, that man's ancestor is the ape:

> Formerly one sought the feeling of grandeur of man by pointing to his divine *origin*: this has now become a forbidden way, for at its portal stands the ape, together with other gruesome beasts, grinning knowingly as if to say: no further in this direction! (D 49)

This represents one of those truths, perhaps the truth, whose consequences are nihilistic: they are the deeds that 'kill God' and thereby eventually destroy our cultural and religious values. And man, or at least the cultured individual, seeing his values and his whole *Weltanschauung* gradually dissolving before his eyes, will perhaps come to see himself as no more than a more complex but unhappy ape. But there is a gulf between deed and the realization of its consequence. In the mean time: 'One therefore now tries the opposite direction: the way mankind is *going* shall serve as proof of his grandeur and kinship with God. Alas this, too, is vain!'[56] Consequently, any optimistic response to Darwin's theory in the sense of looking to man's guaranteed progress up the *scala naturae* is, according to Nietzsche, a grand delusion. So what future, if any, could we look forward to given this theory? What kind of values could it create, if any? And, more importantly, what kind of being does Darwin's theory favour, which would give us a pointer to the way mankind might actually go? These were the areas Nietzsche considered important and were the reasons why I consider Kaufmann's claim that Darwin awoke him 'from his dogmatic slumber'[57] is correct.

6.2.2. *The Future*

Regarding mankind's future, Nietzsche cannot see how mankind, as a species, can now differ from any other species in not being superseded:

[56] D 49. [57] (1974), p. xiii.

The becoming drags the has-been along behind it: why should an exception to this eternal spectacle be made on behalf of some little star or for any little species upon it! Away with such sentimentalities! (D 49)

And, although Nietzsche does not spell it out, it seems to me to follow that, if we take Darwin's theory seriously, it is entirely conceivable that we shall be superseded by some better adapted species to whom we shall be the apes: 'What is the ape to men? A laughing-stock or a painful embarrassment? And just so shall man be to the *Übermensch*: a laughing-stock or a painful embarrassment'.[58] But with Darwin's theory this possible future species will not, according to Nietzsche, be *Übermenschen*, but quite the opposite. And it may be that this future species, if they inherit some of our traits, may decide to terminate our species just as we have done to some others. Or, again, inheriting from us our taste for good meat, they may decide on gastronomic grounds to farm us as fodder for their kitchens; or use us as we use other species for scientific experiments as we will be nearest to them in the *scala naturae*. Of course, all this is highly improbable: if any new and 'favourable' mutation did emerge within our species, given the nature of our species, it would probably meet with various fates none of which would be likely to guarantee the propagation of its advantage. Our species can be extremely jealous! Also, remaining within our own species, there can be no unconditional guarantee for our future. Today we know only too well that a global nuclear war and its after-effects may terminate our species—but not all species: perhaps the cockroach or the ant would survive. And, in Darwin's terms, they would of necessity be the 'fittest' and, in the evaluative language Darwin sometimes slips into, the 'higher' species.[59] We would become just another extinct species for some possible future palaeontologist to puzzle over. Or, again, what if we were to be 'invaded' by some of Fred Hoyle's 'space-bugs' which simply wiped us all out. As Flew remarks in his *Evolutionary Ethics*:

An individual, . . . or a species can perfectly well have many splendid corporeal and mental endowments without this ensuring that it has what is in fact needed for survival: men who are wretched specimens, both mentally and physically, may—and all too often do—kill superb animals; and the

[58] Z, Prologue, 3.

[59] Darwin, however, does admit that some of the 'fittest' would 'be abhorrent to our ideas of fitness' (1975: 437).

genius has frequently been laid low by the activities of unicellular creatures having no wits at all.[60]

Some of the examples I have given may not be probable, and I am being rather unfair to Darwin, but they are possible and illustrate that there are no a priori reasons for us to assume any guaranteed ascent up the Great Chain of Being towards some state of perfection. Indeed, there are no reasons even to assume our continuation as a species. The human species, like any other, is contingent. Given certain natural happenings, what has happened to many other species may happen to us. As we know only too well today, our environment, which is that which we adapt to (or which 'selects'), is under no obligation to remain favourable to us. One does not have to indulge in science fiction to see the unsoundness of that optimism expressed by Darwin in the penultimate paragraph of his *Origin*.

6.2.3. *The Values*

The main thrust of Nietzsche's attack on Darwin and Darwinism, however, is an axiological one: inherent in Darwin's theory is the notion that as survival is what matters, what survives is therefore best. But what kind of values can be derived from this fact? All that can be derived from this is that those variations who procure enough to eat without too much hardship and who procreate the most, will tend to survive. Those who do not will eventually die out. But while this may account for the evolution of barnacles and giraffes and for the emergence of early man, it can hardly give us guiding values or even hope for the continuation of what Nietzsche would consider a truly human life. All it can point to concerns our 'animal' nature. Even the values and pursuits of modern 'developed' countries with their sophisticated technology designed to give us security and happiness, are no more than a mere refinement of our animal nature. As Nietzsche comments:

Yet let us reflect: where does the animal cease, where does man begin? . . . As long as anyone desires life as he desires happiness he has not yet raised his eyes above the horizon of the animal, for he only desires more consciously what the animal seeks through blind impulse. But that is

[60] (1967), 19.

what we all do for the greater part of our lives: usually we fail to emerge out of animality. (SE 5)

Darwin's theory, divested of its unsound optimism, will do little to help us emerge out of animality but will, in fact, when its consequences are understood, help undo the few steps man has taken in the direction of humanity, as Nietzsche sees it. Man has, according to Nietzsche, achieved a degree of true humanity, but, unfortunately, it was a step founded upon an error:

Without the errors that repose in the assumptions of morality man would have remained animal. As it is, he has taken himself for something higher and imposed sterner laws upon himself. (HAH 40)

Through imposing sterner laws upon himself man has, in the process, become more than animal. (However, as animals do not impose laws upon themselves, man must be in some sense distinct from the animals in order to impose laws upon himself!) He has achieved a degree of civilization and distanced himself from the *bellum omnium contra omnes*—at least in some places and for varying periods. However, as this was achieved through an 'error', which is here the belief in the divine origin of morality and human nature, and Darwin's theory shows this to be an 'error', then if we simply remove the error without a means of creating a new non-erroneous morality and view of man as 'humanity' as a replacement, 'we [will] also remove [what] humanity, humaneness, and "human dignity"' we have achieved.[61] Therefore it may come to pass 'that man has emerged from the ape and will return to the ape'.[62] But: 'precisely because we are able to visualize this prospect we are perhaps in a position to prevent it from occurring'.[63] This, I think, is the crux of Nietzsche's 'anti-Darwinism': it seems that Nietzsche himself is the only one who is able 'to visualize this prospect' and therefore 'prevent it from occurring' by creating a new set of values. And he sees that the acceptance of Darwinism can only undo what little humanity, humaneness, and human dignity we have achieved, undo what little distance we have achieved from our animality. This is because the only values that Darwinism can provide concern the survival and propagation of one's group, whether tribal or national, over and against other groups. And this,

[61] GS 115. [62] HAH 247. [63] HAH 247.

for Nietzsche, is tantamount to nihilism: our only values will be expressive of our 'animality', not our 'humanity'. The defining characteristic of our 'humanity', for Nietzsche, is not some 'will to survive' or concern about the biological propagation and survival of the human species. Even the pursuit of happiness as some ultimate panacea is unacceptable to Nietzsche: 'Evolution does not have happiness in view, but evolution and nothing else'.[64] In Nietzsche's view, as life is 'that *which must overcome itself again and again*',[65] if the evolution of humankind is to continue individuals must will perfection through a process of what he calls 'self-overcoming' (*Selbstüberwindung*). This goal must supersede all else. Nietzsche does not want 'Darwinism as philosophy'[66] as rather than encourage the ideal of an evolution towards perfection, it will counteract such an ideal.

6.2.4. *What Kind of Being?*

Nietzsche, being 'able to visualize this prospect', turns towards human history and culture to find a solution to it, so as to 'prevent it from occurring'. The 'goal of all culture', as Nietzsche would like to have it, is 'the procreation of genius',[67] and those whom he sees as geniuses 'are those true *men, those who are no longer animal, the philosophers, artists and saints*; nature, which never makes a leap, has made its one leap in creating them'.[68] It is, therefore, 'the fundamental idea of culture . . . *to promote the production of [these] . . . and thereby to work at the perfecting of nature*'.[69] Nature, as Nietzsche sees it, gives us a pointer to where the goal of humanity lies: in its rare leaps or, as he elsewhere calls them, 'lucky hits',[70] in defiance of Darwin's *natura non facit saltum*. His idea of culture

[64] D 108. [65] Z ii. 12. [66] WP 422. [67] SE 3.

[68] SE 5. But at WS 198, he quotes with approval: 'the fundamental principle that nature never makes a leap'.

[69] SE 5.

[70] This notion of 'lucky hits/strokes' is taken from Lange. Lange used the term *glücklicher Zufall* or 'lucky accident'. See Stack (1983*a*), 166. This seems to be contradicted by his views on the Greeks of whom, as we saw earlier, he claimed 'created many great human beings' and who 'shine in the light of a higher humanity'. Here it was not a question of lucky hits but of a conscious methodology revolving round the notion of *agon*, a notion Nietzsche himself borrows and uses as the paradigm for his answer to nihilism. Perhaps the lucky hits refer to those who came after the Greeks.

is to move from nature to *nurture*, from lucky hit and 'obscure impulse' to 'conscious willing'.[71]

Anyone who believes in culture is thereby saying: 'I see above me something higher and more human than I am; let everyone help me to attain it, as I will help everyone who knows and suffers as I do: so that at last the man may appear who feels himself perfect and boundless in knowledge and love, perception and power, and who in his completeness is at one with nature, the judge and evaluator of things'. (SE 6)

Nietzsche accepts that this is not everyone's notion of what culture is, and comments: '*how extraordinarily sparse and rare knowledge of this goal is*',[72] and 'how dull and feeble is the effect [nature] . . . achieves with the philosophers and artists! How rarely does it achieve any effect at all!'[73] In other words, the 'obscure impulse', even among what philosophers and artists there have been, is still too obscure and what potential there was, was never fully expressed. Nevertheless, what lucky hits nature has so far thrown up on the stage of human history, may one day

live contemporaneously with one another; thanks to history, which permits such a collaboration, they live as that republic of genius of which Schopenhauer once spoke; one giant calls to another across the desert intervals of time and, undisturbed by the excited chattering dwarfs who creep about beneath them, the exalted spirit-dialogue goes on. (UH 9)

Communication across the desert intervals of time is made possible through the medium of culture. It is there one finds one's 'true educators and formative teachers [who] reveal to you what the true basic material of your being is',[74] bringing to consciousness what was obscure impulse. However, such 'liberators' can only indicate and provide the initial spark of inspiration: 'No one can construct for you the bridge upon which . . . you must cross the stream of life, no one but you yourself alone . . . your educators can be only your liberators'.[75] Therefore, 'Culture is liberation'.[76] What one is liberated from is one's animality and the latest fashionable ideas such as Hegel's 'world-process'[77] and other 'parochial' notions: 'It is

[71] SE 6. [72] SE 6. [73] SE 7.

[74] SE 1. Nietzsche's own use of the ancient Greeks is a perfect example of this, as well as his reading of Schopenhauer.

[75] SE 1.

[76] SE 1. *Bildung*, translated here as 'culture', also means 'education'.

[77] UH 9.

parochial to bind oneself to views which are no longer binding even a couple of hundred miles away. Orient and Occident are chalk-lines drawn before us to fool our timidity'.[78] In other words, it is quite possible for Plato or the Buddha to be one of these educators, whereas some contemporary leading thinker may not be. Culture, as Nietzsche sees it, is not bound by space nor time but only by unique individuals. Therefore any talk of a '*goal of humanity* cannot lie in its end but only *in its highest exemplars*'.[79] And this goal of humanity will not be found outside life or in some other world, but only in life itself.

What I have said so far is, of course, mainly early Nietzsche—Nietzsche still under the influence of the German *Naturphilosophie* and Schopenhauer, tinged with the spirit of classical Greece. Nevertheless he did not waver from his notion of what the aim of culture should be: 'A people is a detour of nature to get to six or seven great men'.[80] And, although the triad of artist, philosopher, and saint did not appear in his later writings (the latter two were mostly deemed to have been against life), they were only replaced by a more distant ideal, the *Übermensch*, a kind of extrapolation from life's 'highest exemplars'—a fuller and more complete expression of what they signify, which the later Nietzsche expressed in terms of power. But the type of being he sees being favoured by Darwin's theory, if it is applied to the human species, is the very opposite of this ideal:

> Supposing . . . that this struggle [for existence] exists—and it does indeed occur—its outcome is the reverse of that desired by the school of Darwin . . . namely, the defeat of the stronger, the more privileged, the fortunate exceptions. Species do *not* grow more perfect: the weaker dominate the strong again and again—the reason being they are the great majority. (TI ix. 14)

Nietzsche sees Darwin's theory, at least as applied to human kind, as a reversal of what he sees as the ideal of humanity, of what constitutes a more perfect and evolved human being. The premiss underlying this reversal is his notion that the 'fundamental instinct of life . . . [is] *the expansion of power* . . . [which] frequently risks and even sacrifices self-preservation'.[81] To be actively and fully alive requires that one be 'continually shedding something that

[78] SE 1. No doubt Nietzsche is referring to Hegel's philosophy of history.
[79] UH 9. [80] BGE 126. [81] GS 349.

wants to die'.[82] Thus any restriction or resistance to further change necessitated by life's urge to grow and expand—which is Nietzsche's view—will be detrimental to life itself. But Darwin's fundamental characteristic of life is the instinct of self-preservation—those who survive in the struggle for life being the more evolved and perfect expressions of their type. Consequently Nietzsche concludes that: 'the wish to preserve oneself is the symptom of a condition of distress'[83] and those motivated by such are, according to his premiss, the 'weak', not the 'strong'. Nietzsche's 'strong'—the 'lucky hits', 'geniuses', etc.—are always singular and rare and embody a fuller expression of his notion of life than those who surround them. They are the '*sovereign individual*[s] . . . liberated . . . from morality of custom' [i.e. the group's *mores*], who are 'autonomous' and 'independent'[84] and who 'aspire after a secret citadel where [they are] . . . *set free* from the crowd, the many, the majority'.[85] For them life itself is art: they are both artist and the work of art, Goethe being Nietzsche's most concrete example of this type. But . . .

> The more similar, more ordinary human beings have had and still have the advantage, the more select, subtle, rare and harder to understand are liable to remain alone, succumb to accidents in their isolation and seldom propagate themselves. (BGE 268)

The 'higher types' or 'lucky strokes of evolution' are therefore more likely to 'perish most easily'. What they are cannot be inherited biologically: 'The brief spell of beauty, of genius, of Caesar, is *sui generis*: such things are not inherited. The *type* is hereditary'. The genius is of 'incomparably greater complexity—a greater sum of co-ordinated elements: so its disintegration is incomparably more likely. The "genius" is the sublimest machine there is—consequently the most fragile'. Hence 'the expression "higher type" means no more than this—perish more easily'.[86] The 'lower types' are, unfortunately, more likely to survive and be the great majority, though not always: Goethe and other exemplars did survive; but the fruits of their labours were not passed on through their loins, but through the medium of culture. And it is such fruits that constitute human progress. Nietzsche therefore sees Darwin's theory as an actual threat to human progress as it does not favour the higher types, but the mediocre majority. It emphasizes 'adaptation', which

[82] GS 26. [83] GS 349. [84] GM ii. 2. [85] BGE 26. [86] WP 684.

for Nietzsche implies conforming to accepted *mores*. In his terms it is therefore a symptom of 'weakness' rather than creativity, which requires 'strength'.[87] In Darwin it is the environment which is 'creative' as it 'selects'. Thus external conditions are the primary determinants, not the individual. When, in the human context where the external conditions are social, the individual will be the product of that society, will become a member of the 'herd'. But whilst Nietzsche sees the importance of a stable society as a precondition for the arising of the 'sovereign individual', if the very goal of that society is simply to preserve itself as it is and even look upon any sovereign individual as a threat to its own ends—even as 'evil'—then life, itself, is under threat from a more stultified form of life, even a decaying form of life.

What Nietzsche wants to avoid is the replacement of the old metaphysical and religious values which hold our culture together and represent our 'humanity', our 'cultural evolution', by new scientific ideologies such as Darwinism: he does not want 'Darwinism as philosophy'.[88] Darwinism may point to the biological truth of man's evolution from the ape, but if it were to become a replacement philosophy of man it could only 'destroy the existing evaluations';[89] it cannot create guiding cultural values. At most, as with the rest of science, it can only help deconstruct our past beliefs by 'dissolving all firmly held belief'.[90] In this way the 'horizon clears', leaving the way for those who can to create new cultural values:

> *All* the sciences have from now on to prepare the way for the future task of the philosophers: this task understood as the solution of the *problem of value*, the determination of the *order of rank among values*. (GM i. 17)

Thus 'mediocre minds'[91] such as Darwin's are useful for a while: they prepare the way by undermining the old values rooted in the 'lie' of the two-world system. But mediocre minds which are well suited to scientific work can only create, in human cultural terms, mediocrity: Darwinism as a replacement philosophy of man will, therefore, favour the herd-type of man, the mediocre man who, being enclosed in his narrower animal-like horizon of survival and

[87] GM ii. 12.

[88] WP 422. A modern equivalent might be 'Dawkinsism'! Richard Dawkins, the author of *The Selfish Gene* (1976), *The Blind Watchmaker* (1986), and other works that could be classified as 'scientism', espouses the kind of philosophy that Nietzsche saw as a danger.

[89] WP 422. [90] SE 4. [91] BGE 253.

biological propagation, is more likely to prosper and multiply: 'The mediocre alone have the prospect of continuing on and propagating themselves—they are the men of the future, the sole survivors'.[92] They are Darwin's 'fittest' and, in any Darwinian philosophy, most 'evolved' type representing humanity at its as-yet most progressive and most valuable. Such, for Nietzsche, is the 'naïveté of English biologists'.[93] In the society of his day this culminates in the looming possibility of 'the *democratic* movement [which] inherits the Christian', where the community or herd is now 'the *saviour*'[94] and which breeds the 'perfect herd animal . . . the pygmy animal of equal rights and equal pretensions'.[95] Darwinism, as a philosophy, can lead to the '*collective degeneration of man*'.[96]

6.3. SEARCH FOR A SCIENTIFIC BASIS FOR THE WILL TO POWER

Nietzsche's response to Darwin was part of his overall attitude to the growth and emerging philosophical influence of nineteenth-century science. From the old Newtonian paradigm of the universe as an 'intricate machine'[97] which 'bespeaks an all-powerful Creator',[98] we now encounter the Laplacian version which maintains the intricate machine minus the all-powerful Creator. Laplace's now-famous retort to Napoleon's question: 'M. Laplace, they tell me you have written this large book on the system of the universe, and have never mentioned its Creator', was 'I had no need of that hypothesis'.[99] For Laplace, 'Nature was . . . a complete mechanical system of inflexible cause-and-effect, governed by exact and absolute laws, so that all future events are inexorably determined'.[100] The fundamental units of this machine were the atoms which, whilst varying in shape, were impenetrable and indivisible substances possessed of extension, density, and, when effected by external forces, mobility. In themselves, however, they were inert, lifeless little lumps. Although these external forces were not completely and accurately known, Laplace assumed that in time they would be. When that day came it would then be possible in

[92] BGE 262. [93] GM i. 17. [94] BGE 202. [95] BGE 203.
[96] BGE 203.
[97] Barbour (1966), 36. [98] Ibid. 37. [99] Ibid. 58. [100] Ibid. 59.

principle, if not in actuality, for someone who had all the relevant information, and who possessed 'superhuman intelligence', to calculate with precision the future course of the universe and, by implication, the future of mankind.

After Laplace, we have a shift from the domain of the science of mechanics to a philosophical view known as 'mechanism' or 'mechanistic materialism'.[101] Darwinism fits in with this view in that evolution is also mechanistic: it has no 'inner' direction or goal; the link between organism and environment is mechanistic; and the evolution and survival of an organism is primarily determined by external forces. Consequently:

> The combination of mechanistic materialism and Darwinian evolution seems to present us with a picture of the world as comprised of powerful forces that manifest no purposes. Man is understood as a complex physio-chemical mechanism that is subject to numerous natural forces and an evolutionary process over which he has no control.[102]

Succinctly stated, what we have is a reductionist view of existence in which all life-processes are reduced to the mere movement of atoms, determined by universal laws. Nietzsche saw such a mechanistic view as nihilistic since it deprives human existence of any possible value and meaning:

> A 'scientific' interpretation of the world . . . might . . . be one of the *most stupid* of all possible interpretations of the world, meaning that it would be one of the poorest in meaning. This thought is intended for the ears and consciences of our mechanists who nowadays like to pass as philosophers and insist that mechanics is the doctrine of the first and last laws on which all existence must be based as on a ground floor. But an essentially mechanical world would be an essentially *meaningless* world. Assuming that one estimated the *value* of a piece of music according to how much of it could be counted, calculated, and expressed in formulas: how absurd would such a 'scientific' estimation of music be! What would one have comprehended, understood, grasped of it? Nothing, really nothing of what is 'music' in it! (GS 373)[103]

[101] Bohm (1984), 36–8.
[102] Stack (1983*a*), 186.
[103] At WP 624, Nietzsche says, 'The calculability of the world, the expressibility of all events in formulas—is this really "comprehension"? How much of a piece of music has been understood when that in it which is calculable and can be reduced to formulas has been reckoned up?'

Just as a scientific analysis of a Mozart symphony cannot evaluate it as a work of art or determine what the human being Mozart might have been trying to express in a symphony, mechanism, as a philosophy of life, is quite useless in any evaluation of life, in any attempt to understand what a human being is, or what human goals are *worthy* of being pursued. Nietzsche feared that in his day this mechanistic philosophy, a science for nihilists, was well on its way to becoming the victorious world-view. However, when he read Lange's 'treasurehouse', he 'found a means by which to undermine dogmatic materialism and mechanism': a dynamic theory of nature.[104]

To undermine mechanistic materialism and give his agonistic view of human nature derived from Hesiod and the Greeks the support of a scientific footing, Nietzsche appropriated Boscovitch's dynamic theory of nature.[105]

As for materialistic atomism, it is one of the best-refuted things there are; and perhaps no scholar in Europe is still so unscholarly today as to accord it serious significance ... thanks above all to the Pole Boscovitch who, together with the Pole Copernicus, has been the greatest and most triumphant opponent of ocular evidence hitherto. For while Copernicus persuaded us to believe, contrary to all the senses, that the earth does *not* stand firm, Boscovitch taught us to abjure belief in the last thing on earth that 'stood firm', belief in 'substance', in 'matter', in the earth-residuum and particle atom. (BGE 12)[106]

In Boscovitch's theory of matter,[107] the atomic lumps of inert matter are replaced by *Kraftcentren*: indivisible, dimensionless, point-

[104] Stack (1983*a*), 224. Nietzsche refers to Lange's *Geschichte des Materialismus* as: 'a real treasure-house to be looked into and read repeatedly'. Quoted in Stack (1983*a*), 13, from a letter to von Gersdorff. Stack's chapter 1 is called 'The Treasure-House'.

[105] Stack (1983*a*), 224. As Stack goes on to say: 'What has come to be called "Nietzsche's physics" [by Kaufmann (1974), 262] is, in point of fact, not *his* at all. Virtually every aspect of his examination of the structure of the natural world is derived from the views of Boscovitch and from the physical theories that are examined by Lange. That he has been credited with having developed a physics is testimony to his understanding of the fundamental principles of a rather complex theory'.

[106] Boscovitch was no Pole. He was actually born in what is now Dubrovnic of Serb and Italian parentage.

[107] Nietzsche actually read Boscovitch's *Philosophia Naturalis* in 1873. In a letter to Peter Gast, he refers to Boscovitch as 'the first to demonstrate mathematically that, for the exact science of mechanics, the premiss of *solid* atomic points is an unusable hypothesis'. Quoted in Stack (1983*a*), 39 n. 29.

like 'force-centres'. The stuff that constitutes what we call 'solid matter' is, in fact, more accurately described as a 'constellation of forces', and what we conceive of as 'impenetrability' and 'solidity' are no more than interpretations of what is best described as 'repulsive force'.[108] Yet, according to Nietzsche, in order to make life 'intelligible' which, as we saw, was to be realized on the analogy of our inner world of desires and passions, this dynamic theory of nature 'still needs to be completed: an inner-will must be ascribed to it, which I describe as "will to power," i.e., as an insatiable desire to manifest power; or as the employment and exercise of power, as a creative drive'.[109] Science can only ever be a 'means', it can only 'serve'; it can never 'explain' but only 'describe'.[110] It is up to the creative philosopher-artist to use it, to give value and meaning to what science describes.[111] This is what Nietzsche is attempting here: by adding a primitive *nisus*, a 'creative drive for power', to Boscovitch's *Kraftcentren*, he is putting forward a hypothesis derived from his study of the natural sciences that might help *explain* the natural world, *explain* evolution, and, together with his view of human nature derived from the ancient Greeks, *explain* human history and human nature, as well as form the axiological basis for taking man through this oncoming nihilistic phase of human history. His higher types, those he sees as geniuses and creators must, as a consequence of the demise of the two-world system, be returned to nature, be interpreted as products of the natural world; their urge to create must now have a natural origin, and, in its most fundamental and primitive state, that urge is transposed back into the most basic theoretical units underlying all nature: the *Kraftcentren* which, with Nietzsche's added *nisus*, become *Willens-Punktationen* or 'will-points'.[112] Therefore it is only

[108] See Stack (1981*b*); (1983*a*), 37ff. and 229 n. 11. Stack mentions that Redtenbacher's belief that we understand the physical world of *Kraft* ['force'] on the basis of our consciousness of, and feeling of, our own 'forces' is one that obviously made a deep imprint on Nietzsche's thinking insofar as it is a belief he will appeal to when he seeks to formulate a human interpretation of the physical theory of 'force'. E.g. BGE 36.

[109] WP 619.

[110] GS 112.

[111] In BT 15 and 16 Nietzsche refers to an 'artistic Socrates' who would embody the Dionysian passion of the artist and the Apollinian intellect of Socrates, thereby integrating art and science. The world-view that emerges, being scientifically based, will give 'an anti-metaphysical view of the world—yes, but an artistic one' (WP 1048).

[112] WP 715. See Stack (1983*a*), 171–3.

through what Nietzsche appropriated from Boscovitch and others that we can now make sense of his experiment previously mentioned in *Beyond Good and Evil*: on the basis of human analogy we may hypostatize the material world 'as possessing the same degree of reality as our emotions themselves—as a more primitive form of the world of emotions in which everything still lies locked in mighty unity and then branches out and develops in the organic process'. Our affects, Nietzsche's prime analogate, are seen as the latest fruits in a dynamic continuum whose roots are the forces studied by physics. Consequently there is no matter nor a material world but only various configurations of forces, something more analogous to will struggling with will wherein '*all* efficient force' could be defined as '*will to power*'. And the 'world seen from within, the world described and defined according to its "intelligible character"—it would be "will to power" and nothing else'.[113]

In his published writings this scientific underpinning of his monistic principle of the will to power is only ever hinted at as, for example, his one reference to Boscovitch and the quote from *Beyond Good and Evil* above. Most of his thoughts in this area are found scattered throughout his unpublished notes, revealing that he was occasionally seriously occupied with and reflecting on the scientific theories of Boscovitch and others he had read. But there is no fully worked-out philosophy of nature.[114] What we are left with is the general outline of the principle of the will to power encompassing the whole of existence as a hypothetical explanatory principle. It is proposed to help man reinterpret and understand not only the natural world and human history and institutions but, more importantly, his own self without reference to any realm or world other than the natural world. And, allied with the paradigm of sublimation derived from the Greeks, this notion of the will to power can help man fashion new values and a new morality to replace the now-untenable values rooted in the two-world system.

[113] BGE 36. In WP 689 Nietzsche says: 'The will to accumulate force is special to the phenomena of life, to nourishment, procreation, inheritance—to society, state, custom, authority. Should we not be permitted to assume this will as a motive cause in chemistry too?—and in the cosmic order?'

[114] Stack (1983*a*), and more recently and extensively, Moles (1990), have formulated what can be formulated of Nietzsche's philosophy of nature based upon his unpublished notes.

However, it is to his conception of man as an expression of the will to power that we must now turn.

6.4. MAN AS WILL TO POWER

What emerges from Nietzsche's excursions into the worlds of physics and biology, from his attempt to '"*naturalize*" humanity in terms of a pure, newly discovered, newly redeemed nature',[115] is a view of man as an entirely naturally evolved organism who is best described as an embodied constellation of natural forces, what he calls 'under-wills' (*Unter-Willen*) or 'under-souls' (*Unter-Seelen*),[116] which are continually in flux. What we refer to as the 'body' can therefore be likened to 'a social structure composed of many souls'.[117] Within such a perspective, the old duality of material body and immaterial soul, of *Geist* and *Natur*, drops away, being resolved into what Lange and others called the 'unknown "third"'.[118] The terms 'body' and 'soul' when used by Nietzsche in this context, simply refer to two aspects of a single organized whole—the 'soul' or 'souls' being the inner movements, what we sense as emotions, impulses, etc.; the 'body' being simply a word for the whole nexus. As Stack adequately sums it up:

115 GS 109. 116 BGE 19. 117 BGE 19.

118 Stack (1983*a*), 104. Stack comments that 'Zöllner, du Bois-Reymond, Helmholtz and Lange himself are hesitant to say what this "third" . . . might be and, hence, retain a deep agnosticism about this presumed transphenomenal, transrepresentational "third". For a long time, Nietzsche will also restrain his impulse to say anything about this mysterious "third". Eventually, his own experience and reflections . . . will lead him to guess at the riddle, to proffer his own "hypothesis" . . . he names "the third" *der Wille zur Macht*' (ibid. 104–5). Although 'unknown', it was not, for Nietzsche, another Kantian 'thing-in-itself', not a 'true world' but '*another kind* of phenomenal world, a kind "unknowable" for us' (WP 569). Questions about what 'things-in-themselves' might be like apart from our perception of them are meaningless questions as they imply that some 'thing' can exist, in-itself and property-less, outside all relations with other 'things': 'The properties of a thing are effects on other "things": if one removes other "things", then a thing has no properties, i.e., there is no thing without other things, i.e., there is no "thing-in-itself"' (WP 557). The world 'is essentially a world of relationships' (WP 568); 'we possess the concept "being", "thing", only as a relational concept', making the notion of the '"in-itself" . . . an absurd conception' (WP 583). Nietzsche's heuristic notion of will to power is therefore best understood as a relational concept, it constitutes his understanding of the most primitive and all-embracing relationship between 'things', whether those 'things' be *Kraftcentren*, viruses, affects, people, or nations. The will to power, therefore, is not posited as some Kantian 'thing-in-itself'. It is not a claim to metaphysical truth, even though it can be said to have a metaphysical aspect.

> What we call the 'body' is a symbol for an interplay of forces, a 'colony' of living subjects that have various gradations of power and are subject to a kind of 'division of labour.' From time to time, the 'sovereigns' in this colony change. . . . The self is the body, but the body is a multiplicity of feeling, willing and thinking 'subjects' that comprise, at any stage of life, a hierarchy of *Kräften*. If at different stages of life there are different arrangements of these 'forces', then, in a sense, there are different 'selves.' Insofar as the multiplicities comprising the body are continually changing, and insofar as dominant 'forces' are not constant, the self of an individual is a process, a gradual process in which one bodily self is replaced by another and so on.[119]

A human being can therefore be regarded as a 'body' in the above sense, a body consisting of an organization of 'forces' with various levels of hierarchical activity from the atomic through to what we regard as peculiarly human affects. The whole is not fixed nor does it possess any permanent essence or even a 'will',[120] but is a complex and dynamic process of only relative stability: we are recognizably the 'same' person today as yesterday, but not so the infant and the 80-year-old. Our affects, although they are in constant flux, usually have some habitual pattern more or less peculiar to each person, giving them a recognizable character. Given this picture, in Stack's interpretation it then becomes possible to talk about different phases of this process of 'bodying', of there being different 'selves' even in the 'same' person, an idea that, as we shall see, has obvious affinities with the Buddhist doctrine of *anattan* or 'no-Self'.

To Nietzsche, one very important consequence of such a view of the body is that, from a holistic perspective, given that this body has evolved, there must be some kind of continuity, some relationship between the lower and the higher aspects, between our chemistry and our humanity. And as the genealogy of our humanity can no

[119] (1983*a*), 174–5. To say as Hollingdale does that Nietzsche 'was a thorough-going materialist', whose materialism 'derived . . . from Friedrich Albert Lange's *History of Materialism*' (TI, app. D), seems to misunderstand what Nietzsche gained from Lange: a dynamic theory of nature that attempts to overcome the duality of mind and matter. As Nietzsche himself says: 'There are no eternally enduring substances; matter is as much of an error as the God of the Eleatics' (GS 109). It is a strange materialist who does not believe in the existence of 'matter'.

[120] As we saw earlier, this 'body' is a constellation of 'under-wills', therefore there is no single 'will' or separate faculty called the 'will'. As Nietzsche sees it, 'Willing seems to me to be above all something *complicated*, something that is a unity only as a word' (BGE 19). As such, 'The will to overcome an emotion is ultimately only the will of another emotion or of several others' (BGE 117). The will to power is not some 'thing', but a common and shared *characteristic* of all forces and combinations of forces that constitute the world.

longer be traced to some god but is now understood as being entirely natural, Nietzsche now contemplates the possibility that perhaps even our 'moral, religious and aesthetic conceptions and sensations' may be sublimations of our chemistry. He asks: 'what if this chemistry would end up by revealing that in this domain too the most glorious colours are derived from base, indeed from despised materials?'.[121] He suggests that the hitherto philosophical and religious answers to questions 'about the *value* of existence, may always be considered first of all as the symptoms of certain bodies'.[122] There can no longer be such activity as purely abstract, free-floating, and objective thinking dissociated from the body: 'We are not thinking frogs, nor objectifying and registering mechanisms with their innards removed'.[123] Our thinking, our *mental* activity, is now envisaged as an activity of the body, as an outcome of the various relations, struggles, and movements of our 'under-wills' and 'under-souls' rising to consciousness as thought. What we call 'conscious thinking is secretly directed and compelled into definite channels by [our] instincts'.[124] As such, our thinking and philosophizing cannot be completely dissociated from the body. Rather, they are better understood as particular expressions of it. Future philosophers will now need some 'knowledge of physiology'[125] so as to be able to diagnose moral, religious, and philosophical systems as expressions of, or better 'symptoms' of, the health or sickness of the body. He therefore proposes that the body and physiology are the best starting-points and guides to a new philosophy of man: the

[121] HAH 1. It is often difficult to determine whether Nietzsche is being entirely ironic or not. 'Chemistry' can be taken metaphorically or literally. I would consider it as purposely ambiguous with the literal interpretation being considered a real possibility. In D 119 he wonders whether 'our moral judgements and evaluations . . . are only images and fantasies [analogous to our dreams] based on a physiological process unknown to us'. Interestingly, at the time of writing *Human All Too Human*, Nietzsche relates that: 'A downright burning thirst seized hold of me: thenceforth I pursued in fact nothing other than physiology, medicine and natural science' (EH vi. 3). He obviously considered the study of physiology to be an essential part of any attempt to understand human nature.

[122] GS, Preface, 2.

[123] GS, Preface, 3.

[124] BGE 3. Elsewhere Nietzsche comments that our 'thinking is only the relationship of these drives to one another' (BGE 36).

[125] WP 408. However, Nietzsche reckoned that psychology should become the 'queen of the sciences' (BGE 23). Given the central importance of the affects, drives, etc., in his philosophy of man, this is hardly surprising. It also reminds us that, for Nietzsche, there is no physical–mental dichotomy between physiology and psychology.

body now being a 'much richer phenomenon' than the old soul, being 'even more attractive, even more mysterious', and being 'more tangible' allowing 'clearer observation'.[126]

[126] WP 489, 492, 532, and 659.

7

The Buddha as a 'Profound Physiologist'

Although physics, chemistry, and the other natural sciences are now considered by Nietzsche as indispensable to the new philosopher in any study of man, I think that one has occasionally to treat Nietzsche's comments on the estimation of our chemistry in forming our humanity as being an example of methodological irony. He is not a simple reductionist who regards the highest human achievements as no more than the expressions of complex chemical processes going on in the material body. Such a position would be incongruous as he does not conceive of these processes in terms of reductionist, mechanistic materialism, but as particular and rare constellations of 'forces' expressive of a higher degree of humanity. The constellation 'man' cannot, therefore, be reduced to the mere goings-on in the minute constellations called 'atoms' or in any combinations of atoms. There is a continuity as both the atom and man are interpreted as expressions of the will to power, but the constellation 'man' represents a more complex and evolved—and therefore 'higher'—expression. By drawing attention to the physiological he is simply stressing the new necessity of finding a *natural* as against any metaphysical explanation of human nature, and reminding us that the vastly complex workings of our 'bodies' are relatively unknown—even 'mysterious'—and may play a larger part in our making judgements, etc. than we ever imagined. And, in a manner of speaking, as man has been 'returned to nature', it is primarily the 'body' and its mysterious workings that has produced the highest human creations—what else is there to a human being now that we are entirely natural creations. Therefore the study of the body is essential to any new philosophy of man.

In this context, Nietzsche credits the Buddha as being a 'profound physiologist'[1] as he sought natural causes in his analysis of the human condition and proposed natural remedies for its existen-

[1] EH i. 6.

tial *Ängste*. The Buddha, according to Nietzsche, grasped that the growing state of depression that had arisen among many of his contemporaries had a 'physiological' (natural) origin, due to a combination of 'excessive excitability of sensibility which expresses itself as a refined capacity for pain' and 'an over-intellectuality . . . under which the personal instincts have sustained harm to the advantage of the "impersonal"'.[2] In other words, man has become alienated from his natural, more basic life-affirming instincts. The Buddha's physiological cure for this state was . . .

> life in the open air, the wandering life; with moderation and fastidiousness as regards food; with caution towards all alcoholic spirits; likewise with caution towards all emotions which produce gall, which heat the blood; *no* anxiety, either for oneself or for others. He demands ideas which produce repose or cheerfulness—he devises means for disaccustoming oneself to others. He understands benevolence, being kind, as health-promoting. (A 20)

Nietzsche goes on to say that the Buddha counteracts the harm done to the 'personal instinct', the 'loss of centre of gravity', by redirecting 'the spiritual interest back to the individual *person*', thereby making 'egoism . . . a duty: the "one thing needful", the "how can *you* get rid of suffering" regulates . . . the entire spiritual diet'. The Buddha also warns against such harmful affects as: 'the feeling of revengefulness, of antipathy, of *ressentiment*', because such emotions are 'thoroughly *unhealthy*': they make the body sick. The Buddha, as Nietzsche sees it, replaces the old morality with physiology: this 'is *not* morality that speaks thus, it is physiology that speaks thus'.[3] Hence Nietzsche credits the Buddha with the

[2] A 20. As we saw in Part I, Oldenberg refers to the condition of 'spiritual over-excitement (and) exhaustion of the nervous system' being a common condition among many of the Buddha's contemporary *religieux* (1882: 316). He also considers that the 'Buddha's preaching of deliverance is compared to the work of the physician' (ibid. 191). In the Pāli *suttas* (A-N iv. 340), the Buddha is called a 'physician' (*bhisakka*).

[3] EH i. 6. No doubt much of this is based on Oldenberg. e.g. Oldenberg relates that: 'God and the Universe trouble not the Buddhist: he knows only one question: how shall *I* in this world of suffering be delivered from suffering?' (1882: 130; italics mine). He also relates that 'the decided advantage of moral action over immoral arises wholly and solely from the consequence to the actor himself' (ibid. 289), and that morality is therefore 'the means to an end' (ibid. 289). And, elsewhere: 'The most important part of moral action does not lie according to Buddhist notions in duties which are owing externally, from man to man, . . . but in the scope of his own inner life, in the exercise of incessant discipline . . . The ego . . . here becomes for ethical speculation a determinate power, before which everything external to it

insight that there are only natural causes and origins,[4] there are no supernatural causes or origins, nor a morality based on them. The Buddha's knowledge is not by way of some 'revelation',[5] but comes from an insight into the natural order of things.

While it is true that the Buddha's teachings appeal only to the natural order of things and reckon man himself as his only saviour, what Buddhism considers 'natural' greatly exceeds anything Nietzsche or science would consider natural. The Buddhist cosmos as found in the Pāli *suttas*—an entirely natural cosmos governed by

vanishes into the background as something foreign' (ibid. 305). He then quotes some verses from the *Dhammapada*: 'By thine ego spur on thy ego; by thine ego explore thine ego . . . [379]. For the protection of the ego is the ego; the refuge of the ego is the ego . . . [380] First of all let a man establish his own ego in the good . . . [158]'. The term translated as 'ego' is *attan*. Here, however, *attan* does not refer to the metaphysical 'Self' of the Upaniṣads, but should be translated as 'oneself', 'yourself', 'himself', etc., according to context.

4 Again, the source of this is probably Oldenberg. Once 'the belief in the *Atman* itself had been effaced or lost, . . . as ruler over the world longing for deliverance there remained no more a god, but only the natural law of necessary concatenation of causes and effects. There stood man alone as the sole operative agent in the struggle against sorrow and death; his task was, by the *skilful knowledge of the law of nature*, to aim at gaining a position against it, in which he was beyond the reach of its sorrow-bringing operations' (1882: 323–4, italics mine).

5 The nearest equivalent to our notion of 'revelation' at the time of the Buddha was the concept of *śruti*, literally 'hearing', which when applied to the Veda carried the notion of 'revealed truth'. These texts were handed down from generation to generation, word for word, and were seen as the sacred and authoritative source of Brāhmanical tradition. In denying their authority, the Buddha was also denying the notion of revealed scripture in the sense that what is revealed could not be known through natural means. In a sense the Buddha is a 'revealer', but he only reveals what is open to all who have eyes to see. And what is seen is the natural world as it really is. However, there may be another piece of Buddhist irony in that all Buddhist *suttas* begin with the phrase: *evam me sutam*, 'Thus have I heard', with the implication that what follows was the 'word of the Buddha' or *buddha-vacana*. *Suta* is the Pāli form of Sanskrit *śruta*, a past passive participle meaning 'heard', *śruti* being a feminine noun meaning 'the act of hearing; sound; the Veda'. This correspondence between the Buddhist notion of *śruta/suta* and the Brāhmanical notion of *śruti* would surely not have been lost on the Buddha's contemporaries, especially as many of the interlocutors in the *suttas* were Brāhmans. *Buddha-vacana* therefore replaces Brāhmanical *śruti* and, as I have shown that *buddha-vacana* is essentially what accords with certain natural verifiable principles underlying all Buddhist doctrine, the Buddha may have been implying that real *śruti* is something you can only verify by yourself alone, something each person has to discover for themselves. As Dhp. 276 has it, the Tathāgatas only declare the Way, but 'You yourselves must strive' in order to realize it. Ultimately, one cannot rely upon tradition, sacred or otherwise, but only one's own efforts. As Nietzsche rightly says, Buddhism is a '*religion of self-redemption*' (D 96). Again, the source here is probably Oldenberg, as he refers to Buddhism as a religion 'in which man himself delivers himself' (1882: 52).

natural laws—is full of strange beings, divine and non-divine, who inhabit other worlds and who, when they enter the human world, go about unperceived by ordinary mortals. Even the 'God', Brahmā, who deludedly thinks he created the cosmos with its beings—at least according to the Buddhist texts[6]—comes to be in dependence on natural laws and conditions. Brahmā is therefore a natural being having entirely natural origins, and is subject to the same law of impermanence as all else is. If the Buddha is then to be regarded as a profound physiologist in the sense that his *logos* is only concerned with what is entirely *phusis*,[7] what the Buddha would have regarded as physiological reaches into what Nietzsche and science—and other religions—would regard as the supernatural.

7.1. THE BUDDHIST NATURAL ORDER

To give an outline of the Buddhist view of the natural order of things there is the notion of the *pañca-niyamas*, or the 'five orders' or 'five kinds of natural causal patterns'.[8]

[6] D-N i. 222.

[7] If we take the term *logos* as 'explanation' or 'rationale' then 'physiological' can be taken as an explanation or teaching that appeals only to what is *phusis* or 'natural'. Thus, in principle, and on its own terms, Buddhism is a 'physiological' teaching in this extended meaning of the term as its teachings are primarily focused on the natural processes that go on 'inside' man in relation to the world, and the natural laws that govern them. Given Nietzsche's view of the world as will to power, whether one called Buddhism a physiological or psychological teaching would not matter. And it would be reasonable to refer to the Buddha as a 'profound psychologist', given the centrality of 'mind' (*citta*) and the emphasis on the practice of continual mindfulness and awareness (*sati* and *sampajañña*) of natural processes, within and without, in his teaching.

[8] This listing does not appear in the *suttas* but is a commentatorial systematizing, probably by Buddhaghosa, of types of conditionality found in the *suttas* (see Rhys Davids (1912: 119) and Buddhaghosa's account in his *Aṭṭhasālinī*, trans. Pe Maung Tin as *Expositor*, ii. 360). However, as we shall see, the fifth *niyama* is in need of a little more explanation than the others. A related term, *dhamma-niyāmatā*, does, however, appear once in the *suttas*, but there *dhamma* means 'nature' in the sense of 'natural order' : 'Monks, whether there be an appearance or non-appearance of a Tathāgata, this determination of nature (*dhammaṭṭhitatā*), this orderliness of nature (*dhamma-niyāmatā*) prevails: the relatedness of this to that' (S-N ii. 25). This *sutta* makes it quite clear that all the Tathāgatas or Buddhas do is reveal what is already there, reveal the nature of things summed up in the phrase: 'the relatedness of this to that' (*idappaccayatā*). The *niyamas* represent the universal principle of 'dependent co-arising' (*paṭicca-samuppāda*) operative on five different levels.

1. *utu-niyama*	the physical, inorganic order
2. *bīja-niyama*	the physical, organic order
3. *citta-niyama*	the psychological order
4. *kamma-niyama*	the moral order
5. *dhamma-niyama*	the 'Reality' order

The first four *niyamas* or orders are relatively straightforward. The inorganic order applies to such phenomena as earthquakes and the changing of the seasons; the organic order to changes in seeds and plant-life; the psychological order to the processes of perception and non-volitional consciousness; and the moral order to the relations between volitional actions and their consequent dispositional effect upon the actor. But what the *dhamma-niyama* or 'Reality' order involves seems to require a more accessible account than what tradition tells us. The commentator Buddhaghosa gives an account of the events in the Buddha Vipassin's life as found in the *Dīgha-Nikāya*[9] as an example of the workings of the *dhamma-niyama*, such as the fact that the future Buddha's mother carries him for ten instead of the more usual nine months; that she can have no sensual thoughts about men between conception and giving birth; naturally observes the *pañca-sīla* or 'five precepts' of moral action during this time; gives birth standing up; dies after birth and is reborn in the Tusita *deva*-world. As the *sutta* goes on to say: 'This monks, is the nature of things (*dhammatā*)'.[10] Other writers have other ideas about what the *dhamma-niyama* signifies.[11] However, in my own opinion, the *dhamma-niyama* can be best understood as referring to the natural unfoldment of the activity of an enlightened being in the world, the natural unfoldment of activity informed by 'transformative-insight' or *paññā*, wherein one 'sees and knows things as they really are'. This, I think, makes more sense than ten-month pregnancies![12] In other words post-Enlightenment activity, being rooted in 'transformative-insight', unfolds quite naturally according to a different order of things such

[9] See p. 8 n. 3 of the Rhys Davids' translation. Although it is the previous Buddha, Vipassin, who is mentioned in this context, it is clear that what follows applies to all *bodhisattas* entering their last life before becoming Buddhas.

[10] D-N ii. 12 ff.

[11] See Rhys Davids (1912), Sangharakshita (1991), and Kalupahana (1975).

[12] To see events surrounding the birth of Gotama as the effects of the *dhamma-niyama*—as Buddhaghosa does—is more than problematic. The *Buddha* was 'born' at Bodhgayā some thirty or so years later. It was the 'unenlightened' being Gotama who was born at Lumbini, and being unenlightened only the first four *niyamas* would have been operative.

that a Buddha is completely free from the order of things wherein his actions could be determined in any degree by 'greed' (*rāga*), 'hatred' (*dosa*), or 'delusion' (*moha*). He is said to be free from any unenlightened activity. A Buddha, therefore, or any other person who has attained *bodhi* or 'enlightenment', quite naturally responds to the *dukkha* of others with 'compassionate activity' or *karuṇā*; quite naturally cannot feel ill-will towards anyone regardless of what they do to him; quite naturally responds with 'friendly concern' or *mettā* to all other beings, simply because these are the natural responses from someone who 'sees and knows things as they really are'. I would suggest that it is in such responses as these that we can best see what the *dhamma-niyama* or Reality order represents.

Given this, all five orders can be seen as being unified by the single principle of *paṭicca-samuppāda* or 'dependent co-arising', giving events on each level a 'natural law' (*dhamma*) according to which they unfold. Therefore the whole multidimensional universe comes under this single principle. As the Buddha says: 'Whoever sees dependent co-arising sees the "truth" (Dhamma), whoever sees the "truth" sees dependent co-arising',[13] a clear statement that the highest kind of knowledge attainable concerns the *natural* order of things. And with this perspective, Nietzsche's account of the Buddha's application of natural laws to help his contemporaries overcome their malaise obviously falls short of what Buddhists understand by natural law. Nevertheless, it is quite probable that Nietzsche's idea of the Buddha as a profound physiologist is his own attempt to fit the Buddhist doctrine of dependent co-arising, an account of which he would have read in Oldenberg,[14] to his own historical perspective.

What the relationship between these orders is, how they might interact and influence each other, is not specifically mentioned anywhere in the texts or commentaries. As Guenther comments, Buddhism is so interested 'in man as he appears to himself and the way in which it becomes possible for him to develop spiritually . . . that the external physical world . . . has more or less completely been lost sight of'.[15] Buddhism is almost solely concerned with the *kamma-niyama* or moral order, with our *saṅkhāras* or 'volitional affects', as a way to the Reality order and shows no interest

[13] M-N i. 191–2. [14] (1882), 223 ff. [15] (1959), 144.

whatsoever in any scientific approach to the physical world, apart from subsuming it under the principle of dependent co-arising and seeing it as 'impermanent' (*anicca*) and 'without essence' (*anattan*). The Buddhist spiritual life requires no necessary knowledge of how a cell or the liver works. Yet Nietzsche, with his 'body' as a hierarchy of forces does, on occasions, suggest that it is within the workings of the 'mysterious body' that our fate, unknown to us, is determined. However, as I've said, I interpret such proposals as methodological irony reminding us that we do not know the extent to which such factors, what he calls 'these little things'[16]—such as the food we eat, our metabolism, where we live, our climatic environment—condition how we interpret and interact with the world. In any case, these little things are 'of greater importance than anything that has been considered of importance hitherto', such as the 'merely imaginings': the '*lies* from the bad instincts of sick . . . injurious natures—all the concepts "God", "soul", "virtue", "sin", "the Beyond", "truth", "eternal life" . . .'. We have therefore 'to begin to *learn anew*',[17] and we have to start from that which is tangible and observable, even though not fully known, and that is the 'body' and the 'little things'.

[16] EH ii. 10. See the whole of EH ii on this topic. [17] EH ii. 10.

8

Nietzsche's 'Little Things', the 'Body', and the Buddhist *Khandhas*

8.1. THE 'LITTLE THINGS'

Just as Nietzsche recommends that we begin again and learn anew by paying attention to the 'little things' and the workings of the 'body' in order to determine what formative effect they might have in forming our *Weltanschauungen* (which implies that if we do discover such determinations, we can then begin to *free* ourselves of their influence), Buddhism also considers such factors as important in the development of self-awareness, which is central to the practice of the Buddhist spiritual quest. Both see the relationship between the subject and his environment as reciprocal and mutually conditional, although not necessarily symmetrical.[1] Both want to bring this more into focus in order to create a greater degree of freedom for the subject to develop. On the environment's side we have the objective aspect of Nietzsche's 'little things' and the first of the five Buddhist *khandhas* or 'aggregates', the *rūpa-khandha* or 'aggregate of form' (here understood as the objective world). On the subject's side we have Nietzsche's 'body' or, for our present comparative study, his 'given', our experience of ourselves as embodiments of fluctuating forces—our drives, feelings, emotions, desires, passions, instincts—all of which I will subsume under the

[1] Whether it is the subjects themselves or the environment (which includes parents, society, culture, etc.) that has the larger say in forming the individual depends, for Nietzsche, upon the kind and 'power' of the individual. What he calls the 'herd-types' are seen as hardly more than the product of their environment, and have no real independence of action or thought apart from what has been formed by the environment. The 'higher types', having some independence from the *mores* and attitudes of the herd-type, in other words more power, are able to attain some degree of independence of mind and action. This, as we saw, is the main reason Nietzsche dislikes Darwinism: it favours the herd-type by over-emphasizing the part that the environment plays in determining the 'fittest'. The problem being that in Nietzsche's scheme, his fittest are all to easily swamped by the lowly herd-types.

term 'affects'; and, in the case of Buddhism, the four 'subjective' aggregates: 'feeling-sensation' (*vedanā*), 'apperception' (*saññā*), 'formative forces' (*saṅkhāras*), and 'consciousness' (*viññāṇa*). Both see the environment as in some degree effective in the formation of our subjectivity—our outlook, character, and general disposition—without our usually being aware of it. This can result in us, as subjects, and without any understanding of what we have done, creating a whole *Weltanschauung* about how the world really is, which is no more than a rationalization of the effect the world has had on us.

In both cases, however, these two aspects are not symmetrical, they are not of equal importance. Although Nietzsche acknowledges that we are rather ignorant of the extent of the influence that our environment may have had in conditioning and forming our being as well as our *Weltanschauung*, he nowhere considers that all we have to do in order to become *Übermenschen* is to find and live in the right environment and climate, eat the right kind of food, and simply sit back and passively await a kind of dialectical transformation into an *Übermensch*. One can become an *Übermensch* only by consciously engaging in a process he calls *Selbstüberwindung* or 'self-overcoming', which is essentially the internalization of the will to power, a matter of a struggle or an Hellenic *agon* between the various affects within the individual. The primary aspect is therefore the subject. For Buddhism also the primary aspect involves the subject engaging in a kind of 'self-overcoming', which is a struggle between various affects within the 'aggregate of formative forces' (*saṅkhāra-khandha*). Yet, although the subjective aspect is the primary one, Buddhism recognizes and tries to bring to our awareness that, in our interaction with the world, the world has had a formative effect on our character, and that even our pet *Weltanschauung* may have been formed by the influence our environment has had on us. For example, one may consider oneself a confirmed Christian, Muslim, Hindu, Buddhist, or whatever, when this 'conviction' is no more than the mere accident of one's place of birth, family upbringing, etc. But by becoming aware of this interactive process, we can begin to free ourselves from it and begin to 'learn anew'. Although both consider the environment as initially important, both agree that its influence can and must eventually be overcome. In the past it has influenced, to some degree or other, our present disposition towards the world, and for the future it can either help or hinder 'self-overcoming'. In Nietzsche's case this 'learning anew' is the beginning of a new adventure, but in Buddhism's case this adventure began some 2,500 years ago, and as it already has many helpful insights can therefore offer much guidance to those just setting out on this spiritual adventure. And, ironically enough as we shall see, Buddhism could have more than assisted Nietzsche in forming his path of self-overcoming.

If I had to sum-up the Buddhist path in a word, it would have to be *citta-bhāvanā*,[2] 'mind-cultivation' or 'mind-development' which, as I shall show, has strong affinities with Nietzsche's 'self-overcoming'. Although *citta-bhāvanā* falls into the subjective aspect, what we might call 'mind working on mind', Buddhism has always recognized the importance played by the external conditions one lives under and how they can either help or hinder the path of *citta-bhāvanā*. The most thorough and systematic example of this is found in Buddhaghosa's *Visuddhimagga* or *The Path of Purification*, written in Pāli during the fifth century CE. Not only does Buddhaghosa examine the most beneficial environment for the practice of *citta-bhāvanā*, but also considers the more specific and formative interaction between a type of environment and the character type it tends to produce, which provides a good example of the reciprocal relationship between the objective and subjective aspects mentioned above. In its classification of psychological types, Buddhism recognizes six predominant temperaments: 'greed-temperament' (*rāga-carita*), 'hate-temperament' (*dosa-carita*), 'deluded-temperament' (*moha-carita*), 'faith-temperament' (*saddhā-carita*), 'intelligent-temperament' (*buddhi-carita*), and 'speculative-temperament' (*vitakka-carita*). Each, according to Buddhaghosa, benefits from a particular environment. I shall quote generously his advice to hate- and greed-temperaments on the kind of environment most suited to each as an example of his thoroughness.

[2] *Bhāvanā* is the term that is often translated in the West as 'meditation'. However, its scope extends beyond the practice of 'sitting meditation', a practice specifically aimed at developing *samādhi* or 'meditative concentration' through various mediation practices. What one is trying to 'cultivate' (*bhāvanā*), whether in sitting meditation or in everyday activities, are *kusala* or 'skilful' states of mind such as *mettā* or 'friendliness', *saddhā* or 'confidence', *sati* and *sampajañña* or 'mindfulness and clear comprehension', and other skilful states that provide the necessary conditions for the further development of 'transformative insight' (*paññā*). Thus *nirvāṇa* can be seen as the culmination of *citta-bhāvanā*.

What suits what kind of temperament? A suitable lodging for one of greedy temperament has an unwashed sill and stands level with the ground, and it can be either an overhanging [rock with an] unprepared [dripledge], a grass hut, or a leaf house, etc.; it ought to be splattered with dirt, full of bats, dilapidated, too high or too low, in bleak surroundings, threatened [by lions, tigers, etc.,] with a muddy, uneven path, where even the bed and chair are full of bugs. And it should be ugly and unsightly, exciting loathing as soon as looked at. Suitable inner and outer garments are those that have torn-off edges with threads hanging down all around like a 'net cake', harsh to the touch like hemp, soiled, heavy and hard to wear. And the right kind of bowl for him is an ugly clay bowl disfigured by stoppings and joins, or a heavy and misshapen iron bowl as unappetising as a skull. The right kind of road for him on which to wander for alms is disagreeable, with no village near, and uneven. The right kind of village for him in which to wander for alms is where people wander about as if oblivious of him, where, as he is about to leave without getting alms even from a single family, people call him into the sitting hall, saying 'Come, venerable sir', and give him gruel and rice, but do so as casually as if they were putting a cow in a pen.[3]

And so the text continues in like manner for another half a page. The recommended conditions for the hate-type, are, however, quite the opposite.

A suitable resting place for one of hating temperament is not too high or too low, provided with shade and water, with well-proportioned walls, posts, and steps, with well-prepared frieze work and lattice work, brightened with various kinds of paintings, with an even, smooth, soft floor, adorned with festoons of flowers and a canopy of many-coloured cloth like a Brahmā-god's divine palace, with bed and chair covered with well-spread clean pretty covers, smelling sweetly of flowers, and perfumes and scents set about for homely comfort, which makes one happy and glad at the mere sight of it. The right kind of road to his lodgings is free of any sort of danger, traverses clean, even ground, and has been properly prepared. And here it is best that the lodging's furnishings are not too many in order to avoid hiding-places for insects, bugs, snakes and rats: even a single bed and chair only. The right kind of inner and outer garments for him are of any superior stuff such as China cloth, Somara cloth, silk, fine cotton, fine linen, of either single or double thickness, quite light, and well dyed, quite pure in colour to befit an ascetic. The right kind of road on which to wander for alms is free from dangers, level, agreeable, with a village in which to wander for alms is where people, thinking 'Now our lord is

[3] *Visuddhimaga* of Buddhaghosa: *The Path of Purification*, i. 109–10.

coming', prepare a seat in a sprinkled, swept place, and going out to meet him, take his bowl, lead him to the house, seat him on a prepared seat and serve him carefully with their own hands. Suitable people to serve him are handsome, pleasing, well bathed, well anointed, scented with the perfume of incense and the smell of flowers, adorned with apparel made of variously-dyed clean pretty cloth, who do their work carefully.[4]

And so on with less specific advice for the deluded, faithful, intelligent, and speculative temperaments. These are examples of the thoroughness and attention to detail that the Buddhists give over to what Nietzsche would have recognized as some of his 'little things'.

What emerges from this is a recognition of a formative and reciprocal relationship between the environment and the individual within which the character of a person, and thereby their perspective on the world and responses to life, is to some degree or other formed. By becoming aware of this, the individual can then take steps to undo and counteract his conditioning. For example, the hate-type, through the practice of 'mindfulness' and 'clear comprehension' (*sati* and *sampajañña*), by consciously putting himself into an environment that is the opposite of one that supports his character disposition—that will respond to him in a manner whose tendency would dispose him to become a greed-type—can begin to break down his habitual reactions to the world and, more importantly, his way of seeing the world. In this way his perspective on the world, as well as his experience of himself, will eventually broaden. His mind will then become more malleable and open to change, and some knowledge of the way his own being unfolds in accordance with the principle of 'dependent co-arising' can be gained. In this way Buddhism considers the little things to be of some importance. One need not be a victim of them but can even use them to one's advantage. However, real *citta-bhāvanā* is a matter of mind working on mind, and although the environment can have its role to play at the onset, it becomes less relevant as one progresses.

Nietzsche's corresponding little things, however, seem more an account of his own unsuccessful attempts to find an environment which would alleviate his consistent ailments. Since he was a schoolboy he had suffered vicious and prolonged headaches and attacks of vomiting. Even sunlight was at times so unbearable that

[4] Ibid. 110–11.

he had to wear dark glasses. He eventually was forced into an early retirement at the age of 31 by his recurring illnesses, and then spent much of his time 'in search of the climate in which he would suffer least'[5] in order to carry on writing in relative peace. Therefore, when he says on 'the question of *place* and *climate*' that one should

> Make a list of the places where there have been gifted men, . . . where genius has almost necessarily made its home: they all possess an excellent dry air. Paris, Provence, Florence, Jerusalem, Athens—these names prove something: that genius is *conditioned* by dry air, clear sky—that is to say by rapid metabolism, by the possibility of again and again supplying oneself with great, even tremendous quantities of energy.[6]

This was not so much because all the geniuses he admired happened to be born in climates where the air was dry (Goethe certainly wasn't), but because he found that his symptoms were sometimes alleviated in dry air, especially mountain air. However, he did think that the sea-air of Venice did him good,[7] which is hardly dry. As well as searching for propitious climatic conditions, he also experimented with various kinds of diets as he also suffered from intestinal problems. Yet he found no diet or environment that would sustain his ailing health for very long. Thus his comments on the relation between the German diet and the German spirit are not offered as serious physiology, just Nietzsche grumbling. And, interestingly enough, he once concluded that 'he was convinced that all the physical symptoms "were deeply intertwined with spiritual crises, so that I have no idea how medicine and diet could ever be enough to restore my health"'.[8] However, it may well be that many of these symptoms were no more than the effects of congenital syphilis, which may have been the prime cause of his eventual breakdown. However, we will never really know. What is remarkable about all this is that despite his real physical suffering, he managed to write as he did. Nevertheless, when one compares Nietzsche's account of his little things and their effects on our outlook with the Buddhist account, it is the latter that is more considered and makes more basic psychological sense.

Of far more interest is the comparison between Nietzsche's no-

[5] Hayman (1980), 225.

[6] EH ii. 2. Interestingly, he wrote this in Turin which he had first visited a couple of months earlier because 'I have heard favourable reports of the *dry* air there'. (Quoted from a letter in Hayman (1980), 315.)

[7] Hayman (1980), 225. [8] Ibid. 181.

tions of the 'body' and 'self-overcoming' with the five Buddhist 'aggregates' or *khandhas* and its conception of *citta-bhāvanā.*

8.2. THE 'BODY' AND THE 'AGGREGATES'

As we saw earlier, Nietzsche viewed the person as a constellation of various fluctuating forces whose individual and collective *nisus* was expressed in terms of a striving to overcome all resistance and accumulate more power, i.e., the will to power. This is the 'body', the 'subject as multiplicity'.[9] And although he considers that we know little about the workings of this body and how all these hidden forces effect us, there is little doubt that the important forces are our affects, our 'given'. It is by working on and with the affects that comprises his notion of self-overcoming, that constitutes the accumulative process of qualitatively higher expressions of the will to power, a process that he considers will eventually bring forth his new kind of being, the *Übermensch.* Therefore, although we may know little of the workings of our unconscious 'under-wills', the fact that he considers that whatever goes on in the body terminates as our affects,[10] and that such affects are symptoms of the sickness or health of the body, the fact that self-overcoming is a matter of our working with the affects means that knowledge of the unknown workings of the body is not of immediate or prime importance. Science may aid an athlete by prescribing a diet based upon knowledge of nutrition which helps increase performance. However, the diet in itself will not make an athlete out of anyone. And the athlete can go far without the aid of science. Nietzsche's 'little things', like the Buddhist's, are no more than aids to self-overcoming, and much, if not all, can be achieved without them.

Nietzsche's affects are nothing other than the whole gamut of a person's subjective experience. They include love, pity, enmity, generosity, sexual desire, jealousy, pride, joy, despair, ambition, *ressentiment*, gratitude, cunning, vigour, magnanimity, and many other urges and aspirations. Even conscious activity such as thinking is understood as nothing more than 'the relationship of these drives to one another'.[11] Our intellectual capacity, rather than having some divine source, developed naturally from our evolutionary past, even from things illogical.

9 WP 490. 10 D 119. 11 BGE 36.

> The course of logical ideas and inferences in our brain today corresponds to a process and a struggle among impulses that are, taken singly, very illogical and unjust. We generally experience only the result of this struggle because this primeval mechanism now runs its course so quickly and is so well concealed. (GS 111)

This primeval mechanism that now runs its course and ends as what we experience as a conscious activity, has become, in man, 'instinctual',[12] rather like the workings of the liver. This is why Nietzsche considers we can diagnose ideas as symptoms of the overall health or sickness of the body. Ideas that are 'anti-life' or which affirm another better world than this one, are no more than the intellections of a sick body, a body that has become weary of life, feels impotent, or which has suffered too long.[13] Man is, therefore, nothing other than 'the totality of [his] *drives*'[14] which ebb and flow in a continual flux of becoming, formed, to a greater or lesser degree, by the stimulus afforded by the environment. Our past struggles create an instinctual pattern which unfolds as 'us'—different patterns unfolding as different individuals who, having a common evolutionary past, share the more basic patterns and the more animal-like instincts in common. However, the 'higher type', through self-overcoming, can bring about affects not shared by the common man, can influence the way his being unfolds and add distance between himself and his animal past, and his fellow men. This, for Nietzsche, is how to truly affirm life.

For Buddhism, also, man is 'subject as multiplicity', he is also 'the totality of [his] *drives*'. What he is at any given moment is a psycho-physical complex that has come about as a consequence of his past affective-action which then, in itself, becomes the dispositional basis for present affective-action and so on. This is *saṃsāra*, the continual and habitual 'round'. When Buddhism analyses man into five aggregates or *khandhas* the affective and formative *khandha* is the *saṅkhāra-khandha* or 'aggregate of karmic activities and dispositions', which is simultaneously formative and formed depending upon whether one looks from the present into the future, i.e. how the present will form the future becoming, or from the present to

[12] On Nietzsche's use of this term, see Ch. 12, below.

[13] 'For the condemnation of life by the living is after all no more than the symptom of a certain kind of life' (TI v. 5). 'It was suffering and impotence—that created all afterworlds' (Z i. 3).

[14] D 119.

the past, i.e. how the present comes to be formed in dependence upon past karmic action. In the latter case the *saṅkhāras* are the 'results' (*vipākas*) of former 'actions' (*kammans*) which, given similar present circumstances, become the *saṅkhāras* that predispose us to act in a similar manner in the present. And, acting in a similar manner in the present sets up similar predispositions for the future. Therefore, unless man can change the pattern of his *saṅkhāras* as 'karmic activities'—change their 'constellation' to use a Nietzschean term—can change his affective life, he will not develop spiritually but will remain very much as he is or become even more spiritually degenerate.

That the *saṅkhāra-khandha* is the methodologically cardinal *khandha*, a fact that is often overlooked, is brought out in the *Saṃyutta-Nikāya*:

And why, brethren, do you say '*saṅkhāras*'? Because they compose [*abhisaṅkharonti*] a compound [*saṅkhata*]. That is why, brethren, the word '*saṅkhāras*' is used. And what compound do they compose? They compose a compound which is the body in order to be endowed with a body; compose a compound which is feeling in order to be endowed with feeling; compose a compound which is apperception in order to be endowed with apperception; compose a compound which is the karmic activities [*saṅkhāras*] in order to be endowed with dispositions [*saṅkhāras*]; compose a compound of consciousness which is consciousness in order to be endowed with consciousness. They compose a compound, brethren. Therefore the word '*saṅkhāras*' is used. (S-N iii. 87)

In other words the present individual, who is conceived of as a compound of five aggregates of body, feeling, apperception, dispositions, and consciousness, each of which is also a compound, comes to be so composed by the formative activities of his past *saṅkhāra-khandha*, his past 'karmic activities' (*saṅkhāras*) or, we could say, past 'willings'. 'Self-overcoming' is therefore an activity carried out between the various 'forces' (*saṅkhāras*) that constitute the *saṅkhāra-khandha*. It is this *khandha* that forms the volitional aspect of the person,[15] and since that volitional aspect is conceived

[15] At S-N iii. 60, the *saṇkhāra-khandha* is defined as 'the six seats of "will"' (*sañcetanā*) or better 'willing', the 'willing' being sixfold as *sañcetanā* responds to all six avenues of sense-experience—the 'mind' (*manas*) being regarded as a 'sense' (*indriya*). Each affect can therefore be seen as a particular 'will'. The *saṅkhāras*, as affects, can therefore be regarded as a collectivity of particular 'wills' in the sense of Nietzsche's 'under-wills'.

of as a multiplicity of 'forces', what we have is a multiplicity of what we could call 'wills'. Past karmic activities (*saṅkhāras*) become present 'predispositions' (*saṅkhāras*),[16] which predispose present 'willing' to 'will' in a particular manner which, in turn, sets up future dispositions, and so on. Not only do they set up the future dispositional aspect of the *saṅkhāra-khandha*, but they also 'compose' the other future *khandhas*, in other words compose what kind of being we will become in the future.[17] As this process is considered to span many lifetimes, what is 'reborn' is not some unchanging 'self' or soul, but these dispositional *saṅkhāras*, a particular configuration of predispositions. In a sense, one could say that it is only a kind of predisposition to 'will' that continues from life to life.

This is as much as we can derive from the *suttas* concerning the *saṅkhāra-khandha*, that, in its active aspect, it can be conceived of as a plurality of wills. However, if we ask what these wills are we have to turn to the various Abhidhammas, which 'filled in' the *saṅkhāra-khandha* with the variety of emotions and affects found in the *suttas*. What emerges is a list of what Nietzsche would have classified as affects or 'wills'. In terms of unskilful (*akusala*) affects we have 'hate' (*dosa*), 'envy' (*issā*), 'selfishness' (*macchariya*), 'greed' (*lobha*), 'opinionatedness' (*diṭṭhi*), 'conceit' (*māna*), 'mental obduracy' (*thīna*), 'vindictiveness' (*kodha*), 'resentment' (*upanāha*), 'hypocrisy' (*makkha*), 'lack of confidence' (*asaddhā*), 'lust' (*sineha*), 'sexual infatuation' (*pema*), etc. Curiously, in the lists of skilful (*kusala*) affects, some of those one would expect to find such as 'friendliness' (*mettā*), 'compassion' (*karuṇā*), 'sympathetic joy' (*muditā*), 'generosity' (*dāna*), do not appear in all the Abhidhamma lists. In fact the first and the last affects do not appear in any. The skilful affects listed are 'confidence' (*saddhā*), 'greedlessness' (*alobha*), 'hatelessness' (*adosa*), 'non-viciousness' (*ahiṃsā*), 'vigour' (*viriya*), 'diligence' (*apamāda*), 'equanimity' (*upekkhā*), 'alertness' (*passaddhi*), etc. In the Theravādin Abhidhamma we also have 'agility' (*lahutā*), 'elasticity' (*mudutā*),

[16] As is obvious from the above, the term *saṅkhāra* can mean 'karmic-activity' in some contexts, and the 'dispositions' or 'tendencies' set up as a result of such 'karmic-activity' in others. Past 'karmic-activities' become present 'predispositions', which dispose one to 'karmic activity' in the present, which sets up future dispositions, and so on. If one gets stuck in this loop, that is *saṃsāra*.

[17] However, as we saw earlier, the environment one is born into will also have its part to play. Nevertheless, the way in which one responds to that environment will be an expression of the *saṅkhāras* as dispositions.

'adaptability' (*kammaññatā*), 'proficiency' (*pāguññatā*), and 'uprightness' (*ujukatā*) of 'consciousness' (*viññāṇa*) and 'body' (*kāya*), the latter being all the skilful factors collectively, not the physical body.[18] *Cetanā* or 'will' is listed as one of the 'omnipresent mental factors' (*sabba-citta-sādharaṇas*) meaning that it is a constant factor present, in some degree, in every experience. However, it would be a mistake to see *cetanā* as something separate from the various affects listed above. It is always present because it is an integral aspect of each and every affect, in the sense that it is a characteristic of *being* an affect. It is not that one feels generous then *cetanā* comes along and provides the necessary 'will' to *be* generous. Generosity *is* an affect, a drive, a *saṅkhāra*, and is, therefore, a particular case of 'willing'. Given this, we therefore have a correspondence in kind between Nietzsche's view of man as 'the totality of [his] drives', which is his 'body', and the Buddhist conception of man as being primarily an embodied collection of *saṅkhāras* or, one could say, 'drives'.

[18] See Guenther (1959), 54.

9

'God's Shadow' and the Buddhist 'No-Self' Doctrine

At the beginning of book 3 of the *Gay Science*, using an image taken from Max Müller's *Selected Essays*,[1] Nietzsche tells us:

> *New Struggles*—After [the] Buddha was dead, his shadow was still shown for centuries in a cave—a tremendous, gruesome shadow. God is dead; but given the way of men, there may still be caves for thousands of years in which his shadow will be shown.—And we—we still have to vanquish his shadow too. (GS 108)

One of the main forms that God's shadow takes is the deeply held belief that there are 'eternally enduring substances'.[2] References to these can be found in a variety of forms throughout Nietzsche's writings, and include the notions of soul, essence, ego, will, self, subject, being, thing-in-itself, matter, atom. As he considers that such 'shadows of God ... darken our minds',[3] they need to be banished. Banishing these shadows is what Nietzsche terms the 'de-deification of nature', an attempt 'to "*naturalize*" humanity in terms of a pure, newly discovered, newly redeemed nature',[4] a nature free of man's 'erroneous articles of faith'.[5]

As is often Nietzsche's way, he does not offer any standard philosophical arguments for why such notions are erroneous, but uses what he terms '*historical philosophizing*',[6] which relies more on anthropology and other sciences than on abstract reasoning. For example, concerning arguments for and against the existence of God:

[1] Müller (1881), 271. Müller refers to a story involving the Chinese pilgrim Hsüan Tsang, of 'an extraordinary cave where [the] Buddha had formerly converted a dragon [i.e. a *nāga*], and had promised his new pupil to leave him his shadow, in order that, whenever the evil passions of his dragon-nature should revive, the aspect of his master's shadowy features might remind him of his former vows'.

[2] GS 109. See also GS 110.

[3] GS 108. [4] GS 109. [5] GS 110. [6] HAH 2.

Historical refutation as the definitive refutation.—In former times, one sought to prove that there is no God—today one indicates how the belief that there is a God could *arise* and how this belief acquired its weight and importance: a counter-proof that there is no God thereby becomes superfluous.—When in former times one had refuted the 'proofs of the existence of God' put forward, there always remained the doubt whether better proofs might not be adduced than those just refuted: in those days atheists did not know how to make a clean sweep. (D 95)

In Chapter 4 we saw one example of Nietzsche's idea of the de-deification of nature: that the belief in survival after death in another world, and thereby the foundation for the notion of the soul, arises through an '*error* in the interpretation of certain natural events, a failure of the intellect',[7] in this instance primitive man's misinterpretation of his dreams. In showing how primitive man misunderstood his dreamlife, Nietzsche—following some anthropologists of his day—thinks he has found the natural source of the arising of the two-world framework, a framework he thinks subsequently became the model for all religious, metaphysical, and even scientific thinking. Other examples of this de-deification of nature are found scattered throughout Nietzsche's works, where nature is 'redeemed' by simply depositing the sources of the above 'eternally enduring substances' back into man's lap—man being the only 'creator'. For example, Nietzsche finds 'God's shadow' in the syntax of grammar:

I fear we are not getting rid of God because we still believe in grammar. (TI iii. 5)

The 'error' here is to mistake the structure of the sentence as a reflection of reality, of thinking 'that in language [one] possessed knowledge of the world',[8] whereas, in fact, we had simply developed a 'bad habit of taking a mnemonic, an abbreviated formula, to be an entity, finally as a cause, e.g., to say of lightning "it flashes" '.[9] Or to understand that the ' "I" is the condition, "think" is the predicate and conditioned—thinking is an activity to which a subject *must* be thought of as cause'.[10] But for Nietzsche, if one attends to what actually happens, one would see the truth 'that a thought comes when "it" wants, not when "I" want', the 'I' or 'subject' being 'only an assumption, an assertion'.[11] The 'I' or 'subject' 'is not something given, it is something added and invented and projected

[7] GS 151. [8] HAH 11. [9] WP 548. [10] BGE 54. [11] BGE 17.

behind what there is',[12] and has no real existence outside the formal syntax of the sentence. Or, as he puts it elsewhere, 'there is no "being" behind doing, . . . "the doer" is merely a fiction added to the deed'.[13]

The culprit who is to blame for these 'errors' is reason: '"Reason" is the cause of our falsification of the evidence of the senses. In so far as the senses show becoming, passing away, change, they do not lie'. It is what 'we *make* of their evidence that first introduces a lie into it, for example the lie of unity, the lie of materiality, of substance, of duration'.[14] As an example of the origin of the error of mistaking what is merely 'similar' for what is 'equal', Nietzsche presents us with his own example of natural selection:

> *Origin of the logical:*— How did logic come into existence in man's head? Certainly out of illogic, whose realm originally must have been immense. Innumerable beings who made inferences in a way different from ours perished; for all that, their ways might have been truer. Those, for example, who did not know how to find often enough what is 'equal' as regards both nourishment and hostile animals—those, in other words, who subsumed things too slowly and cautiously—were favoured with a lesser probability of survival than those who guessed immediately upon encountering similar instances that they must be equal. The dominant tendency, however, to treat as equal what is merely similar—an illogical tendency, for nothing is really equal—is what first created any basis for logic.
>
> In order that the concept of substance could originate—which is indispensable for logic although in the strictest sense nothing real corresponds to it—it was likewise necessary that for a long time one did not see nor perceive the changes in things. The beings that did not see so precisely had an advantage over those that saw everything 'in flux'. At bottom, every high degree of caution in making inferences and every skeptical tendency constitute a great danger for life. No living beings would have survived if the opposite tendency—to affirm rather than suspend judgement, to err and *make up* things rather than wait, to assent rather than negate, to pass judgement rather than be just—had not been bred to the point where it became extraordinarily strong. (GS 111)

He also considers the notion of the subject to arise from a similar mistake: 'The "subject" is the fiction that many similar states in us are the effect of one substratum: but it is we who first created the "similarity" of these states; our adjusting them and making them

[12] WP 481. [13] GM i. 13. [14] TI iii. 2.

similar is the fact, not their similarity'.[15] The notion of being is another such 'substratum; there is no "being" behind doing, effecting, becoming; "the doer" is merely a fiction added to the deed—the deed is everything'.[16] Thus notions such as subject, ego, being, are merely the creations of 'a conceptual synthesis',[17] a synthesis of what is in fact a continually fluctuating multiplicity of states under a single, static concept that is then misunderstood as the bearer and cause of such states. However, although grammar and reason may provide a framework for producing such 'conceptual mummies',[18] it is man's desire for power and control over all that seems strange and threatening to him that is the real force behind the creation of these notions:

In the formation of reason, logic, the categories, it was *need* that was authoritative: the need, not to 'know', but to subsume, to schematize, for the purpose of intelligibility and calculation. (WP 515)

Man wants to deny what his actual experience reveals: 'Death, change, age . . . growth', that all is *becoming*.[19] He *wants* existence to reflect the dictum: 'What is, does not *become*; what becomes, *is* not'.[20] Out of man's basic need for security and urge for power and control over chaotic nature, including his own, man, the creator, out of compulsion spins his deceptive web of 'conceptual mummies' over existence, thereby creating what he erroneously believes

[15] WP 485. One wonders to what extent Nietzsche might have been influenced by either Hume or Buddhism, or perhaps both, in these matters. Hume (1978), bk 1, sect. 6 'Of Personal Identity', offers a similar critique of the self. For example, Hume says that the 'self or person is not any one impression, but that to which our several impressions and ideas are suppos'd to have a reference. If any impression gives rise to the idea of self, that impression must continue invariably the same, thro' the whole course of our lives; since self is suppos'd to exist after that manner. But there is no impression constant and invariable'. When Hume enters 'most intimately into what I call *myself*, I always stumble on some particular perception or other . . . I never can catch *myself* at any time without a perception, and never can observe anything but the perception'. There again, he would have read in Oldenberg: 'We are accustomed to realize our inner life as a comprehensible factor, only when we are allowed to refer its changing ingredients, every individual feeling, every distinct act of the will, to one and an ever identical ego, but this mode of thinking is fundamentally opposed to Buddhism. Here as everywhere it condemns that fixity which we are prone to give to the current of incidents that come and go by conceiving a substance, to or in which they might happen. A seeing, a hearing, a conceiving, above all a suffering, takes place: but an existence, which may be regarded as the seer, the hearer, the sufferer, is not recognized in Buddhist teaching' (1882: 253–4).

[16] GM i. 13. [17] WP 371. [18] TI iii. 1. [19] TI iii. 1. [20] TI iii. 1.

to be the '*real world*',[21] a world where he finds a special place for himself in the hierarchy of being. The fundamental self-deception, here, is that 'instead of seeing in logic and the categories of reason means toward the adjustment of the world for utilitarian ends ... one believed one possessed in them the criterion of truth and *reality*'.[22] But, according to Nietzsche, when one realizes 'all that has begotten these assumptions, is passion, error, and self-deception ... [and that these are] the foundation of all extant religions and metaphysical systems', then, Nietzsche rather sweepingly claims, 'one has refuted them!'[23] But although man has created a purely fictitious world of 'eternally enduring things' for himself out of his own weakness in the face of reality as it is, i.e. a world of becoming, nevertheless

> It is through *errors* as to its origin, its uniqueness, its destiny, and through the *demands* that have been advanced on the basis of these errors, that mankind has raised itself on high and again and again 'excelled itself'. (D 425)

It is because man 'saw himself only incompletely ... placed himself in a false order of rank in relation to animals and nature ... invented ever new tables of goods and always accepted them for a time as eternal and unconditional',[24] because he 'has taken himself for something higher and imposed sterner laws upon himself' and was thereby able to restrain and 'tame' his animal nature, that man has actually become more than an animal. Without such 'errors ... man would have remained animal'.[25] But, as man begins to awaken to the truth of these errors a danger emerges: 'If we removed the effects of these ... errors, we should also remove humanity, humaneness, and "human dignity"'.[26] Therefore, when man emerges from these errors, he has to

> take a *retrograde step*: he has to grasp the historical justification that resides in such ideas, likewise the psychological; he has to recognize that they have been most responsible for the advancement of mankind and that without such a retrograde step he will deprive himself of the best that mankind has hitherto produced. (HAH 20)

Man has to understand the truth these errors reveal, the truth of *becoming*, the truth that he is not 'an *aeterna veritas* ... something

[21] WP 521. [22] WP 584. [23] HAH 9.
[24] GS 115. [25] HAH 40. [26] GS 115.

that remains constant in the midst of all flux', but, just like any other natural phenomenon, is something that has *become*.[27] And if man can realize the truth that he has actually become more than an animal, and that he did so without any divine intervention or influence, but solely through his own efforts, then it follows that he can become more than he is at present. What he therefore needs is a view of himself and nature that will help him become more, a view that for Nietzsche will be characterized by his notion of the will to power: 'the ultimate ground and character of all change'.[28]

Although we will not find any examples of what Nietzsche calls '*historical philosophizing*' in the Pāli texts, nevertheless, there is an example of advancing natural causes for the belief in a creator God which parallels Nietzsche's example above. In the *Dīgha-Nikāya*, the Buddha says:

> There are . . . some recluses and brāhmans who declare as their doctrine that all things began with the creation by a God [*issara*], or by a Brahmā. I have gone to them and said: 'Reverend sirs, is it true that you declare that all things began with the creation by a God, or by a Brahmā?' 'Yes', they replied. Then I asked: 'In that case, how do the reverend teachers declare that this came about?' But they could not give me an answer, and so they asked me in return, and I replied:
>
> 'There comes a time, friends, sooner or later after a long period, when this universe devolves. At this time of contraction, most beings are reborn in the Ābhassara Brahmā world. There they dwell, mind-made, feeding on rapture, self-luminous, moving through the air, glorious—and they stay like that for a very long time.
>
> 'But the time comes, sooner or later after a very long period, when this universe begins to re-evolve. In this expanding universe an empty palace of Brahmā appears. And then one being, from the exhaustion of his life-span or of his merits, falls from the Ābhassara realm and arises in the empty Brahmā palace. There he dwells, mind-made, feeding on rapture, self-luminous, moving through the air, glorious—and he stays like that for a very long time.
>
> 'Then in this being who has been alone for so long there arises unrest, discontent and worry, and he thinks: "Oh, if only some other beings would come here!" And other beings, from the exhaustion of their life-span or of their merits, fall from the Ābhassara realm and arise in the Brahmā palace as companions for this being. There they dwell, mind-made . . . and they stay like that for a very long time.
>
> 'And then, friends, that being who first arose there thinks: "I am

[27] HAH 2. [28] WP 685.

Brahmā, the Great Brahmā, the Conqueror, the All-Powerful, the Lord, the Maker and Creator, Ruler, Appointer and Orderer, Father of All That Have Been and Shall Be. These beings were created by me. How so? Because I first had this thought: 'Oh, if only some other beings would come here!' That was my wish, and then these beings came into this existence!" But those beings who arose subsequently think: "This, friends, is Brahmā, Great Brahmā . . . Father of All That Have Been and Shall Be. How so? We have seen that he was here first, and that we arose after him."

'This being that arose first is long-lived, more beautiful and powerful than they are. And it may happen that some being falls from that realm and arises in this world. Having arisen in this world, he goes forth from the household life into homelessness. Having gone forth, he, by means of effort, exertion, application, earnestness and right attention attains such a degree of mental concentration [*ceto-samādhi*] that he thereby recalls his last existence, but recalls none before that. And he thinks: "That Great Brahmā, the Conqueror . . . he made us, and he is permanent, stable, eternal, not subject to change, the same for ever and ever. But we who were created by that Brahmā, we are impermanent, unstable, short-lived, fated to fall away, and we have come into this world"'. (D-N iii. 28–30)

Here we have a rather satirical account of a Buddhist parallel to Nietzsche's 'natural philosophizing' concerning the origins of the belief in a creator God, but here the 'error in the interpretation of certain natural events' concerns a recluse's meditation experience—which, within the Indian context is a purely natural event—rather than that of a dream. The Buddhists, however, add a double irony in that they do not actually deny that there is a being who actually thinks he is the 'Father of All That Have Been and Shall Be', and that, in higher states of meditative consciousness, a mystic can actually meet him, just that 'God' simply suffers from grand self-delusion![29]

Although 'God', in the form of Brahmā, was still around in the Buddha's day, the Buddha also encountered what could be called the Indian version of 'God's shadow' in the various views and doctrines of his contemporaries, some of whom, the *samaṇas*, had, like himself, rejected the authority of the Vedic tradition where

[29] Not only that, but according to Buddhist cosmology, there are seven realms beyond this Brahmā, all of which are classed as mundane as they form part of *saṃsāra*. At A-N iv. 89, the Buddha says that for seven aeons of the universe's evolution and devolution he did not come back again to this world, but when the universe began to re-evolve again, he seven times won Brahmā's empty palace, and became the Great Brahmā. So presumably Gotama—or whoever he was in those previous lives—also suffered from such grand self-delusion!

God in various forms was to be found.[30] Many of these shadows are found in the lists of *diṭṭhis* or 'speculative views' found in the *Brahmajāla Sutta* or 'Net of Brahmā Discourse' of the *Dīgha-Nikāya*. From the sixty-two 'speculative views' that are listed there, the only ones that that are of interest here are those which postulate some form of 'eternalism' (*sassatavāda*). These can be categorized as those views postulating some notion of a two-world framework, one realm of which is eternal and is either occupied by the Great Brahmā, as we have seen, or instead by many eternal gods. The other realm is our ordinary impermanent world occupied by ordinary mortals, who seem doomed to remain so for ever. These views are called 'partial-eternalism' (*ekacca-sassatavāda*), and have their source in the practice of meditation giving rise to the memory of a previous life in some other divine realm. The account, above, of how the belief in Brahmā as a creator god arose is found here. However, it is not only meditation experience that can give rise to such eternalistic views; they can also arise though 'logical reasoning' (*takka*) and 'investigation' (*vīṃaṁsa*):

> Here, a certain recluse or Brāhman is a logician, an investigator. He declares his view, hammered out by reason and investigation, following his own flight of thought, he argues: 'That which is called "eye", "ear", "nose", "tongue", and "body"—that is a Self [*attan*] that is impermanent, unstable, subject to change. But that which is called "mind" [*citta*], or "mentality" [*manas*], or "consciousness" [*viññāṇa*]—that is a Self that is permanent, stable, eternal, not subject to change, and will remain the same eternally. (D-N i. 21)

Other eternalists believe that both the Self and the world are eternal. Again, these views arise either through meditation experience, wherein some are said to remember their previous existences through forty aeons (*kappas*) of the evolution and devolution of the universe, which amounts to millions of lives, and so conclude that the Self and world must be eternal as they are always present, or through logical reasoning and investigation as in the above

[30] Other gods, who at one time have held some kind of 'Supreme Being' status in the Brāhmanical tradition and are mentioned in the Pāli *suttas*, are Varuṇa, Pajāpati, Inda (Indra), and Issara (Īśvara). For an account of these see Gonda's essay, *The Concept of a personal God in ancient Indian religious thought*, in Gonda (1975). Olivelle (1996: 411), in his 'List of Names', mentions that Pajāpati ('Lord of Creatures') 'is the creator god *par excellence* in the Brāhmaṇas and the Upaniṣads' Perhaps by the time the Buddha appears Brahmā had become more popular, at least in the Ganges basin.

quote. They all conclude: 'Though those beings roam and wander [through existence], pass away and re-arise, yet the "Self" and the world remain the same, just like eternity itself'. Other views assert an eternal Self that is either 'conscious' (*saññin*) after death, or 'unconscious' (*asaññin*), or both conscious and unconscious, or neither conscious nor unconscious. These latter views are further expanded by claiming that this eternal Self is either material, or immaterial, both, or neither; finite, or infinite, both, or neither; of uniform perception, or diversified perception, both, or neither; exclusively happy, or exclusively miserable, both, or neither. Given this rather stereotyped categorization, one can see how sixty-two different views are arrived at.

The *sutta* offers no direct arguments to contradict or undermine these views, but has the Buddha simply declaring that he understands these 'view-points (*diṭṭhiṭṭhāna*) thus assumed and misapprehended', as well as what future destinations they will lead to within *saṃsāra*. He alone knows that which transcends them all, i.e. *nirvāṇa*. Such views the Buddha sees as arising in dependence upon a misinterpretation of experience, and even though that experience includes states of heightened consciousness experienced through meditation, it is nevertheless deemed by the Buddha to be 'the experience of those who do not know and see, the worry and vacillation of those immersed in thirst'. The Buddha, therefore, is refuting these views by claiming to understand their psychological origins in a manner not too dissimilar from Nietzsche's, except that the Buddha is relying only on his own direct experience.

Although there are no direct references to the Upaniṣads or to the notion of *brahman* in the Buddhist *suttas*,[31] we can find instances of the Buddhist response to the substantialist ontology of the *ātman/brahman* doctrine of the early Upaniṣads. Briefly stated, the *ātman/brahman* doctrine is a doctrine of an immanent and transcendent absolute, variously called *brahman,* the 'Self' (*ātman*), the 'Person' (*puruṣa*), the 'Immortal' (*amṛta*), and sometimes simply 'this All' (*sarvam idam*), implying the whole universe.[32] For example, in the *Bṛhadāraṇyaka Upaniṣad* we have the following:

[31] As individual Upaniṣads were assigned to one of the three (later four) Veda(s), when the Buddhist texts refer to the three Veda(s) they may well have included the Upaniṣads indirectly, if not by name.

[32] As Olivelle states (1996: notes, p. 297), 'the term [*sarva*] . . . is used to indicate not all things in the universe but a higher-level totality that encompasses the universe'. The following quotes from the Upaniṣads are taken from Olivelle (1996).

In the beginning this world was just a single body (*ātman*), shaped like a man [*puruṣa*]. He looked around and saw nothing but himself. The first thing he said was, 'Here I am!' and from that the name 'I' came into being. (1. 4. 1)

It then occurred to him: 'I alone am this creation, for I created all this.' From this 'creation' came into being. Anyone who knows this prospers in this creation of his. (1. 4. 5)

One should consider [all activities] as simply his Self (*ātman*), for in it all these become one. This same Self (*ātman*) is the trail of this All, for by following it one comes to know this All, just as by following their tracks one finds [the cattle]. Whoever knows this finds fame and glory. (1. 4. 7)

In the beginning this world was only *brahman*, and it knew only itself (*ātman*), thinking: 'I am *brahman*.' As a result, it became this All. Among the gods [*devas*], likewise, whosoever realized this, only they became this All. It was the same among the seers and among humans. . . . If a man knows 'I am *brahman*' in this way, he becomes this All. Not even the gods are able to prevent it, for he becomes their very Self (*ātman*). (1. 4. 10)[33]

Now this Self (*ātman*) is a world for all beings. (1. 4. 16)

For when there is a duality [*dvaita*] of some kind, then the one can smell the other, the one can see the other, . . . hear . . . greet . . . think of . . . perceive the other. When, however, the All has become one's very Self (*ātman*), then who is there for one to hear [etc.] and by what means? (2. 4. 14; repeated at 4. 5. 15)

The radiant and immortal person [*puruṣa*] in the earth and, in the case of the body (*ātman*), the radiant immortal person residing in the physical body—they are both one's Self (*ātman*). It is the immortal; it is *brahman*; it is this All. (21. 5. 1) [*This last sentence is repeated at the end of verses 2–14*]

All these—the priestly power, the royal power, worlds, gods, beings, this All—all that is nothing but this Self [*ātman*]. (4. 5. 7)

However, I have preferred the refrain 'this All' for his 'this Whole World' and 'the Whole', and replaced 'self' with 'Self'.

[33] Reading this section of the *Bṛhadāraṇyaka*, it is rather obvious that the 'creation myth' quoted above from the *Dīgha-Nikāya*, that is proffered as the main explanation for the arising of the belief in a creator God, is a tongue-in-cheek Buddhist parody of this Upaniṣadic account. For example, in the *Bṛhadāraṇyaka*, it is *brahman* rather than Brahmā who finds himself becoming lonely: 'He found no pleasure at all; so one finds no pleasure when one is alone. He wanted to have a companion. Now he was as large as a man and woman in close embrace' (1. 4. 3). From this union, creation issues forth. However, it is rather odd that *brahman*, which is usually regarded as the impersonal Absolute, seems here to become rather personal.

In the *Chāndogya Upaniṣad* we have:

Brahman, you see, is this All. (3. 14. 1)

The finest essence here—that constitutes the Self [*ātman*] of this All; that is the truth; that is the Self (*ātman*). And that's how you are, Śvetaketu. (6. 8. 7; 6. 9. 4; 6. 10. 3; 6. 11. 3)

Plenitude [also the 'I', the Self (*ātman*)], is below ... above ... in the west ... in the east ... in the south ... in the north. Indeed [they] extend over this All. (7. 25. 1–2)

The standard simile of this immanent absolute is that of salt dissolved in water: the salt is not seen, yet, like 'absolute Being' [*sat*], it permeates the whole and gives it one taste,[34] a simile adopted by the Buddhists for their own ends.[35]

That the Buddha sometimes responded to these ideas in an almost satirical manner can be seen from a couple of passages from the *suttas*. For example, in the *Sabba Sutta* the Buddha states what he understands by 'the All':[36]

Brethren, I will teach you 'the all.' ... It is the eye and visual objects, ear and sounds, nose and scents, tongue and savours, body and things tangible, mind and objects of mind. That, brethren, is called 'the all.'

Whoso, brethren, should say: 'Rejecting this all, I will proclaim another all,—it would be mere talk on his part, and when questioned he could not make good his boast ... because ... it would be beyond his scope to do so. (S-N iv. 15)

Here, the Buddha is obviously addressing a topic that was of general interest among his contemporary *religieux*, and I would understand 'the all' here as referring to something comparable with 'this All' of the above Upaniṣads, which is also a synonym for the *ātman*/*brahman*. I would suggest that the Buddha's conception of 'the all', above, assumes the Upaniṣadic notion of 'this All'. And, being an explicit rejection of it, is therefore a rejection of the *ātman*/*brahman* doctrine since the latter conception implies a metaphysical something over and above what he teaches as 'the all'. The Buddha, here, also rejects any possibility of knowledge beyond 'the all' for epistemological reasons: 'it would be beyond his scope to do

[34] *Chāndogya Upaniṣad*, 6. 13. 1–3.

[35] One of the 'eight strange and wonderful things about the mighty ocean' is that it 'is of one taste, the taste of salt, even so, monks, this Dhamma is of one taste, the taste of freedom [*vimutti*]' (Ud. 56).

[36] *Sabba* in Pāli, *sarva* in Sanskrit.

so', which I would take as implying that the *ātman/brahman* as conceived of in the Upaniṣads could not be an object of knowledge. For example, in relation to the six senses and their objects, which constitute the Buddhist 'all' above,[37] the *Chāndogya Upaniṣad* conceives of an *ātman* over and above this 'all' as the agent for whom the senses (including the mind [*manas*]) are mere instruments.[38] In the *Kaṭha Upaniṣad* we have the 'secret and eternal *brahman*', the single Inner Self [*antarātman*] within every being [which] adapts its appearance to match that of each, of all things . . . yet remains quite distinct'.[39] The Buddha, however, in contrast to the Upaniṣadic view states that the 'all' is 'without Self' (*anattan*).[40] Given what these *suttas* have to say about the 'all', I would suggest that it is some views such as those found in the Upaniṣads that the Buddha is rejecting here as 'mere talk', as these views can all be subsumed under the Upaniṣadic notion of 'this All' thought to be beyond 'the all' mentioned by the Buddha.

Elsewhere,[41] in the same group of *suttas*, the Buddha refers to the 'conceit' (*maññita*) of 'being the all or in the all or coming from the all', which, again, I would understand as being directed at some of the Upaniṣadic views quoted above: 'If a man knows "I am *brahman*" in this way, he becomes this All'; 'In the beginning this world was only *brahman*, and it knew only itself (*ātman*), thinking: "I am *brahman*." As a result, it became this All. Among the gods, likewise, whosoever realized this, only they became this All. It was the same among the seers and among humans'; '*Brahman*, you see, is this All'. The Buddha is therefore dismissing such views as mere conceits, although, as we saw above, such views may very well spring from meditation experiences of a mystical kind, but these experiences are considered by the Buddhists to be misconstrued by the yogic practitioners, resulting in conceited views such as that one is 'the All', or 'I am *brahman*'.

There may also be a touch of irony about what the Buddha, in

[37] It must be remembered that the scope of possible objects of the 'mind-sense' or *manas* goes quite beyond the scope of what modern Western philosophy and psychology would consider as part of their field, i.e. other worlds and beings, clairaudience, clairvoyance, etc. Such aspects of the human condition are considered normal in both Buddhist and other contemporary systems. They all belong to the domain of the 'senses' (*indriyas*), which includes the 'mind-sense' (*mano-indriya*).

[38] 8. 12. 4, with slight modification to Olivelle's trans.

[39] 5. 6 and 9, with slight modification to Olivelle's trans.

[40] S-N iv. 28.

[41] S-N iv. 23.

some other *suttas* from this group, says about 'the all'. Rather than, as in the Upaniṣads, identifying the goal as gaining knowledge of 'the All', or becoming one with 'the All', the Buddha teaches that one should abandon 'the all' by 'fully knowing and comprehending it' as, 'without fully knowing and comprehending it . . . without detaching himself from, without abandoning the all, a man is incapable of extinguishing *dukkha*'. 'The all' is said to be 'on fire with the blaze of lust, hatred and stupidity, the blaze of infatuation, the blaze of birth, decay, sorrow and grief, woe, lamentation and despair'.[42] 'The all' is therefore to be abandoned as it is *dukkha*. Could the Buddha here have in mind the Upaniṣadic notion that *ātman* 'consists of bliss' (*ānanda-maya*),[43] alluding to the fact that rather than being bliss, 'the All' is quite the opposite![44]

In the *Alagaddūpama Sutta* or 'Discourse on the Parable of the Water-Snake',[45] the Buddha refers to the six *diṭṭhiṭṭhānāni* or 'six grounds of speculative views'—which are all regarded as *micchā-diṭṭhis* or 'wrong-views'—the sixth of which is a clear allusion to the Upaniṣadic notion of the identity of the *ātman* with 'the All', here called the 'world' (*loka*):[46] 'That which is the world, that is the *attan*. After dying I will become permanent, lasting, eternal, not liable to change . . . he regards this [world] as: "this is mine, this I am, this is my *attan*"'. Two of these last three phrases may reflect their Upaniṣadic origins: 'this I am' (*eso 'ham asmi*) reflects the phrase 'I am this' (*ayam asmi*) from the *Bṛhadāraṇyaka Upaniṣad*, which is in relation to knowing the *ātman*,[47] and the phrase 'this is my Self' (*eso me attā*) reflects the phrase 'this is my Self' (*eṣa ma ātmā*) found in the *Chāndogya Upaniṣad*.[48] Norman also adds that 'The phrase *eso 'ham asmi* "I am that" is the *tat tvam asi* "Thou art that" of the Upaniṣada [*sic*] looked at from the point of view of the first person

[42] S-N iv. 18–20. At Itv 3–4 there is a similar treatment of 'the all' which concludes with the verse: 'Who, having known the all in all its parts, | And who finds no pleasure in any of it, | By full comprehension of the all | He truly escapes all *dukkha*.

[43] *Taittirīya Upaniṣad*, 2. 8 and elsewhere.

[44] Under the doctrine of the four 'perversions' (*vipallāsas*) of 'apperception' (*saññā*), 'mind' (*citta*), and 'view' (*diṭṭhi*), there is the *vipallāsa* of seeing that which is *dukkha* as pleasant, and that which is 'without-self' (*anattan*) as 'the Self' (*attan*). (See A-N ii. 52.)

[45] M-N i. 130ff.

[46] Regarding the term *loka*, the PED says the term is used to denote 'the comprehensive sense of "universe"', or, we could say, 'this All' (*sarvam idam*).

[47] 4. 4. 12.

[48] 3. 14. 3–4.

instead of the second person'.[49] The implication of these views is brought out when the Buddha asks:

If a person were to gather or burn or do as he pleases with the grass, twigs, branches and foliage in the Jeta Grove, would it occur to you: The person is gathering us, he is burning us, he is doing as he pleases with us?

'No, Lord'. What is the reason for this? 'It is that this, Lord, is not our *attan*, not what belongs to the *attan*'. (M-N i. 141)[50]

Here the Buddha is being very ironic about the Upaniṣadic metaphysics of the *ātman*: if 'everything here is what the *ātman* is',[51] then the *ātman* must also be these twigs and branches. If someone burns these twigs and branches they must therefore be burning the *ātman*. And, if that *ātman* is our true Self, then our true Self is being burned. Yet, when these twigs and branches are being burned, what is our experience? Is there any part of us that feels it is being burned? No. Therefore it does not make much sense to claim 'that which is the world, that is the *attan*'.[52]

At other times, the Buddha is rather more straightforward in his dealing with Upaniṣadic essentialist ideas. For example, in the *Śvetāśvatara Upaniṣad* we have the notion of the 'all-pervading *ātman*, which is contained [in the body], like butter in milk'.[53] In the *Dīgha-Nikāya*, the Buddha, no doubt with this image in mind, says that although from 'milk we get curds, from curds butter, from butter ghee, and from ghee cream of ghee . . . when we have milk, we do not speak of curds, of butter, of ghee or of cream of ghee, we speak of milk'.[54] In other words, when we have milk there is only milk, there is no unseen substantialist essence of that milk which is butter. To posit a trans-empirical and unchanging essence, 'butter', behind the appearance of milk is to fall into the extreme view of 'eternalism' (*sassatavāda*). The Buddhist view, the 'Middle Way' (*majjha-magga*), expressed in the doctrine of 'dependent co-origination', is to see that without milk there can be no curds, without curds there can be no butter, etc. There is a continuity of

[49] Norman (1981), 23. The phrase 'thou art that', meaning that one's essential being, the *ātman*, is one with the universal *ātman* or *brahman*, is found at *Chāndogya Upaniṣad*, 6. 8. 7 and elsewhere.

[50] No doubt some intellectually astute Brāhman would not have acquiesced so easily as the Buddha's audience did here.

[51] *Bṛhadāraṇyaka Upaniṣad*, 4. 5. 7.

[52] S-N iv. 23. See also Norman (1981) on this point.

[53] 1. 16. [54] D-N i. 201.

conditional arising, represented here by the process from milk to cream of ghee, but within this process there is no thing that remains unchanged. 'Milk' is simply a name we give to an aspect of this particular process that arises in dependence upon conditions. When it is present, we talk about 'milk', and do not ask what happens to the 'milk' when 'it' becomes curds, or what happens to the 'curds' when 'they' become butter. To do so, from a Buddhist point of view, would be to fall in with the 'wrong view' (*micchā-diṭṭhi*) of 'eternalism' (*sassatavāda*) expressed in the Upaniṣads.

Elsewhere in the Upaniṣads, the *ātman*, among other things, is said to be 'made of consciousness' (*vijñāna-maya*), and, passing at death from one embodied form to another, is compared to a caterpillar passing from one blade of grass to another.[55] In the Buddhist texts, we have a Buddhist monk called Sāti, who thought that the Buddha actually taught this kind of Upaniṣadic doctrine: 'just this one and the same "consciousness" (*viññāṇa*, Skt. *vijñāna*) runs on [unchanged] and is reborn again and again'.[56] The Buddha isn't too pleased at this and censures him, telling him that he has never taught such a doctrine:

> Misguided man, in many discourses have I not stated consciousness to be dependently arisen, since without a condition there is no arising of consciousness. (M-N i. 258)

Sāti's error was to think that it was the 'self-same' (*anañña*) consciousness that transmigrates,[57] that consciousness was some unchanging essence equivalent to the Upaniṣadic *ātman* that, despite phenomenal change, remains in essence unchanged from life to life.

The Buddhist alternative to this form of essentialism is found in its principle doctrine of 'dependent co-arising' (*paṭicca-samuppāda*), which states that all phenomena—including the goal of *nirvāṇa* itself—come to be only in dependence upon other conditions, conditions that are themselves dependent upon other conditions *ad infinitum*. In the above quote this is expressed as 'without a condition there is no arising of consciousness'. The universe as presented by the Buddhists is a universe of pure *becoming*, without a trace of any 'eternally enduring substances', whether they be the

[55] *Bṛhadāraṇyaka Upaniṣad*, 4. 4. 3–5.

[56] M-N i. 256ff.

[57] As Collins (1982) says 'The point here is not to deny that consciousness is in any way the vehicle of rebirth, but only to deny that it is a *changeless* subject of experience and action' (104; see also 213ff).

Upaniṣadic *ātman* or *brahman*, 'consciousness' (*viññāṇa*), the *jīva* or 'soul' of the Jainas,[58] the seven eternal and indestructible 'substances' (*kāya*) taught by Pakudha Kaccāyana, a contemporary of the Buddha,[59] or any other 'substance' for which similar claims are made. None of these are considered by the Buddhists to stand outside this universal law of dependent co-arising: if everything comes to be in dependence upon other conditions, then there can be no 'Self' (*ātman*), 'soul' (*jīva*), 'consciousness', or 'substance' (*kāya*) of any kind that can be considered to be eternal, unchanging, or autonomous. All this is summed up in the Buddhist *anattan* or 'no-Self' doctrine, which I would understand as this principle of dependent co-arising applied to the Upaniṣadic *ātman* doctrine: if the Upaniṣads had chosen the term *jīva* or 'soul' as their unchanging essence, then the Buddhists would in all probability have formulated an *ajīva* or 'no-soul' doctrine. The fact that the Buddhists formulated an *anattan* or no-Self doctrine probably indicates that the term *ātman* was the most popular term among those who held some 'eternalist doctrine' (*sassatavāda*), who held some theory of an 'eternal enduring substance'. The Buddhist goal of *nirvāṇa*, which replaces the Upaniṣadic goal, is spoken of in quite the opposite terms, as 'a designation meaning "no-Self" (*anattan*)'.[60] *Nirvāṇa* is therefore not some eternally enduring substance or Self, but is in fact a state of liberation (*vimutti*) attained through insight into the

[58] In Jainism, the individual *jīva* or 'soul' has a natural state of unlimited 'insight' (*darśana*), 'knowledge' (*jñāna*), 'energy' (*vīrya*), and 'happiness' (*sukha*), but this is not actualized because of being weighed down by particles of *karman*, which results in the *jīva* becoming embroiled in *saṃsāra*. When liberated from *karman*, it ascends to the summit of the cosmos where it dwells eternally in its natural state. See Frauwallner (1973), i. 199 ff. The Buddhist texts, however, make no direct comment on this *jīva* or 'soul' doctrine. The only references to the *jīva* in the Pāli texts are restricted to the oft-repeated question as to whether the *jīva* is the same as or different from the body. However, the Buddha never gives a direct answer but simply replies that such questions do not conduce to leading the religious life (see S-N ii. 51). Therefore there is no corresponding *ajīva* or 'no-soul' doctrine in Buddhism, only an *anātman* doctrine. Nevertheless, the *anātman* doctrine does imply that there is no *jīva* as the Jainas conceive of it.

[59] See D-N i. 56. Pakudha Kaccāyana postulated that there were seven eternal and indestructible substances: the four elements (referred to as *kāyas*), 'pleasure' (*sukha*) and 'pain' (*dukkha*), and the 'soul' (*jīva*). For comments on the correspondences between this theory and the philosophy of Empedocles, see Jayatilleke (1963), 267 ff. Again, there are no direct refutations of this doctrine in the any of the Pāli texts, but one assumes that it would have been dismissed as being merely the product of logic and reason, as similar views were deemed.

[60] Vin. v. 86.

very fact that there is no such thing as a Self, that there are no eternally enduring substances, that all things arise in dependence upon conditions.[61] When the Buddha was asked 'How does one abandon speculation about the "Self"', he replies that one can only abandon all such speculations by 'knowing and seeing' that all the conditions and factors, both subjective and objective, that create and constitute our total experience are 'without Self'.[62] Attachment to such doctrines will only bring one *dukkha*,[63] or, as Nietzsche puts it, they will 'darken our minds'.[64]

Like Nietzsche, Buddhism is also aware of the beguiling nature of language, and the part it plays in the creation of such 'conceptual mummies' as the *ātman* or the soul or the atom. For example, in the *Dīgha-Nikāya*, the Buddha states that although he may refer to such entities as the 'gross acquired self' (the 'self' of ordinary mortals in this world, and other *kāma-loka* or 'sensuous worlds), the 'mind-made acquired self' (the 'self' of the *devas* of the divine realms or *rūpa-loka*), or the 'formless acquired self' (the 'self' of the *devas* of the higher divine realms or *arūpa-loka*), he sees that 'these are merely names, expressions, turns of speech, designations in common use in the world, which the Tathāgata uses without misapprehending them'.[65] When a person with 'transformative insight' uses terms such as 'I' and 'mine' he does so in a merely conventional sense,[66] without being beguiled into assuming, to use Nietzsche's phrase, that when he says 'I think' there is an '*I* who thinks'.[67] He is not misled by concepts and the structure of language. Just as such notions are simply concepts applied to and imposed upon what is in fact a plurality of events, what Nietzsche calls a 'conceptual synthesis',[68] Buddhism also regards such notions in a similar manner:

> For just when the parts are rightly set,
> The term 'chariot' is used,
> So, when the five *khandhas* are present,
> There is the convention 'being'. (S-N i. 135)

[61] 'He who sees dependent co-arising, sees the Dhamma. He who sees the Dhamma sees dependent co-arising' (M-N i. 191–2), Dhamma being understood here as 'truth'.
[62] S-N iv. 148.
[63] M-N i. 137.
[64] GS 109.
[65] D-N i. 195–202. [66] S-N i. 14. [67] BGE 16. [68] WP 317.

The five *khandhas* or 'aggregates' of 'body', 'feeling', 'apperception', 'formations', and 'consciousness' are, of course, themselves merely concepts applied to what is an ever-changing plurality of events. The notion 'being' (*satta*) is simply a 'synthetic concept' applied to the whole.

That Nietzsche was to some extent aware of the Buddhist position, is witnessed in the *Will to Power*, where he notes that Buddhism has a

> lack of categories not only for a 'world in itself', but an insight into the erroneous procedures by means of which this whole concept is arrived at. 'Absolute reality', 'being-in-itself' a contradiction. In a world of becoming, 'reality' is always only a simplification for practical ends, or a deception through the coarseness of organs, or a variation in the tempo of becoming. (WP 580)

Whether it is God in the form of Yahweh, Allah, the 'God of Love', Brahmā, Prajāpati, *brahman*, the Absolute, or 'God's shadow' in the form of the soul, *ātman*, *jīva*, atom, 'thing-in-itself', ego, substance, both Nietzsche and Buddhism agree that such notions are fictions. Using Nietzsche's language, both claim that there are no 'eternally enduring substances' of any kind, that there is no essence to man.[69]

[69] HAH 57.

10

'The Will to Power' and 'Thirst'

In the *Will to Power*, Nietzsche envisages the cosmos as 'a monster of energy, without beginning, without end, . . . a creating and destroying play of forces, . . . an eternal becoming that must return eternally'.[1] This is Nietzsche's '*Dionysian* world', the world as '*will to power*'. Within this world, man is a particular and discrete embodiment of this will to power, a particular configuration of a 'play of forces' emerging at a distinct point in the evolution of the natural world. Man is therefore a product of a world that precedes him. Buddhism, on the other hand, has never had a philosophy of nature, nor has it felt it necessary to have any definite view on the ultimate origins of man or the cosmos. In the *Dīgha-Nikāya*, we are presented with a general cosmological picture of a kind of beginningless cosmos—in that the Buddha says that the beginning of *saṃsāra* cannot be 'conceived of' (*anamatagga*) nor 'known' (*paññāyati*)[2]—which continually cycles through immense aeons (*kappas*) of 'devolution' (*saṃvaṭṭa*) and 'evolution' (*vivaṭṭa*).[3] Within this general cosmological picture, regardless of whatever period the cosmos is in, there are always unenlightened beings around in some realm or another, who could be said to 'return eternally' somewhere within *saṃsāra*—provided that they never attained *nirvāṇa*. However, within this cosmology, the only play of forces with which Buddhism is directly concerned are those that constitute unenlightened beings, not the forces that constitute the natural world. Therefore, any comparative study of Nietzsche's notion of will to power and the Buddhist notion of *taṇhā* will of necessity revolve around one particular embodiment of forces: man.

Stack mentions that Nietzsche's 'emphasis upon the centrality of "urges", "cravings", and "drives" in man that are said to be derived from a more primitive form of "affect" (= will to power)

[1] WP 1067. See also Stack (1983*a*), 265 ff. [2] S ii. 178 ff.
[3] See D-N i. 14, iii. 84 ff; A iv. 89.

suggests something analogous to the Buddhist concept of *tṛiṣṇā*'.[4] Stack bases this suggestion on the notion of *taṇhā* found in D. T. Suzuki's *Mysticism: Christian and Buddhist.*[5] He also mentions that 'Although there is no direct evidence that Nietzsche appropriated this basic notion [of *taṇhā*] in Buddhism, he was more than familiar with oriental thought (e.g., through Schopenhauer, the works of his friend, Paul Deussen—*Das System des Vedānta* and *Die Philosophie der Upanishads*—and through other studies or works, especially the Hindu *Laws of Manu*)'.[6] Schopenhauer does indeed compare 'willing . . . to an unquenchable thirst',[7] although he never mentions the Buddhist notion directly. However, in the works of Deussen[8] there are no references to the Buddhist notion of *taṇhā*, nor do we find any in the *Laws of Manu.* The most direct reference to *taṇhā* from Nietzsche's oriental sources that could be contrasted with his will to power would be Oldenberg's reference to the three forms of *taṇhā*: 'the thirst for pleasures, the thirst for being, the thirst for impermanence',[9]— the 'thirst for impermanence', as we saw, being a mistranslation of *vibhava-taṇhā*, which actually means 'thirst for non-existence'.[10]

As Nietzsche's notion of will to power has its paradigm in Hesiod's notion of *Eris* or Strife, I will use the notion of *Erōs* as found in Plato's *Symposium* as a paradigm for *taṇhā.*[11]

10.1. *TAṆHĀ* AND *ERŌS*

In the *Symposium*, Socrates makes the interesting point that as *Erōs* desires beauty and 'one desires that which one lacks', *Erōs* therefore 'lacks and does not possess beauty'.[12] Hence *Erōs* represents a state of desiring that which one lacks. As for the full nature

[4] (1983*a*), 265. *Tṛiṣṇā* [*tṛṣṇā*] is the Sanskrit of Pāli *taṇhā*.

[5] (1957), 94–5.

[6] (1983*a*), 265.

[7] (1969), i. 312. See also i. 327 and 389.

[8] See Deussen (1906 and 1912).

[9] (1882), 211.

[10] See end of Section 3.3.

[11] Interestingly, he could also have used the paradigm of *Erōs*, and indeed alludes it on occasions, e.g. at TI ix. 23 and 24. See Kaufmann (1974), ch. 8. Nietzsche also 'nominated Plato's *Symposium* as his *Lieblingsdichtung*, or favourite poetry, at the time of his graduation from Schulpforta' (Tejera (1987), 94).

[12] *Symposium*, 199e–201b.

of *Erōs*, Socrates' 'guide' Diotima informs him that 'the truth is that we isolate a particular kind of *Erōs* and appropriate for it the name of *Erōs*, which really belongs to a wider whole, while we employ different names for other kinds of *Erōs*'.[13] When Socrates asks for examples of some other kinds of *Erōs*, Diotima gives the examples of 'love of money or of physical prowess or of wisdom' and 'poetry',[14] which are all *Erōs* under different names, in the sense that they all share the characteristic of *Erōs*. *Erōs* can therefore be understood as a 'generic concept [which] embraces every desire for good and for happiness'.[15] It is not, therefore, to be identified with only one particular drive or affect, but is a characteristic shared by many drives, including the more spiritual. Diotima also makes a Hesiod-like distinction in alluding to the nature of *Erōs*, in that 'procreation can be either physical or spiritual'.[16] The former brings forth children whilst the latter creates beauty of mind and character, even wisdom, 'Wisdom [being] one of the most beautiful things'.[17] Yet this latter *Erōs* is not some completely dissimilar affect, but can be understood as the 'spiritualization' or 'sublimation' of the former—to use Nietzsche's terms.[18] Therefore, we can say that it is the actual object desired that informs one of the *kind* and quality of *Erōs*: an attractive body is the object of one kind of *Erōs*, i.e. physical love, and a beautiful state of mind is the object of another kind of *Erōs*, i.e. spiritual love. But what about *taṇhā*? How can *taṇhā* be modelled on this Socratic notion of *Erōs*?

10.2. THE TERM *TAṆHĀ*

Anyone acquainted with either the Pāli *suttas* or the Theravāda tradition as a whole, who was asked for an opinion on the spiritual status of *taṇhā*, usually translated as 'craving', would most likely answer along the lines that *taṇhā* is entirely antithetical to the Buddhist spiritual quest, the *brahmacariya,* and is almost akin to the Christian notion of original sin, in the sense that no one is born

[13] Ibid. 205b. [14] Ibid. 205d. [15] Ibid. 205d. [16] Ibid. 206b.
[17] Ibid. 204b.
[18] Using this term to cover *Erōs*'s 'ascent' from the more basic love of physical beauty to love of that beauty which is 'absolute, existing alone with itself, unique, [and] eternal' (ibid. 210a–211b).

without it. As the second of the Four Noble Truths tells us, *taṇhā* is the cause of *dukkha* or 'suffering and unsatisfactoriness', the first Noble Truth, and the cessation of *taṇhā*, the third Noble Truth, is synonymous with *nirvāṇa* itself, the very goal of Buddhist practice. *Taṇhā* is said to be the 'seamstress' that 'sews one just into this ever-becoming rebirth';[19] it is that by 'which this world is smothered, enveloped, tangled like a ball of thread, covered as with a blight, twisted up like a grass-rope, so that it overpasses not *saṃsāra*, the Downfall, the Way of Woe, the Ruin';[20] it is likened to an 'arrow . . . thickly smeared with poison'.[21] Selecting certain passages from the Pāli *suttas*, one can build up a view of *taṇhā* as completely unwholesome and anti-spiritual, which is more or less how *taṇhā* is presented in standard Buddhist writings. Notwithstanding this reprobation of *taṇhā*, there are also passages that present *taṇhā* in a more neutral and even in a positive light. When these are taken into consideration, what emerges is a more balanced view of *taṇhā*, a view that, like Nietzsche's will to power, can be said to have both destructive and creative potential. *Taṇhā* can become the 'seamstress' that 'sews one just into this ever-becoming rebirth', yet it can be shown that without *taṇhā* there would be no Buddhist spiritual life—no *brahmacariya* or 'pursuit of excellence'—and therefore no Buddhas.

Taṇhā is literally 'drought' or 'thirst' and, as the *Pali–English Dictionary* informs us, 'is found mainly in poetry, or in prose passages charged with emotion. It is rarely used in the philosophy or the psychology'. Figuratively, it means 'craving, hunger for, excitement, the fever of unsatisfied longing'. Given its poetic pedigree, *taṇhā* can be said to be a term that appeals more to the imagination than reason, and this may be why it is hardly mentioned in the lists and abstract permutations of the later technical, not to say arid, literature of the Abhidhamma. To those who heard the word from the mouth of the Buddha or one of his disciples, *taṇhā* no doubt evoked an acute pathos which the translation 'craving' miserably fails to do. Given the poetic pedigree of the term, I will attempt to show that *taṇhā* is best understood as a metaphor that conveys the general condition of unenlightened existence: a state of being whose general condition is the existential ground out of which arise the various strivings for gratification and fulfilment. In other words,

[19] A-N iii. 399–400. [20] A-N ii. 209–10. [21] M-N ii. 259–60.

taṇhā is not so much a specific affect or emotion, but, just as *Erōs* is said to be a 'generic concept [which] embraces every desire for good and happiness', can be understood more generally as a generic concept for the affective ground underlying the whole of saṃsāric existence[22] (which, of course, would include every desire for good and happiness). It can therefore be understood as an attempt to characterize, in a single metaphor, the general condition of being in the world, as well as providing the primary reason why we experience *saṃsāra* as ultimately *dukkha* or 'unsatisfactory'. In other words, as *saṃsāra* cannot *fully* quench our 'thirst', it must appear to one who fully understands this (i.e. an *ariya*) as *dukkha*.

10.3. THE COSMOLOGICAL PERSPECTIVE

In the *Aggañña Sutta*, which is as near as Buddhism comes to having a kind of Genesis, during the 'devolution' cycle of the cosmos, most beings are said to be reborn in the Ābhassara Brahmā world, where they are said to 'dwell, mind-made, feeding on delight, self-luminous, moving through the air, glorious'. They remain in this condition for 'a very long time'. However, all things being impermanent, the ordinary world begins to evolve again, and those self-luminous beings, as a result of their 'merit' (*puñña*) running out, tumble down the Buddhist version of the Great Chain of Being and eventually hover around the now evolving earth. As the Buddha tells it to Vāseṭṭha:

> At that period, Vāseṭṭha, there was just one mass of water, and all was darkness, blinding darkness. Neither moon nor sun appeared, no constellations or stars appeared, night and day were not distinguished, nor months and fortnights, nor years or seasons, and no male and female, beings being reckoned just as beings. And sooner or later, after a very long period, savoury earth spread itself over the waters where those beings were. It looked just like the skin that forms itself over hot milk as it cools. It was the colour of fine ghee or butter, and it was very sweet, like pure wild honey.

[22] I use the word 'ground' here in the sense of a 'primary condition', or 'fundamental principle' that attempts to characterize life in general. If one takes one of Flew's (1979) definitions of metaphysics, as 'an attempt to characterize existence or reality as a whole', then we could say that *taṇhā* is a metaphysical notion in this sense.

> Then some being of a greedy nature said: 'I say, what can this be?' and tasted the savoury earth on his finger. In so doing, he became taken with the flavour, and *taṇhā* arose in him. Then other beings, taking their cue from him, also tasted the stuff with their fingers. They too were taken with the flavour, and *taṇhā* arose in them . . . And as a result their self-luminance disappeared . . . the sun and moon appeared, night and day were distinguished, months and fortnights appeared, and the year and its seasons. To that extent the world re-evolved. (D-N iii. 84–5)

The once self-luminous beings continue their 'fall', becoming coarser and coarser as they become more and more entangled in the world, until they eventually create the kind of troubled and divided world that surrounds us today, peopled by people like us, driven by all sorts of affects. And, as we can see, it is *taṇhā* that replaces the infamous bite of the infamous apple, causing the world to re-evolve—a kind of Buddhist version of the Fall—but here the apple is replaced by what seems to be one of those delicious Indian sweets, and the Fall is only a part of a cycle that endlessly repeats itself. We also notice that *taṇhā* arose not in the mind of a crude, biologically conditioned being, but in the mind of a *deva*, a divine 'self-luminous' being. Elsewhere, the Buddha declares that *taṇhā* is the 'fuel' (*upādāna*) that links one life with the next,[23] implying that *taṇhā* is the ground condition for existing anywhere within the Buddhist cosmos. One could perhaps say that just as the will to power is the all-pervasive and fundamental characteristic of the Nietzschean cosmos, so *taṇhā* is the all-pervasive and fundamental characteristic of the Buddhist cosmos.

10.4. *TAṆHĀ* AS THE MOST 'PRIMITIVE FORM OF AFFECT'

Although it is not directly stated in the *suttas*, there are passages that, when combined with the view of *taṇhā* above, suggest that *taṇhā* can also be understood in the terms with which Nietzsche characterizes the will to power: as the most 'primitive form of affect' from which 'all other affects are only developments'.[24] For example, in the *Aṅguttara-Nikāya* we have:

[23] S-N iv. 400.

[24] WP 688. In other words, the will to power is understood by Nietzsche to be a characteristic even of the most primitive forms and elements of existence. As we

Monks, a first beginning of *bhava-taṇhā* cannot be known [*paññāyati*] before which one could say *bhava-taṇhā* did not exist, it has since come to be. (A-N v. 116)

Although this *sutta* mentions *bhava-taṇhā,* one of a group of three *taṇhās* mentioned in the *suttas*, and not *taṇhā per se*, I think it is rather obvious that *bhava-taṇhā* is the most general and basic of the three, and is synonymous with *taṇhā per se. Kāma-taṇhā* is 'thirsting' after specifically sensual experiences and is therefore an aspect of the more general *bhava-taṇhā,* which is 'thirsting' after any form of being or experience or object. If we assume that existence does not have an inherent Freudian 'Death Wish', then the third *taṇhā*, *vibhava-taṇhā* or 'thirsting after non-existence', is more likely to be the outcome of the continual frustration of *bhava-taṇhā* and *kāma-taṇhā. Vibhava-taṇhā* would therefore correspond to Nietzsche's '"last will" of man, his will to nothingness',[25] or, we could say, 'thirst for nothingness'. As Nietzsche adds, 'man would rather will *nothingness* than *not* will'.[26] We could therefore paraphrase this and say that man would rather thirst after nothingness than not thirst at all: 'thirst', being the most general condition of being in the world, man has no choice not to thirst.

Given the cosmological role of *taṇhā*—that it is the primary and affective condition that sets in motion another cycle of the Buddhist cosmos, and is therefore the primary condition out of which all other affects can be understood as developments—and that, like the cosmos itself, its beginning is said to be unknowable, we have a clear affinity between *taṇhā* and Nietzsche's characterization of the will to power as the most 'primitive form of affect' from which 'all other affects are only developments'.

10.5. *TAṆHĀ* AS A METAPHOR

What is said of *taṇhā* having no knowable first beginning, is also said of 'spiritual ignorance' (*avijjā*).[27] Commenting on these two *suttas*, Buddhaghosa asks: 'But why does the *bhagavant* [i.e. the Buddha] give the exposition of *saṃsāra* with those two things as

have evolved from these earlier forms, our present affects can be said to be 'developments'. However, we must remember that primitive nature is understood on the basis of *human* analogy, not the other way round.

[25] GM iii. 14. [26] GM iii. 28. [27] A-N v. 113ff.

starting points?' He provides his own answer: 'Because they are the principal causes of *kamman* that lead to happy and unhappy destinies'.[28] Unlike some other religions such as Christianity and Islam, Buddhism does not posit any particular point in time when the universe first came into being, or even that it ever did, let alone posit any first cause. Therefore, even these two principal causes are not in any manner *causa sui*, but are 'conditionally connected' [*idappaccayā*],[29] not otherwise. 'But', as Buddhaghosa adds, 'there is a figurative [*pariyāya*] way in which [they] can be treated as the root cause [of *saṃsāra*]. What way is that? When [they are] made to serve as a starting point in an exposition of *saṃsāra*'.[30] In other words, they are methodologically foremost in that they represent the basic and general condition of unenlightened saṃsāric existence, as well as being the last saṃsāric tendencies to be eroded before attaining Arahantship or complete Buddhahood. In this sense, in one form or another, they characterize the whole of saṃsāric existence, from its most primitive and crude depths to its most refined heights. They can, therefore, be said to be there from the very beginning until the final end of *saṃsāra*. One could even say that, conjoined, these two are the twin pillars that support the whole edifice of *saṃsāra*. *Taṇhā*, therefore, according to this account, is clearly not some particular affect among other affects, but is best understood as a metaphor—a *voluntaristic* metaphor—that attempts to capture the most pervasive affective characteristic of saṃsāric existence. Moreover, if we take these two *suttas* from the *Aṅguttara-Nikāya* at face value, it appears that *taṇhā*, as *bhava-taṇhā*, is even more fundamental than *avijjā* or 'spiritual ignorance', in as much as *taṇhā* is said to be 'nourished' by *avijjā*, but not vice versa, making *taṇhā* more fundamental than even *avijjā*. However, both are said to be conditionally dependent, which implies that we can understand *taṇhā* and *avijjā* as the affective and cognitive aspects of the one state. In other words, there is a conditional interdependence between affective state and *perceived world* which cannot be experientially separated. To use an image from the *suttas*, they are like two sheaves of reeds stacked together, which depend upon each other for support.[31] The two sheaves of reeds in this case are *nāma-rūpa* or 'mind and body' and *viññāṇa* or

[28] Vsm. 525. Note that *taṇhā* here is said to lead to 'happy destinies' as well as unhappy ones.
[29] A-N v. 116. [30] Vsm. 525. [31] S-N ii. 114.

'consciousness', which means that 'consciousness' or 'discernment' (*viññāṇa*) is conditionally dependent upon the affects, and vice versa—taking *nāma* or 'mind' as comprising *vedanā* or 'feeling-sensation', *saññā* or 'apperception', and the *saṅkhāras* or 'formative forces', which is where the affects are found. This interdependence can also be seen elsewhere in the *suttas*, where the Buddha exhorts his monks to cultivate concentration (*samādhi*): 'A *bhikkhu* who is concentrated knows (*pajānāti*) things as they really are (*yathā-bhūta*)'.[32] The state of *samādhi* here implies much more than the term 'concentration' can convey. It implies the cultivation of the four levels of *jhāna* or 'meditative absorption', states of psychic integration attained through meditation (*bhāvanā*), which consist of purely skilful affects. Therefore, 'knowing things as they really are', or, as the *suttas* also phrase it, 'seeing and knowing things as they really are' (*yathā-bhūta-ñāṇa-dassana*),[33] can only come to be in dependence upon the development of the state of *samādhi*, implying the development of the skilful affects, which clearly illustrates the interdependence of the cognitive 'knowing' (*ñāṇa*) and 'seeing' (*dassana*)), and the affective (*samādhi*). Given this interdependence of *taṇhā* and *avijjā*, and that, as both Vasubandhu and Matilal have argued[34] *avijjā* is not simply an absence of 'knowledge' (*vijjā*), but must, in some sense represent a 'view'—in this case a 'wrong-view' (*micchā-diṭṭhi*)—then *taṇhā*, like the will to power, will always be accompanied by a perspective,[35] whether conscious or unconscious, that in some sense informs and directs the search for satisfaction, whether immediate or long term. And as there is the possibility that such views and ideas can be modified by experience, there is also the possibility that if these views become 'right-views' (*sammā-diṭṭhis*) then *taṇhā* can eventually quench its 'thirst'.

10.6. DEPENDENT CO-ARISING AND *TAṆHĀ*

That *taṇhā* can be understood as a general condition rather than a specific affect can also be seen in the most common twelve-membered *nidāna* chain of *paṭicca-samuppāda*. Here, it is said that

[32] S-N iii. 13; v. 414. [33] S-N ii. 30; A-N ii. 19, and elsewhere.
[34] Pruden (1988–90), 419ff.; Matilal (1985), 319ff.
[35] See GM iii. 12, and WP 481.

in dependence upon our 'contact' (*phassa*) with the world, *vedanā* or 'feeling-sensation' arises; in dependence upon *vedanā* there arises *taṇhā*; and in dependence upon *taṇhā* arises *upādāna* or 'clinging', which results in becoming even more bound up in saṃsāric activities. However, I do not consider *taṇhā* here to refer to a *particular* affect arising in dependence upon 'feeling-sensation', but a term for a *general* condition: it is, as Buddhaghosa puts it, a 'figurative' (*pariyāya*) expression for the primary and general condition of our being in the world, from which spring the manifold affects that arise through our contact with the world.[36] For example, if a heterosexual man encounters a very attractive woman, this will probably give rise to a pleasurable feeling-sensation, which in turn can form the condition for the arising of affects such as 'lust' (*rāga*), 'infatuation' (*pema*). Whereas, if we encounter someone who tells us that we are stupid, then the feeling-sensation is more likely to be unpleasant, which in turn forms the condition for the arising of affects such as 'aversion' (*paṭigha*) or 'hatred' (*dosa*). The response to feeling-sensation is going to be a particular affect, and *taṇhā* here, as I suggest, is not so much a particular affect, but is best understood figuratively, or metaphorically, as the general condition from which there can arise all manner of affects, including, as we shall see, what Buddhism regards as 'skilful' affects, the kind of affects cultivated as part of the spiritual life.

Given what has been said so far about *taṇha*, it is clear that *taṇhā* is not to be understood simply as a state of 'craving', as one affect among others, but is a term that expresses the most general and basic condition of being an inhabitant of *saṃsāra*—or even the cosmos itself—regardless of whether that level of being within *saṃsāra* is 'primitive' or exalted. This is why, as the second of the Four Noble Truths, it is regarded as *the* cause of all forms of *dukkha*, from physical suffering to the most refined longings of the *devas* and *brahmās*, and its quenching is synonymous with attaining *nirvāṇa* itself.

[36] According to a footnote in Rhys Davids' translation of the *Mahānidāna Sutta* (D ii. 55), Buddhaghosa, in his commentary on this *sutta*, does indeed make a distinction between *vaṭṭa-mūlabhūtā purima-taṇhā* or 'primary *taṇhā* which is the root of *saṃsāra*', and *samudācāra-taṇhā* or *taṇhā* in action'. However, my point is that it is always a particular affect such as 'lust' or 'aversion' that arises at this point, not *taṇhā*, even in the form of '*taṇhā* in action'. One could say that 'lust' is a particular form of '*taṇhā* in action', but this is just saying that '*taṇhā* in action' is always some particular affect, that all the affects are expressions of *taṇhā per se*.

10.7. SKILFUL AND UNSKILFUL *TAṆHĀ*

Although, as I've said, the common and traditional view of *taṇhā* is of a state antithetical to the Buddhist spiritual life, there are a couple of little-known and, as far as I am aware, almost completely ignored passages which indicate that *taṇhā* also has a more wholesome aspect.

In the *Aṅguttara-Nikāya* we have the statement: 'He abandons *taṇhā* by means of *taṇhā*'.[37] But here we are just presented with the bare statement, with no suggestion as to what 'by means of *taṇhā*' might imply. However, in the *Saṃyutta-Nikāya* we have an illustration that can help us. There the Brāhman Uṇṇābha asks Ānanda:

What is it, master Ānanda, for which the life of excellence is lived under the recluse Gotama?

For the sake of abandoning 'desire' [*chanda*], Brāhman, the life to excellence is lived under the Exalted One. (S-N v. 271 ff.)[38]

When asked whether there is any practice for abandoning this *chanda*, Ānanda replies that *chanda* is to be abandoned by developing the four *iddhi-pādas* or 'paths to power', the first of which is *chanda-samādhi* or 'concentration of will'.[39] Uṇṇābha retorts: 'That he should get rid of one *chanda* by means of another *chanda* is an impossible thing'. Ānanda then asks Uṇṇābha whether, before setting out to visit him, he had the *chanda* to visit him, and when he arrived at the Park, whether that *chanda* was not now abated? Uṇṇābha agrees that this is the case.

Very well then, Brāhman . . . That monk who is an Arahant, in whom the *āsavas* are destroyed, who has reached perfection, done what had to be done, laid down the burden, reached the highest good, who has outworn the fetters of becoming and is freed by perfect knowledge [*sammadaññā*]—that *chanda* which he previously had to attain

[37] A-N ii. 146: *taṇhaṃ nissāya taṇhaṃ pajahati.*

[38] Mrs Rhys Davids draws attention to this passage as an important example of the way in which the notion of 'extinction of desire' needs qualifying (1912: 222 f.). *Chanda* means 'impulse, excitement; intention, resolution, will; desire for, wish for, delight in' (PED), and, as Mrs Rhys Davids also points out, is often a synonym of *taṇhā*.

[39] See also M-N i. 480 and ii. 173 for *chanda* as the necessary 'will' to strive and attain *paññā*. As the PED says of *iddhi*: 'there is no single word in English for Iddhi, as the idea is unknown in Europe. The main sense seems to be "potency"'.

Arahantship, now that Arahantship is won, that appropriate *chanda* is appeased.

The *chanda* to be 'abandoned' (*pahāna*), which the commentator construes as *taṇhā*,[40] is to be abandoned by means of developing the 'appropriate' [*tajja*] *chanda*, which, here, is the *chanda* or 'desire' for Arahantship. And, as the text tells us, this 'appropriate' *chanda* is not said to be simply abandoned at the attainment of Arahantship, but is said to be 'appeased' [*paṭippassaddha*], or, we could say, satisfied and fulfilled. Consulting other texts, we could say that the *chanda* to be abandoned is the *chanda* whose objects are, for example, mundane existence,[41] the body[42], or the *chanda* associated with malevolence[43] or sensuality,[44] or which replaces either *rāga* or *lobha* as one of the three 'unskilful roots'.[45] These forms of *chanda*, which are said to be unskilful, as they can never be fully appeased, must inevitably result in 'frustration' (*dukkha*). Therefore, we can say that it is these and similar unskilful forms of *chanda* that are to be abandoned, and the way to abandon them is by cultivating a skilful form of *chanda*, the *chanda* for Arahantship, which I would associate with other 'appropriate' forms of *chanda*, such as 'striving in the ways of the Dhamma' (*dhammapadesu chanda*),[46] 'striving after skilful ways of being' (*kusala-dhamma-chanda*),[47] and 'rousing one's will (*chanda*) to prevent the arising of evil, unskilful states of mind . . . to overcome evil unskilful states of mind that have arisen . . . to bring into being skilful states of mind . . . [and] for the increase, abundance, development and consummation of skilful states of mind that have arisen'[48]—which, following the *Vibhaṅga*, I will refer to as *dhamma-chanda*.[49] It is only these latter forms of *chanda* that can ever become fully appeased, making the important point that not all our willing and desiring must inevitably end in *dukkha*, and that the right kind of willing and desiring is essential to the Buddhist spiritual path.

As the commentary on the above *sutta* tells us that the initial

[40] See n. 4 in Woodword's trans. of S-N and also Rhys Davids' note on *chanda* in 1910 trans. of As, p. 244.

[41] Therī 14 (*bhave chanda*); Sn 866 (*lokasmin chanda*).

[42] M-N i. 500; Sn 203 (*kāye chanda*).

[43] S-N ii. 151 (*vyāpāda-chanda*).

[44] D-N i. 156, 246, etc. (*kāma-chanda*).

[45] M-N i. 119. [46] S-N i. 202. [47] A-N iii. 441.

[48] D-N ii. 312–13. [49] *Vibhaṅga*, 208.

chanda to be abandoned is to be understood as *taṇhā*, and elsewhere the terms *chanda* and *taṇhā* are clearly interchangeable,[50] and given that what has been said above about *chanda* could be paraphrased as 'He abandons *chanda* by means of *chanda*', we can fill out the statement 'He abandons *taṇhā* by means of *taṇhā*' by saying that if *taṇhā* is to be abandoned it can only be so by means of cultivating 'appropriate' *taṇhā*, which is a form of *taṇhā* that can be 'appeased'. Although there are no such terms in the *suttas* as 'thirsting after Arahantship', or 'thirsting after the Dhamma',[51] the notion that *taṇhā* can have *nirvāṇa* as its object is found in the post-canonical *Nettippakaraṇa*:[52]

There are two kinds of *taṇhā*: skilful [*kusala*] and unskilful [*akusala*]. Unskilful *taṇhā* leads to *saṃsāra*, skilful *taṇhā* is for abandoning, which leads to diminishing [of saṃsāric activities]. (87)[53]

As the text goes on to tell us, quoting a passage from the *Majjhima-Nikāya*, such skilful *taṇhā* is synonymous with an 'eager desire [*pihā*] to enter the peaceful sphere that the *ariyas*, who having realized it by themselves, dwell in'.[54] Thus, having 'liberation of mind' (*ceto-vimutti*) due to the 'fading away of [unskilful] desire' (*rāga-virāga*) as its object, such *taṇhā* is skilful,[55] and, in the manner of *chanda*, can therefore be said to be eventually appeased.

[50] The *chanda* which is synonymous with *taṇhā* is probably the one referred to in the statements: 'all mental states [*dhammas*] are rooted in *chanda*' (A-N iv. 339 and v. 107), and '*chanda* is the root of *dukkha*' (S-N iv. 328), statements where one would usually expect to find *taṇhā*. The *chanda* in these passages would therefore correspond to the more general condition of unenlightened existence. Also, in what is probably the earliest formulation of 'dependent co-arising' (Sn 862–72), it is *chanda* that arises in dependence upon 'pleasant' (*sāta*) and 'unpleasant' (*asāta*) sensations (which here replace the more usual *vedanā* or 'feeling-sensation'), not *taṇhā*, as is the case in all other formulations.

[51] At D-N ii. 58, we do find the term *dhamma-taṇhā* but here it means 'thirsting after mental states' as it is in a list of six *taṇhās*, each connected with the objects of the six senses. It is also listed in this latter sense in the first book of the Abhidhamma Piṭaka, the *Dhammasaṅgaṇī*, among the *akusala-dhammas* (Dhs. 1059).

[52] The 'Guide-treatise', translated from the Pāli by Ñāṇamoli as *The Guide*. It is not so much a commentary on the *suttas*, but a 'guide' for commentators on how to interpret the *suttas*. It was probably written around the 2nd or 1st cents. BCE.

[53] Author's translation. As A-N v. 276–7 informs us, the compound term 'leads to diminishing' (*apacayagāmin*) is explained as the practice of the ten precepts of skilful action, e.g. abstention from harming living beings, sexual misconduct, lying, slanderous speech, bitter speech, idle babbling, coveting, ill-will, and the only 'positive' precept, cultivating 'right view' (*sammā-diṭṭhi*).

[54] M-N iii. 218. See also M-N i. 303–4, which adds that one then sets up a longing (*pihā*) for 'unsurpassed emancipation' (*anuttara vimokha*).

[55] Netti. 87.

The Pāli commentator Buddhaghosa also understands *taṇhā* as having a wholesome aspect:

just as . . . [a] cow, through her *taṇhā* for cold water, starts drinking cold water, which gives her satisfaction and allays her torment, so the worldly man in the grip of *bhava-taṇhā* performs actions of various kinds beginning with abstention from killing living beings. This leads to happy destinies and gives satisfaction because it is free from the burning defilements and, by bringing him to a happy destiny, allays the torment of suffering [that would be experienced] in those unhappy destinies.[56]

Buddhaghosa points out that the spiritually ignorant person is like a thirsty cow who tries to slake her thirst by drinking hot water, 'which gives no satisfaction', and represents unskilful action leading to continual frustration and sorrow (*dukkha*). Given this example of the thirsty cow, we can therefore say that 'getting rid of *taṇhā* by means of *taṇhā*' implies that *taṇhā* can only be appeased by becoming *skilful*, only by thirsting after those things that, from the Buddhist point of view, can actually bring real satisfaction. In other words, *taṇhā*, as the general condition of unenlightened existence, can only be appeased by taking up the Buddhist *brahmacariya* or 'pursuit of excellence', whose goal is *nirvāṇa*. And we can also add that, as with *Erōs*, it is the objects thirsted after that determine whether *taṇhā* is either skilful or unskilful, or simply neutral. And given that the terms *chanda* and *taṇhā* are often synonyms, we could say that skilful *taṇhā* would therefore correspond to those skilful forms of *chanda* previously mentioned, which I will subsume under the general term *dhamma-chanda*, the active desire or will to attain spiritual ends.

It is also interesting to note that two affects closely related to *taṇhā*—*rāga* and *kāma*—also have this twofold aspect.[57] For example, we have the terms *dhamma-rāga* or 'desire for the Dhamma',[58] and *dhamma-kāma* or 'love of the Dhamma',[59] both of which are understood as skilful affects to be developed. Yet *rāga* is listed as one of the three *akusala-mūlas* or 'roots of unskilfulness' from which other secondary unskilful affects are said to develop, and is,

[56] Vsm. 525. The 'happy destinies' (*sugatis*) refer to future lives in some *deva-lokas* or 'heavenly worlds'.

[57] *Rāga* means 'love, affection, vehement desire for, interest in, desire for', etc; *kāma* means 'desire for, longing after, love (especially sexual love or sensuality), affection' etc.

[58] A-N iv. 423; v. 345.

[59] A-N v. 24, 27, 90, 201; Sn 92.

as far as I am aware, almost always considered an unskilful affect, as is *kāma*. *Rāga* and *kāma*, therefore, like *taṇhā* and *chanda*, can also be said to have their skilful and unskilful aspects, can also be said to form the affective aspect of the Buddhist path, and, when their objects are 'appropriate', can be said to eventually find satisfaction.

Another little-known distinction made in the *suttas* which also has relevance here, is that between the *āmisa* or 'carnal' affects and the *dhamma* or 'spiritual' affects, which is a direct parallel to that of the unregenerate and regenerate aspects of *Erōs*.[60] For example, there is both a carnal or unregenerate and a spiritual or regenerate kind of 'longing' (*esanā*), 'searching' (*pariyesanā*), and 'power' (*iddhi*). Although no examples are given to illustrate this distinction, I would conjecture that, for example, 'longing' in its *āmisa* form is for material objects and pleasures, whereas 'longing' in its *dhamma* form would have spiritual objects in mind. For example, with regard to 'searching' (*pariyesanā*), there is elsewhere the distinction between the 'ignoble search' (*anariyā pariyesanā*) and the 'spiritual search' (*ariyā pariyesanā*), the former being the search for 'Sons and wife . . . women slaves and men slaves . . . goats and sheep . . . gold and silver' etc., the latter being the search for *nirvāṇa*.[61] Interestingly, in a not-so-well-known example of 'dependent co-arising', we have: '*taṇhā* is conditioned by "feeling-sensation" [*vedanā*], "searching" [*pariyesanā*] is conditioned by *taṇhā*, "acquisition" [*lābhā*] is conditioned by "searching", and so on until we finally end up with "other bad and unskilful states"'.[62] Given that we have both an ignoble and a noble *pariyesanā*, an unregenerate and a regenerate *pariyesanā*, and we also have a skilful as well as an unskilful *taṇhā*, *taṇhā per se* can be said to be the condition out of which *both* kinds of searching can arise (or both kinds of *rāga* or *kāma* or *chanda*), that condition being labelled either skilful or unskilful depending upon the kind of objects being sought. Therefore, it can be said that neither *taṇhā*, *rāga*, *kāma*, *pihā*, *esanā*, *pariyesanā*, nor *chanda* are intrinsically unskilful, ignoble, or unregenerate, but it is the objects sought after that

[60] See A-N i. 93 ff. and Itv. 98. *Āmisa* means: '1. originally raw meat; hence prevailing notion of "raw, unprepared, uncultivated" . . . 2. "fleshy, of the flesh" (as opposed to mind or spirit), hence material, physical; generally in opposition to *dhamma*' (PED). As *dhamma* in this context is obviously concerned with the spiritual life, the parallel, especially with *Erōs*, is obvious.

[61] M-N i. 162 ff. [62] D-N ii. 58–9.

inform us whether they are either skilful or unskilful, noble or ignoble, generate or unregenerate. Given this, we could say that there are four conditions of *taṇhā*: (1) as the affective ground of existence, or simply *taṇhā per se*, which is ethically neutral, but which can give rise both to skilful and to unskilful affects; (2) unskilful *taṇhā*, when it is the general condition for the arising of unskilful affects; (3) skilful *taṇhā*, when it is the general condition for the arising of skilful affects; (4) the 'appeasement' of *taṇhā*, or, we could say, the 'quenching' or even 'satiation' of *taṇhā*, which is *nirvāṇa*.[63] *Taṇhā per se* is simply the general condition out of which all kinds of affects, both skilful and unskilful, can arise. When those affects are skilful, we can say that the general condition out of which they arise is skilful; when unskilful, the general condition is unskilful. Given that Buddhist doctrine teaches that all things come to be only in dependence upon conditions, and that, as I see it, *taṇhā per se* has no ethical apriority, this raises the interesting question as to the conditions under which *taṇhā* can be said to become either skilful or unskilful.

In Section 10.5, '*Taṇhā* as a Metaphor', we saw that besides *taṇhā*, *avijjā* or 'spiritual ignorance' also had no knowable or perceptible 'first beginning'. Further, according to Buddhaghosa, *taṇhā* and *avijjā*, 'being the principle causes of *kamman*', 'can be treated as the root cause [of *saṃsāra*]', and, methodologically, can therefore be 'made to serve as the starting point in an exposition of *saṃsāra*'—which, like *taṇhā* and *avijjā*, has no knowable beginning. As *taṇhā* and *avijjā* are so fundamental and are so inextricably linked—one cannot have one without the other—within the individual they can be understood as the basic affective and cognitive aspects that inform experience, which implies that how one sees and understands one's self and the world is influenced by one's affective state, and one's affective state is in turn influenced by the way one sees and understands one's self and the world. As we saw above, according to Buddhaghosa, they are 'conditionally connected' [*idappaccayā*]. Yet if *taṇhā* can be skilful as well as unskilful, and skilful activity is spiritual activity, then 'spiritual ignorance' (*avijjā*) cannot be the cognitive counterpart of skilful *taṇhā*, whose object is *nirvāṇa*. The cognitive counterpart of skilful *taṇhā* must be something like 'right view' (*sammā-diṭṭhi*), the first member of the

[63] *Nirvāṇa* can also mean 'quenched'. See PED under *nibbuta*.

Noble Eightfold Path. Further, if *taṇhā per se* has no knowable beginning, and is simply the general condition that all beings find themselves in the world, it would be rather absurd to hold them all culpable for being in a condition of *taṇhā*. And, as spiritual ignorance (*avijjā*) is *taṇhā's* beginningless cognitive counterpart, then beings cannot be held responsible for being born in the condition of spiritual ignorance either, implying that spiritual ignorance is also an ethically neutral state. To do otherwise would be to hold all beings culpable for not being born fully fledged Buddhas from that 'unknowable beginning', which is clearly absurd. Given this, we can draw up a correspondence between the various forms of *taṇhā* and their cognitive counterparts:

taṇhā per se	corresponds to	*avijjā* or 'spiritual ignorance'
unskilful *taṇhā*	corresponds to	*micchā-diṭṭhi* or 'wrong view'
skilful *taṇhā*	corresponds to	*sammā-diṭṭhi* or 'right view'
taṇhā 'appeased'	corresponds to	*vijjā* or 'wisdom' (i.e. *nirvāṇa*).

The question as to how *taṇha* can become either skilful or unskilful can therefore be linked to the question as to how wrong views and right views arise. However, as this list of correspondences is not found as such in the Pāli texts, I will put this question into a kind of Nietzschean evolutionary setting.

10.8. *TAṆHĀ* IN AN EVOLUTIONARY SETTING

As *taṇhā per se* is the general existential condition we find ourselves in, it is the source from which spring the various means of seeking some form of gratification and purpose in life. Using Buddhist traditional terms, we can see this search for gratification as expressive of the two 'root' affects of *rāga* or 'desire' in general, and *dosa* or 'aversion', the former being the basic response to that which appears attractive, the latter to what appears threatening. Together with their cognitive aspect, *moha* or 'bewilderment', these form the three *akusala-mūlas* or 'unskilful-roots' of existence. As Buddhism is concerned solely with spiritual development, these *akusala-mūlas* are always regarded ethically as hindrances not only to the individual, but, in their cruder forms, to civilized society itself. Notwithstanding this, for the purposes of this illustration, I will transfer them from their traditional conception and view them from the perspective of a non-moral evolutionary setting, as the most general and basic natural forces that were necessary for the evolution and survival of early man: *rāga* as the urge to acquire the necessities for survival; *dosa* as the aggressive drive needed when one is acquiring those necessities in a contest with others, as well as to defend one's possessions and family/tribe against aggressors. As *moha* is the dimness of the bewildered mind in relation to the truth of the spiritual life, it is simply the general state of mind that the other affects inhabit. In early man it would be a state of mind with very limited horizons: eating, copulating, hunting, basic co-operation with other members of the tribe and, in moments of quiet consciousness, perhaps the first glimmerings of 'why?'. The view that simply satisfying basic needs will ever quench *taṇhā* would be in Buddhist terms a *micchā-diṭṭhi* or 'wrong view'. But because *taṇhā* cannot be fully satisfied with such, some will eventually experience this as an unsatisfactory state of affairs (*dukkha*), and will therefore seek out more satisfying ways of living—other views on life—which can lead eventually, at least in some instances, to the emergence of more developed and civilized societies. As life in such a society, at least for some, is not so dominated by the ends of pure survival and satisfying basic needs, there will arise the necessary freedom for more co-operative and cultivated social interaction to arise, providing the necessary conditions for a wider range of more purely human and cultivated responses and affects to emerge. Such a progression is compatible with the general Buddhist doctrine of *paṭicca-samuppāda*: affects arise in dependence upon conditions. Therefore, within such conditions, more developed and civilized affects can emerge—including those which Buddhism would regard as being to some degree skilful—as well as their interrelated cognitive counterparts expressed in such cultural forms as literature, philosophy, art, religion. Some of these forms would embody to some degree what Buddhism would recognize as *sammā-diṭṭhi* or 'right view', in that they would 'understand that it is good to be generous, make offerings and sacrifices; that both good and evil actions will bear fruit and have consequences; that there is this world and the other world', etc.[64] Such a state of affairs

[64] M-N iii. 72. This is 'right view with taints [*āsavas*]', which does not seem to have *nirvāṇa* as its goal, but is instead a means of creating the necessary 'merit' (*puñña*), or one could say 'conditions', for a better and happier life in the future to arise, whether in this life or the next. As 'right view with taints' also includes the acknow-

can arise out of the fact that man is driven by his 'thirst' for satisfaction and meaning in life, and that, as long as he has not seen the way to satisfy his deeper longings, in other words, as long as right view has not arisen, he will continually experience dissatisfaction (*dukkha*), which, in turn, is the primary condition for the search to continue.

All this, however, is contingent. Buddhists are in complete accord with Nietzsche regarding mankind's 'progress', in that Buddhism also has no notion of any divinely ordained and necessary progress up through the Great Chain of Being, or any of its modern secular counterparts. Apart from natural forces, the main factors in the nexus of conditions within which human development and progress can be said to happen are the all-too-fickle human desires and aspirations: the greater freedom offered by more civilized societies also gives the opportunity for base unskilful affects to arise, which create various unwholesome ideologies such as fascism, racialism, despotism, and express themselves in religious bigotry and intolerance, etc. Therefore at times and for various reasons, the crude and atavistic urges—primitive *rāga* and *dosa*—erupt under conditions such as war and social strife, and, in the process, being framed in rationalized ideologies, become much more destructive and inhuman than the *rāga* and *dosa* counterparts found among the 'beasts'. As long as *moha* or 'bewilderment' is still present, all kinds of 'wrong views' can emerge, and there is the permanent possibility of falling victim to these atavistic urges. Nevertheless, all things being contingent, the more civilized affects can be seen as arising in dependence upon the more primitive urges: the fact that the more basic urges cannot fully satisfy *taṇhā* will inevitably result in the arising of *dukkha*, and as long as there is *dukkha* man will keep searching for something more. As long as some keep searching, there is the possibility that they will find something, but there is also the possibility that some will give up and decide that it is all just human vanity, and settle into an annihilationist creed. The greater freedom offered by civilized so-

ledgement that there are 'good and virtuous recluses and Brāhmans in the world who have realized for themselves by direct knowledge and declare this world and the other world', a view that obviously includes non-Buddhist recluses, one could see this as the Buddhist view of the ideal society, which upholds the doctrine of *kamman* and the importance of the spiritual life. These would be the ideal conditions for those who seek out 'right view without taints', which is 'transcendental' (*lokuttara*) and Ariyan, and has *nirvāṇa* as its goal.

ciety offers a greater range of objects to respond to and, therefore, a correspondingly greater potential for the development of more peculiarly human and even spiritual affects and institutions to emerge. As no form of existence short of *nirvāṇa* can quench our thirst, some will find even the most civilized and cultured forms of life, including the accepted religious forms, *dukkha*, and will therefore venture out on the 'Ariyan quest' (*ariyā pariyesnā*) and search for that which, according to Buddhism, will finally quench our thirst: *nirvāṇa*. Yet without the initial attempts of primitive *rāga* and *dosa* to find security and satisfaction, civilization as we know it would not have arisen,[65] and the very conditions necessary for spiritual development in the Buddhist sense would not have arisen. After all, without *taṇhā* there would be no existential *Angst* (*dukkha*), and without existential *Angst* there would be no search for an answer to the human predicament, and without such a search there would be no Buddhas.

Having outlined this broad overview of *taṇhā*, we can now look at the kind of affinities that such a view shares with Nietzsche's will to power.

10.9. THE AFFINITIES

Perhaps the most general characteristic shared by both Nietzsche's will to power and *taṇhā* is that both dispense with any theistic or transcendental being or force in their accounts of man and his place in the world. Both provide *naturalistic* grounds, which, although in themselves are neither inherently 'good' nor 'evil', can be made to bear the double nature of Hesiod's *Eris* goddess: both, under certain conditions, can become brutal and inhuman; yet, under other conditions, can provide the necessary impetus for the eventual creation of an *Übermensch* or a Buddha. Both *taṇhā* and the will to power can also be said to have cosmic significance, in that both are said to have no known beginning, and both permeate all levels of their respective cosmologies, from the most primitive levels to the

[65] Nietzsche makes much of this point, that what we regard as 'good' and 'spiritual' could not have arisen without the previous 'bad'. See BGE 229 and Nietzsche's unpublished essays, GCS and HC in vol. ii of *The Complete Works of Friedrich Nietzsche*, ed. Levy (1911). However, as we saw previously in the footnote to Hesiod's poem on *Eris*, this was also Kant's view.

most exalted. However, Buddhism does talk of *taṇhā* as ceasing at the attainment of *nirvāṇa*, whereas Nietzsche sees no final state wherein the will to power finally ceases.

Taṇha can become either skilful or unskilful, and, as we saw earlier, Nietzsche also covers a similar distinction, although not explicitly stated, in his notion of will to power. The will to power in its crude and primitive human form is concerned with conquering others, cruelty, tyranny, crude egotism, etc. Yet he sees the only possible way of dealing with this aspect of existence is not to crush it—which would be equivalent of the will to power turning against itself—but to follow Hesiod's example and use its very nature to overcome itself by rechannelling the affects. Following Hesiod, he sees that the will to power can be seen as having a dual nature, an unregenerative aspect and a regenerative aspect, or, using Buddhist terminology, an *āmisa* or *anariya* or unskilful form and a *dhamma* or *ariya* or skilful form. The regenerate form is what he calls *Selbstüberwindung* or 'self-overcoming', which is not concerned with overcoming externals or conquering others but with overcoming the unregenerate side of one's nature, for example the *need* to make others feel one's power, or the *need* to take one's revenge. In the case of Buddhism, I have tried to make a similar case for *taṇhā*, also using an ancient Greek model—that of *Erōs* from Plato's *Symposium*. Unskilful *taṇhā* is unregenerate and would correspond to the will to power in its unregenerate form. *Taṇhā*, when it becomes skilful—in other words when it becomes cognizant of a way to satisfy its deeper and more truly human and spiritual desires and 'needs'—can be said to become *dhamma-chanda*, the active desire or will to strive and fulfil those deeper desires. Skilful *taṇhā* or *dhamma-chanda* would then correspond to the will to power in its regenerate aspect. This regenerate will to power manifests in practice as the drive to self-overcoming, and I would propose that when *dhamma-chanda* manifests in practice it is what the *suttas* call *citta-bhāvanā* or 'mind-development'. Both *taṇhā* and the will to power can be said to share the common ground of a state of 'striving': the will to power to 'vent itself' and attain some temporary gratification; *taṇhā* to express itself in an affective form to temporarily gratify itself. This striving, in the case of Buddhism, is said to be finally 'quenched' (*nibbuta*) in *nirvāṇa*; but Nietzsche does not seem to envisage some ultimate state wherein the will to power ceases its continual striving. Indeed, he talks of an 'Eternal Recurrence', a kind of eternal *saṃsāra* without *nirvāṇa*.[66] However, perhaps it is only a certain aspect of striving that is quenched in *nirvāṇa*. As one *sutta* tells us,[67] the Dhamma was something that even the Buddha, after his Enlightenment, 'reverenced and honoured', implying, perhaps, that some further aspect of *dhamma-chanda* is not fully quenched in *nirvāṇa*, or even *parinirvāṇa*. But I will look into that in Chapter 11.

Just as there is no will to power apart from the affects—'The will to overcome an affect is ultimately only the will of another affect or of several others'[68]—I would also suggest that there is no abstract *taṇhā* apart from the affects. What we are referring to in both instances is a general characteristic of being in the world: the continual 'need' to strive and attain certain objects and ends, whether those ends be material, political, psychological, or spiritual. Both the will to power and *taṇhā* are therefore best understood as metaphors—voluntaristic metaphors that, using Nietzsche's words, attempt to make life 'intelligible'.

Yet nothing is guaranteed. Both the will to power and *taṇhā* can lead to the most brutal and cruel forms of society, just as they can lead to a flowering of civilization. What makes for the difference in the Buddhist context is a matter of 'seeing' (*dassana*), a kind of

[66] Although much has been written about the 'Eternal Recurrence', like Magnus (1978) and many others I would be inclined to interpret Nietzsche's Eternal Recurrence as an existential imperative in the manner of Kant's categorical imperative. It is a 'test': if one can affirm life when confronted with the prospect of one's life being eternally repeated—'*not* to a new life or a better life or a similar life . . . [but just] this identical, self-same life' (Z iii. 13)—without being psychologically crushed, without any desire or hope of ever escaping to some other world or of finally becoming extinct, then one passes the test: one affirms life unconditionally and is thereby a suitable candidate for *Übermenschlichkeit*. This more psychological interpretation is favoured by reading Nietzsche's statements on the Eternal Recurrence from his published works. However, his unpublished works show that he would have liked it to be also a cosmological doctrine, 'the most *scientific* of all possible hypotheses' (WP 55, see also 1063). He also links this view with his idea of what a 'European form of Buddhism' might be like: 'existence as it is, without meaning or aim, yet recurring inevitably without any finale of nothingness: "*the eternal recurrence*". This is the most extreme form of nihilism: the nothing (the "meaningless") eternally'. This seems to point to a form of Buddhism that has no *nirvāṇa* but only an eternally recurring *saṃsāra*—a strange form of Buddhism! Nietzsche also sees this European form of Buddhism as being a product of 'the energy of knowledge and strength'. Stack remarks: 'A European form of Buddhism? This from a thinker who has, in general, condemned Buddhism as a nihilistic faith' (1983*a*: 46). For an interesting discussion on the Eternal Recurrence, see Stack (1983*a*), and Clark (1990), ch. 8.

[67] A-N ii. 20–1. [68] BGE 117.

'epistemic shift'. The condition for the arising of this 'epistemic shift' is a form of *dukkha*: becoming aware of the fact that the life one is leading is not satisfactory as it is not satisfying deeper needs. This dissatisfaction then becomes the condition whose aspect allows a certain freedom to 'see' new opportunities. In Nietzsche's case, the reason for the shift from the unregenerate to the regenerate is not so clear, apart from the fact that one continually strives for more power, and that any achievement must eventually be felt as unsatisfactory.

11

'Self-Overcoming' and 'Mind-Development'

11.1. SELF-OVERCOMING

In *Twilight of the Idols* Nietzsche comments:

> There is a time with all passions when they are merely fatalities, when they drag their victim down with the weight of their folly—and a later, very much later time when they are wedded with the spirit, when they are 'spiritualized'. (TI v. 1)

One can deal with this 'folly' either stupidly or intelligently. The stupid way, for Nietzsche, is exemplified in the Sermon on the Mount from the New Testament: 'If thy eye offend thee, pluck it out', which he understands as an ordinance to '*exterminate* the passions and desires merely in order to do away with their folly'. To Nietzsche this itself is 'merely an acute form of folly', a folly shared by 'all the moral monsters [who] are unanimous that "*il faut tuer les passions*"'.[1] It is folly because 'the Christian who follows that advice and believes he has killed his sensuality is deceiving himself: it lives on in an uncanny vampire form and torments him in repulsive disguises'.[2] No affect can be annihilated, but, if denied some outlet, will become 'internalized' and assume a secondary form, for example *ressentiment* or 'righteous' hatred of those who allow their sensuality a freer expression. However, I'm not concerned here with chasing the proto-Freudian 'uncanny vampire form[s]', but want to concentrate on what Nietzsche sees as the intelligent response to the folly of the passions. Again, he turns to the Greeks as an example:

[1] TI v. 1. 'The passions must be killed' but to attempt this is to attempt 'to attack life at its roots'.

[2] WS 83. Nietzsche here is referring to the same quote from the Sermon on the Mount.

Greek prudence.—Since the desire for victory and eminence is an inextinguishable trait of nature, older and more primitive than any respect for and joy in equality, the Greek state sanctioned gymnastic and artistic contest between equals, that is to say marked off an arena where that drive could be discharged without imperilling the political order. With the eventual decline of the gymnastic and artistic contest the Greek state disintegrated into inner turmoil. (WS 226)

The Greeks, following Hesiod's example, found a method of dealing with the combative drives which allowed them expression[3] and, in the case of the artistic *agon*, created some of the jewels of Western culture. As we saw in the *Symposium*, which is one of those jewels, the Greeks also tried to deal with our sensual passion in the form of *Erōs* in a less barbaric manner than 'castration', which Nietzsche understood as Christianity's 'cure' for the passions.[4] The *Symposium* is also the link between Hesiod's method of dealing with potentially destructive affects for the sake of social stability and government and the further development of more civilized life-forms, and the conscious application of that method in the form of Nietzsche's *Selbstüberwindung* or 'self-overcoming'. Socrates' account of the possible sublimation of *Erōs* from its cruder physical expression into a pursuit of the Forms of Beauty and Truth has nothing to do with the stability of the state or society, but is solely concerned with the transformation of the individual from a relatively crude state of being into one who naturally expresses beauty of mind and character. As Nietzsche was well aware of this,[5] it is strange that his comments about Socrates focus mainly on other Dialogues where Socrates' attitude to the passions is more disparaging and is considered by Nietzsche to be a prime example of 'folly'. It is strange because the model in the *Symposium* accords in principle with Nietzsche's notion of 'self-overcoming', rather

[3] Elsewhere, in WC, p. 375, Nietzsche comments: 'Nature, [with the Greeks,] isn't denied but merely *ordered*, restricted to specific days and religious cults. This is the root of all spiritual freedom in the ancient world; they sought to release natural forces moderately, not to destroy them or suppress them'.

[4] TI v. 1 and 2.

[5] At TI ix. 22 he says, contrasting Plato's view of 'procreation' with Schopenhauer's view that 'in beauty he sees the procreative impulse *denied*', that 'the divine Plato (—so Schopenhauer himself calls him) maintains a different thesis: that all beauty incites to procreation—that precisely this is the *proprium* of its effect, from the most sensual regions up into the most spiritual'.

than Socratic folly. For example, Nietzsche refers to the transformation of sensuality by the sight of beauty into, as in the case of Schopenhauer, 'the energy of contemplation and penetration'.[6] He also comments: 'As for the "chastity" of philosophers . . . this type of spirit clearly has its fruitfulness somewhere else than in children',[7] and that 'Making music is another way of making children'.[8] These views are clearly influenced by the *Symposium*: 'there are some whose creative desire is of the soul [not of the body], and who long to beget spiritually [not physically]', and what they beget 'is wisdom and virtue'.[9] Perhaps this lack of admission of Socratic influence is because Nietzsche considered the *Symposium* to be Plato's own work before he was corrupted by the decadent Socrates:

> Compare Plato, who was diverted by Socrates. Attempted characterization of Plato *apart from* Socrates: tragedy—profound view of love—pure nature—no fanatical renunciation. The Greeks were evidently *on the point* of discovering a *type of man still higher* than any previous type when they were interrupted by the snip of the shears. (SW 194)[10]

Therefore I would assume that the intelligent method of dealing with the passions found in the *Symposium*, which may or may not be solely the work of Plato, was considered by Nietzsche to be snipped by the shears of Socratic folly.

Selbstüberwindung or 'self-overcoming' is related to Nietzsche's other notions of *Sublimierung* or 'sublimation', *Vergeistigung* or 'spiritualization' and *Selbstaufhebung—Aufhebung* being a term that defies translation by a single English word:[11] as Kaufmann observes, Nietzsche uses it with its Hegelian sense in mind of a dialectical process involving 'a simultaneous preserving, cancelling,

[6] GM iii. 8. [7] GM iii. 8. [8] WP 800.

[9] *Symposium* 209a. Kaufmann also points this out: commenting on the creative aspect of the will to power, he says that it 'is full of allusions to Plato's *Symposium*, which, almost certainly, suggested these ideas to him' (1974: 249).

[10] See also HAH 261. Nietzsche comments in GM iii. 25 'Plato, the greatest enemy of art Europe has produced'. This is no doubt the Plato of the Republic and the Laws, the corrupted Plato who, because 'he appears to have suffered terribly from the non-fulfilment of his nature . . . towards the end of his life his soul became full of the blackest gall' (HAH 261). Here Nietzsche also comments: 'It is no idle question whether, if he had not come under the spell of Socrates, Plato might not have discovered an even higher type of philosophical man who is now lost to us for ever'.

[11] e.g. Kaufmann consistently translates *Selbstaufhebung* as 'self-overcoming'; Stack, however, translates it as 'self-suppression'.

and lifting up'.[12] However, in Nietzsche's usage the lifting-up is not necessarily to something higher. Unlike Hegel's *Geist*, whose dialectical movement is progressive and hierarchical, Nietzsche's basic force, the will to power—at least when human consciousness enters the process—can degenerate: man has evolved from the ape, but may also degenerate back into the ape.[13]

As an example of Nietzsche's dialectic of *Selbstüberwindung* as a historical process, we have the Christian 'concept of truthfulness that was understood ever more rigorously' with each succeeding generation, until it was eventually 'translated and sublimated [*sublimiert*] into a scientific conscience, into intellectual cleanliness at any price'—the price being the death of God—leaving us the 'heirs of Europe's longest and most courageous self-overcoming [*Selbstüberwindung*]'.[14] The modern scientist expresses the 'same' will to truth as the old religious ascetic, but one formed within a different cultural *Weltanschauung* wherein the old notions of Truth have been 'cancelled' and 'overcome' by a new form of the will to truth. Yet, as is clear from what I said about the advent of nihilism, within a historical context this dialectical process of overcoming or sublimating does not itself offer any guarantee of man's future progress: as we saw earlier, a nihilistic catastrophe might well be the eventual result of this particular *Selbstüberwindung*. What is needed to overcome nihilism is the conscious application of this process by the individual to his own self in the manner of Plato's sublimation of *Erōs*. As Nietzsche sees it, no doubt with Hegel in mind, 'the future of man [is dependent upon] his *will*', as this is the only way 'to make an end of that gruesome dominion of chance and nonsense that has hitherto been called "history"'.[15] The natural processes of *Selbstüberwindung* or *Selbstaufhebung*, which are in Nietzsche the forms of the will to power, left to themselves may simply produce 'chance and nonsense', even though there are the occasional 'lucky hits'.

Although self-overcoming as consciously taken up by the individual is the central theme of Nietzsche's answer to nihilism, it is not sufficiently worked out; he has left no clear, detailed account of

[12] Kaufmann (1974), 236. For a discussion of the relationship between Hegel's *Geist* and Nietzsche's will to power as cosmic dialectical processes in relation to their respective notions of *Aufhebung* and *Sublimieren*, see Kaufmann (1974), ch. 8, and Stack (1983*a*), 74 n. 9.

[13] HAH 247.

[14] GS 357. For other exx. see WP 667 and HAH 1.

[15] BGE 203.

how self-overcoming is to be achieved, left no guiding examples of his method or methods. We have only suggestions, hints, and rough sketches. For example, as self-overcoming is concerned with transforming aspects of our nature into higher forms we must have some account of what those higher forms might be. Yet all we have from Nietzsche are a few examples scattered throughout his writings, coupled with the general rule that whatever is higher represents an expression of a greater quantum of power[16] relative to the lower. He does give us some clues scattered here and there, but only clues. However, despite the unfinished nature of his account, it is nevertheless possible to construct an overall outline of his central theme of self-overcoming.

In order to assess what Nietzsche regards as a 'greater quantum of power', I will take some of his specific examples as a model by which to determine the general direction and goal of self-overcoming, and to determine also what a 'greater quantum of power' is in terms of the affects, i.e. what affects are supposed to express a greater quantum of power than others. As examples, we have:

Sexual-desire/sensuality	⇒	love (*Liebe*)/love of beauty
revenge	⇒	justice and gratitude
enmity	⇒	*agon*: seeing value of having enemies
urge to punish guilty	⇒	forgiveness
judging others	⇒	mercy (*Gnade)*
tyranny	⇒	law-giving/self-discipline
lust for power/to conquer	⇒	philosophy/knowledge
enjoying hurting others	⇒	rejoicing at the joy of others

The affects on the right represent an 'overcoming' and 'sublimation' of those on the left, represent the expression of a greater quantum of power:[17]

all these motives, whatever exalted names we may give them, have grown up out of the same roots as those we believe evilly poisoned;... Good actions are sublimated evil ones; evil actions are coarsened, brutalized good ones. (HAH 107)

[16] In D 108, Nietzsche comments that: 'Only if mankind possessed a universally recognised *goal* would it be possible to propose "thus and thus is the *right* course of action": for the present there exists no such goal'. However, he does think one can '*recommend* a goal', which would entail imposing a new moral law upon oneself. Later, Nietzsche proposed his 'universally recognised goal'—the *Übermensch*—with his new morality of 'self-overcoming'.

[17] The sources for these examples are respectively: TI v. 3 and GM iii. 16; HAH 44; TI v. 3; D 202; GM ii. 10; HAH 261 and TI ix. 38; BGE 6 and WP 423; AOM 62.

It is only the 'moral fanatic, who believes that the good can grow only out of the good and upon the basis of the good'.[18]

These examples also reveal Nietzsche's conception of what he considers true morality, the 'naturalization' of morality which is a '*healthy* morality' because it affirms life.[19] Thus his notion of a new morality rests upon self-overcoming: an action is 'moral' if it is concerned with self-overcoming, concerned with transforming a 'bad' affect into a 'good' affect, or if it simply expresses the latter. However, I will come back to this later. The 'bad' is what is to be overcome, and scouring Nietzsche's writings for other examples of what he deems bad we have: petty envy, vengefulness, covert revengefulness, pity, wrath, choler, the various lusts, lack of integrity, lack of control of instincts, lying, *ressentiment*, hatred, humility, fear, inertia, deception, and fanaticism. In contrast to these are what Nietzsche considers 'good': honesty, bravery, courage, sense of justice, strength of character, mastery of wrath and revenge, self-control, discipline, patience, unpretentiousness, magnanimity in victory, gratitude, independence of mind, love, intellectual stoicism, non-attachment to one's opinions, the courage for an *attack* on one's convictions, healthy egoism, instinct for freedom and contempt for all great vanities. If there are only natural causes and in our evolutionary history 'everything has become',[20] including what we regard as our virtues which 'are really refined *passions*',[21] what are we to make of the relationship, if any, between what Nietzsche considers good and what he considers bad? Are the good simply sublimations of the bad; are they the overcomings of the latter? Or is it the case that at least some of these goods are just as natural to our affective constitution as sexual desire is, but only emerge under certain conditions?

One can understand what Nietzsche is trying to achieve: he proposes that all our affects, both the bad and the virtuous, have natural origins, are even our own creations in the sense that they are the products of human interaction and willing. And when he puts on his psychologist's hat and peers, with his penetrating gaze, into the history of the human psyche in the light of its now evolutionary past, he sees an underlying trait characteristic of all nature which he calls 'the will to power', *the* fundamental and most pervasive characteristic of life. From this perspective he considers that

[18] WS 70. [19] TI v. 4. [20] HAH 2. [21] WP 255.

many of our inherited Christian virtues, rather than reflecting our affirmation of life, in fact reveal our weaknesses in the face of life. Yet these virtues are also created by our will to power, but what they reveal to Nietzsche is the will to power of the weak, those who can only gain some feeling of power by condemning life in the world, by revenging themselves on all that is natural and instinctual and affirms life. As a compensation, they create a fictitious higher world that can only be attained, at death, by way of their virtues. Not only that, but desiring their sick revenge on those who affirm life, those who are not so weak in the face of life, they create a hell where the unvirtuous are thrown at death to suffer eternally. Commenting on the 'crude blunder' of Dante, who 'placed above the gateway of his hell the inscription "I too was created by eternal love"', Nietzsche adds: 'there would be more justification for placing above the gateway to the Christian Paradise and its "eternal bliss" the inscription "I too was created by eternal *hate*"'.[22] The root cause of such creations is weakness in the face of life, and whatever virtues and theology arise as a consequence of this weakness are no more than symptoms of the will to power become morbid, become sick. Some of the virtuous become so sick that they actually resent what relatively healthy expressions of life they encounter, and try to cunningly undermine them, infect them with their invented virulent virtues that attack relatively healthy, albeit some times crude, forms of life.[23] But, given this scenario, it is too simplistic to say: 'Good actions are sublimated evil ones; evil actions are coarsened, brutalized good ones' (which, here, implies a chicken and egg relationship between the good and evil). How does one sublimate 'weakness'? How does one sublimate 'sick' affects such as *ressentiment*? One can imagine the crude but

[22] GM i. 15. Nietzsche then goes on to ask: 'For *what* is it that constitutes the bliss of this Paradise?' and quotes 'the great teacher and saint' Thomas Aquinas: '*Beati in regno coelesti videbunt poenas damnatorum,* ***ut beatitudo illis magis complaceat***', which Kaufmann translates as 'The blessed in the kingdom of heaven will see the punishments of the damned, *in order that their bliss be more delightful for them*'. However, Kaufmann adds, 'To be precise, what we find in *Summa Theologiae,* III, *Supplementum,* Q. 94, Art. 1, is this: 'In order that the bliss of the saints may be more delightful for them and that they may render more copious thanks to God for it, it is given to them to see perfectly the punishment of the damned'. Nietzsche was obviously quoting from memory.

[23] At AOM 224, Nietzsche comments: 'for youthful, vigorous barbarians Christianity is *poison*; to implant the teaching of sinfulness and damnation into the heroic, childish and animal soul of the ancient German . . . is nothing other than to poison it'.

healthy being sublimated into the refined and more healthy. Using this analogy, the only course for sick affects such as *ressentiment* would be for them to lose their sickness and be resolved back into the crude but relatively healthy condition they were in before catching (or inventing) the virus. Then they could be sublimated. This would entail a classification into primary and secondary affects: the crude but healthy and the sick, with the former comprising the basic raw material fit for sublimation. This would make sense of some of what he says about Hellenic culture: the Greeks gave the crude and even brute-like affects a playground rather than try and crush them or make them out to be somehow evil. There is no urge to castrate them, which only drives them underground where they become vampires who suck the blood of life. The Greeks keep the crude material of life alive and under some control. But how did they produce artistic *agon* from gymnastics? Is this possible?

Sublimation itself, as Nietzsche conceives it, seems, as I have said, a little simplistic: a matter of 'affect A' becoming 'affect B', a straightforward and uncomplicated continuum from one to the other, the 'same' energy transformed into an enhanced form. But if, for example, the energy that constitutes sexual desire is overcome and sublimated into 'love', and the latter represents a greater quantum of power than the former, where does the 'extra' power come from? Was there some 'hidden', potential energy associated in some way with, or having some affinity with, sexual desire that was not being actualized? Nietzsche, referring to 'the "chastity" of the philosophers',[24] claims that in such instances 'the greater energy . . . *uses up* the lesser', implying that 'affect A' (the sexual drive) is 'used up' by the activity of an already existing and stronger 'affect B' (the urge to artistic creation) to produce 'affect C' which, in contrast, represents a greater quantum of power. Chastity is a necessary condition for the more enhanced creative drive to give fully of itself, as sexual activity will decrease the necessary tension required for the creative urge fully to manifest. Thus, in this example, it is not the case of a single transformative continuum between 'affect A' and 'affect B', but a matter of the energy available as sexual desire being used up for a higher end for which a necessary condition is another higher affect—the impulse towards that end—

[24] GM iii. 8.

which already exists in some degree. This raises the problem of where the higher affect comes from in the first instance if it is not also the sublimation of some other drive? One can see an analogous connection between the impulse to artistic creation and sexual desire as in the *Symposium*, and as is alluded to by Nietzsche above: in both instances there is the urge to create and bring something into the world. But is the latter simply the higher form of the former? Or is it that the suppression of the former is a necessary condition for the emergence of the latter—the latter being present to some degree or other in the psyche, or perhaps as one of Nietzsche's 'under-wills' lurking under the surface of consciousness ready to emerge given the operative conditions? Or is it as the Buddhists would say, that given certain conditions certain more exalted affects are likely to come into being? However, there are no clear answers to these questions in Nietzsche's writing, so I shall now consider what else Nietzsche has to say about dealing with the drives and affects.

Practically all Nietzsche's reflections and advice on how one can work on and with our affects and so 're-create' ourselves are found in a few extended dicta in *Daybreak* and one in *Twilight of the Idols*. First, he considers that we have so far been blind to the possibility of self-development:

> *What we are at liberty to do.*—One can dispose of one's drives like a gardener and, though few know it, cultivate the shoots of anger, pity, curiosity, vanity as productively and profitably as a beautiful fruit tree on a trellis; one can do it with the good or bad taste of a gardener . . . one can also let nature rule and only attend to a little embellishment and tidying-up here and there; one can, finally, without paying any attention to them at all, let the plants grow up and fight their fight out among themselves . . . All this we are at liberty to do: but how many know we are at liberty to do it? (D 560)[25]

[25] Interestingly enough, in the Republic we have: 'to say that it pays to be just is to say that we ought to say and do all we can to strengthen the man within us, so that he can look after the many-headed beast like a farmer, nursing and cultivating its tamer elements and preventing the wilder ones growing' [589a–b]. What Nietzsche says here puts other seemingly deterministic and anti-free-will statements into context. When he says that 'The individual is, in his future and in his past, a piece of fate' (TI v. 6), he is implying that the individual, being unaware of his actual 'liberty', becomes a victim of chance happenings, i.e. 'a piece of fate'. It does not imply that the individual can have no directive influence on what he will become. Elsewhere in TI (ix. 49) he makes this clear. He says of Goethe: 'he disciplined himself to a whole, he *created* himself'.

'Disposing of one's drives like a gardener' requires 'weeding', 'pruning' and cultivation through 'nourishment'. With respect to weeding and pruning, he gives us a few hints as to his gardening methods.

> First, one can avoid opportunities for gratification of the drive, and through long and ever longer periods of non-gratification weaken it and make it wither away. [Secondly] one can impose upon oneself strict regularity in its gratification: by thus imposing a rule upon the drive itself and enclosing its ebb and flood within firm time-boundaries, one has then gained intervals during which one is no longer troubled by it—and from there one can perhaps go over to the first method. Thirdly, one can deliberately give oneself over to the wild and unrestrained gratification of a drive in order to generate disgust with it and with disgust to acquire a power over the drive: always supposing one does not do like the rider who rode his horse to death and broke his own neck in the process—which, unfortunately, is the rule when this method is attempted. Fourthly, there is the intellectual artifice of associating its gratification in general so firmly with some very painful thought that, after a little practice, the thought of its gratification is itself at once felt as very painful. . . . Fifthly, one brings about a dislocation of one's quanta of strength by imposing on oneself a particularly difficult and strenuous labour, or by deliberately subjecting oneself to a new stimulus and pleasure and thus directing one's thoughts and plays of physical forces into other channels. . . . Finally, sixth: he who can endure it and finds it reasonable to weaken and depress his *entire* bodily and physical organization will naturally thereby also attain the goal of weakening an individual violent drive: as he does, for example, who, like the ascetic, starves his sensuality and thereby also starves and ruins his vigour and not seldom his reason as well.—Thus: avoiding opportunities, implanting regularity into the drive, engendering satiety and disgust with it and associating it with a painful idea (such as that of disgrace, evil consequences or offended pride), then dislocation of forces and finally a general weakening and exhaustion—these are the six methods. (D 109)

He goes on to say that the fact '*that* one *desires* to combat the vehemence of a drive at all, however, does not stand within our power', as 'at bottom it is one drive *which is complaining about another*'. The intellect, here, is simply the 'blind instrument' at the service of a particular drive. Yet he also says that in such a 'struggle . . . our intellect is going to have to take sides', which is rather odd if it 'is only the blind instrument of *another drive*'. This notion of intellect is similar to Hume's notion of reason in the *Treatise*, where 'Reason is, and ought only to be the slave of the passions'. For Hume, abstract reasoning, although a mere 'slave', can be an aid to action by trying to determine what the consequences of certain actions are likely to be, and those consequences, being generally subsumed under 'the prospect of pain or pleasure', will help us 'choose'. But, as Hume adds, ''tis evident in this case, that the impulse arises not from reason, but is only directed by it'.[26] I imagine that it is something akin to Hume's view of the role of reason that Nietzsche has in mind here, especially as he says elsewhere, almost paraphrasing Hume, that 'All drives are connected with pleasure and displeasure . . . and there is no drive which does not anticipate pleasure in its satisfaction'.[27] Reason, although itself a mere slave of the passions, has a part to play in self-overcoming by presenting, in the abstract, the possibilities for action. And, as Nietzsche says elsewhere, the quality of the intellect will effect the outcome.[28] If reason, intellect or consciousness had no part to play in self-overcoming, we would surely continue to be the mere victims of chance—a prospect that Nietzsche wishes to put an end to through self-overcoming.

In *Twilight of the Idols* (ix. 41) Nietzsche refers to pruning the affects by subjecting certain drives to 'iron pressure, so as to permit another to come into force, become strong, become master'. The weeding and the pruning are therefore concerned with the 'cancelling' aspect of self-overcoming. But here, unlike Hegel's *Aufhebung* mentioned above, there is no preserving or lifting-up—we are not talking about 'affect A' becoming 'affect B'—but of creating room for 'affect B' to come into its own through the action of 'affect C', and of 'affect A' simply 'wither[ing] away'. We are speaking here of *conflict*, not simple continuity, with 'affect A' being suppressed by 'affect C' which, rather like 'spirit' (*thūmos*) in Plato's tripartite soul, takes sides. But, if we regard one of the affects as higher, as representing a greater quantum of power, why is there such a struggle? Indeed, if the lower wins, does not that make it the higher as it must obviously express a greater quantum of power! Perhaps

[26] Hume (1978), II. III. iii. Hume's account in sect. iii of the relation between reason and the passions certainly has affinities with Nietzsche's various statements on the subject. And it is far more illuminating than Nietzsche's.

[27] TL 181. Also: 'Knowledge can allow as motives only pleasure and pain' (HAH 34); 'Without pleasure no life; the struggle for pleasure is the struggle for life. Whether an individual pursues this struggle in such a way that people call him *good*, or . . . *evil*, is determined by the degree and quality of his intellect' (HAH 104).

[28] HAH 104.

one sees that a particular drive has more potential for creative human fulfilment than the other, and so wants to cultivate it, which requires giving it room to flourish and the necessary nourishment. But this would be making axiological judgements that presuppose some standard for judgement to take place against, and this is hardly the work of a 'blind instrument'. Yet, perhaps the contrast between the drives creates the conditions from which to judge: the conflict itself may create a new perspective—a kind of 'epistemic shift'—within which judgement can be made in favour of the higher. This epistemic shift, unlocked by the tension, proffers the promise of something more exalted and satisfying, 'the scent of a kind of *pleasure* we have not known before, and as a consequence there arises a new *desire*'.[29] On the other hand:

> *Overcoming of the passions.*—The man who has overcome [*überwunden*] his passions has entered into possession of the most fertile ground; like the colonist who has mastered the forests and swamps. To *sow* the seeds of good spiritual works in the soil of the subdued passions is then the immediate urgent task. The overcoming itself is only a *means*, not a goal; if it is not so viewed, all kinds of weeds and devilish nonsense will quickly spring up in this rich soil now unoccupied, and soon there will be more rank confusion than there ever was before. (WS 53)

Here, it is a matter of planting some 'good spiritual works' in the 'subdued' (*bezwungenen*) and now-fertile soil. But where do the seeds come from here? If the only seeds we have available are the very '*drives* which constitute [our] being', and of these 'we can scarcely name even the cruder ones: their number and strength, their ebb and flood, their play and counterplay among one another',[30] then to 'sow the seeds of good spiritual works' is going to be a rather hit-and-miss affair. Perhaps the choosing of seeds is where the intellect has its Humean role? Or does a seed arise in the form of a 'new *desire*' as when we get 'the scent of a kind of *pleasure* we have not known before'?[31] Is this what Nietzsche has in mind when he says that the healthy and potentially higher type, like any animal, 'instinctively strives for an optimum of favourable conditions under which [they] can expend all [their] strength and achieve [their] maximal feeling of power'?[32]

On the question of the 'nourishment' of our drives, Nietzsche comments that 'the laws of their *nutriment* remain wholly unknown

[29] D 110. [30] D 119. [31] D 110. [32] GM iii. 7.

to [us]'. What nutriment they have had so far 'is therefore the work of chance':

> our daily experiences throw some prey in the way of now this, now that drive, and the drive seizes it eagerly; but the coming and going of these events as a whole stands in no rational relationship to the nutritional requirements of the totality of the drives: so that the outcome will always be twofold—the starvation and stunting of some and the overfeeding of others. (D 119)

The result is that as we are now we are mere 'accidents'; what we have become is the result of mere chance encounters. Yet, when it comes to what we are to do about all this and take responsibility for what we will become, what little advice Nietzsche has given above raises more questions than it answers. We do not know too much about the forces that constitute our being; apart from the term *Übermensch*, we have no clearly spelt-out goal except that whatever it is it should represent a greater quantum of organized power; and we are not quite sure about the kind of nourishment the particular drives we may wish to cultivate need. Are we to rely here on 'instinct' alone? Is this where 'the scent of a kind of *pleasure* we have not known before' comes in? Nevertheless, at least the first step for Nietzsche's spiritual aspirant is quite clear: he has to 'become master over his wrath, his choler and revengefulness, and his lusts', as any attempt 'to become master in anything else, is as stupid as the farmer who stakes out his field beside a torrential stream without protecting himself against it'.[33] Nietzsche also calls this 'the *first* preliminary schooling in spirituality': we have to learn

> *not* to react immediately to a stimulus, but to have the restraining, stock-taking instincts in one's control. Learning to *see*, as I understand it, is almost what is called in unphilosophical language 'strong will-power': the essence of it is precisely *not* to 'will', the *ability* to defer decision. All unspirituality, all vulgarity, is due to the incapacity to resist a stimulus—one *has* to react, one obeys every impulse. (TI viii. 6)

Thus we know the first step and at least have an idea of the kind of drives that have to be subdued. However, the relationship of 'learning to *see*' being an aspect of the condition of one's being may be fruitful. I shall look at that later.

With this and the 'bad' affects listed above, we now have a good

[33] WS 65.

idea of the kind of affects that are to be suppressed. And as to what is to be cultivated we can assume that the list of 'good' affects points the way, even though we are rather ignorant as to how to bring them into being if they do not form part of our affective constitution at present. We will need to be 'honest', especially with ourselves; we will need 'self-control' and 'patience' and also 'courage'. Then 'independence of mind' and 'intellectual stoicism', tempered with an undogmatic and unattached stance to our own opinions and views. And 'love' and 'justice' are to be cultivated. From this it seems there are two kinds of affects necessary for self-overcoming: the stoical kind which stand in relation to what has to be overcome, and the affects that are to be cultivated within this fertile soil. But it is still not clear how we are to go about developing the latter if 'the laws of their *nutriment* remain wholly unknown to [us]' and we are not quite sure where they come from in the first instance. But, as Nietzsche reminds us, nothing is certain in this new venture, as we are, as yet, only 'our experiments and guinea pigs'[34] and cannot be entirely sure where we are going. I shall end this discussion with an attempted model.

To picture what Nietzsche is trying to express from the various glimpses of his often uncompleted thoughts, a Hegelian-like dialectical model may help. Hegel has his central concept of *Geist* which, in its Absolute form, is the Idea of Freedom. In its actual but incomplete and concrete form it is that Idea as found to some degree expressed in the world. There is therefore a creative tension set up between the ideal and the real, between the potential and the actual, which provides the necessary ground out of which an 'epistemic shift' can occur. This epistemic shift occurs in some individual allowing them to see the incompleteness of the previous expression, and who can then 'posit' a more complete expression of the Idea of Freedom which, whilst 'suppressing' the old, creates a fuller expression of it in the new. Thus a dialectic between the ideal and its actual expressions can continue until, as Hegel envisages it, the tension is finally resolved when the actual completely expresses the potential. In Nietzsche's case the will to power replaces *Geist*, and the tension in this case is between a fundamental *nisus* to express a greater quantum of organized power and the present state of organized power: whatever one is, there is always some at

[34] GS 319.

least potential urge to go beyond that state, to overcome one's present limitations. Or, looking at this from another perspective, one could say that the tension between the potential and the actual is experienced as a lacking of something we know not what: a feeling of being unfulfilled, of being dissatisfied with one's life, a state of being that the Buddhists would recognize as *dukkha*. This dialectical tension can then give rise to a search for a solution, which, under certain conditions can lead to an epistemic shift, a new way of seeing oneself and the world, a parallel to what Nietzsche calls 'Learning to *see*'. This epistemic shift or new way of seeing provides the necessary condition for a new affect or configuration of affects to come into being, in other words a greater quantum of power manifests. A new 'self' emerges, at least temporarily. In Hegel's system the dialectic unfolds towards a definite end determined by the Idea of Freedom. In Nietzsche's case we have the ideal of the *Übermensch* posited by Nietzsche, but this is no pre-formulated, a priori goal: in Nietzsche's view nothing is predetermined: the will to power can go astray, can become sick and attack itself, with whatever potential man had never becoming actualized.

Both also rely upon certain individuals, those within whom the epistemic shift occurs, showing the way forward. In Hegel's case these are the 'world-historical individuals';[35] in Nietzsche's the artists and philosophers and, to some degree, certain religious types. However, as far as Nietzsche is concerned, such higher types as we have had so far are no more than 'man's *lucky hits*'.[36] No doubt with Hegel in mind he says: 'No, the *goal of humanity* cannot lie in its end but only *in its highest exemplars*',[37] these highest exemplars being the 'lucky hits' whom nature 'has made its one leap in creating'.[38] It is these 'accidents' of blind nature that reveal to Nietzsche humanity's future course as well as the general processes involved in bringing them about, for example the kind of culture they were nourished by. So it is necessary to capture that 'obscure impulse' of nature and replace it 'with a conscious willing'.[39] This obscure impulse has been determined by Nietzsche to be the will to power. However, trying to determine the way ahead will be something of an experiment.

Hegel has his notion of the 'unhappy consciousness'[40] as a

[35] See Taylor (1975), 392–3. [36] GM iii. 14. [37] UH 9.
[38] SE 5. [39] SE 6. [40] See Taylor (1975), 159–61.

conflict-ground, a necessary tension for the dialectic from which springs a search to ease the tension. For Nietzsche, as the will to power is also 'the *instinct for freedom*',[41] the counterpart is a feeling of being in a prison from which there springs 'a search for means of escape', which opens the possibility of discovering 'a new path which no one knows'.[42] Thus we have the tension necessary for some kind of Nietzschean dialectic to evolve: the *nisus* of existence creating a tension within the individual between what he is and what he can become, between a certain configuration of forces which is his old self and an emerging dissatisfaction felt as a result of some unfulfilled *nisus* seeking to express itself, a kind of 'psychic mutation'. Or, as he also suggests, the stimulus may come from outside, in some cultural context—perhaps the sight of something beautiful—from which there 'arises in us the scent of a kind of *pleasure* we have not known before, and as a consequence there arises a new *desire*',[43] the expression of which would elevate us. The potential outcome would entail a new configuration of forces, a new self, which expresses a greater quantum of power than the previous one. And even though this fuller expression may be only momentary, it will reveal to one the direction one's life should take. But if one never found such nutrition or a way out of the tension, one might simply be tortured by such tension and never find a resolution. So, according to Nietzsche, those who have done so (apart from the Greeks) relied more on luck than design. But in doing so they become exemplars of a kind. What they held human and valuable are our beacons. Thus we are left with the idea that our 'nourishment' is to be found within what higher expressions of culture we have—'Culture is liberation'[44] —and it is left to each to find his own source of inspiration. Nietzsche gives his own, personal example:

> Let the youthful soul look back on life with the question: what have you truly loved up to now, what has drawn your soul aloft, what has mastered it and at the same time blessed it? Set up these revered objects before you and perhaps their nature and their sequence will give you a law, the fundamental law of your own true self. Compare these objects with one another, see how one competes, expands, surpasses, transfigures another, how they constitute a stepladder upon which you have clambered up to yourself as you are now; for your true nature lies, not concealed deep within you, but immeasurably high above you, or at least above that which

[41] GM ii. 18. [42] HAH 231. [43] D 110. [44] SE 1.

you usually take yourself to be. Your true educators and formative teachers reveal to you what the true basic material of your being is, something in itself ineducable and in any case difficult of access, bound and paralysed: your educators can be only your liberators. (SE 1)

This is Nietzsche's tribute to his 'liberator' Schopenhauer, whose work *The World as Will and Representation* started the young Nietzsche in the direction of philosophy. Thus, apart from a general outline of the factors and hints involved in self-overcoming, we are at length left to find our own way. The process does seem rather sketchy and bereft of any clear and definite goal—a matter of experiment and trial and error. And we are still left with questions like: 'What does it mean to say that to "love" requires a greater quantum of organized power than to hate?' And: 'How does the world look from such a perspective; can it tell us anything about the way the world is actually constituted?'

Turning to the Buddhist notion of *citta-bhāvanā* or 'mind-cultivation', it does seem, ironically enough, that the Buddhists are on to a similar theme. But, having worked out their notion of self-overcoming—i.e. *citta-bhāvanā*—more systematically, with practical methods to follow it through, one could employ Buddhism as a means of filling-in and completing Nietzsche's sketchy outline.

11.2. *CITTA-BHĀVANĀ*

The Buddhist notion of self-overcoming is most clearly expressed in the *Dhammapada*:

Though he may conquer a thousand times a thousand men in battle, yet he indeed is the noblest victor who would conquer himself. (Dhp. 103)

The real battle for 'power' is within the individual. As Nietzsche says man is a war, which is 'a war against oneself', and the basic weapons in this war are 'self-control [and] self-outwitting'.[45] Both Nietzsche and Buddhism agree that the primary forces within this battle are the various drives and passions that we are. And just as in Nietzsche's account of self-overcoming there are two aspects—a 'suppression' aspect and a 'nourishing' or 'cultivating' aspect—so, too, with the Buddhist notion of *citta-bhāvanā* or 'mind-

[45] BGE 200: 'the war which [man] *is*'.

cultivation'. However, the term *citta-bhāvanā* connotes far more than its translation as 'mind-cultivation' suggests.

The term *citta* is often translated as 'thought', and although in later more philosophical texts this is usually what it means, here, and in the Pāli texts generally, the term has affective, conative, and cognitive aspects quite beyond what we in the West might mean by 'thought'. Even the more common translation as 'mind' is insufficient, as in Buddhism 'mind' is not in any manner distinct from 'emotion' or 'will'. For example, in the Abhidhamma tradition what we would call an emotion such as jealousy is termed a *cetasika*, usually translated as 'mental event', i.e. an event happening which is an aspect of a *citta*. But even this is only a manner of speaking since in the Theravāda Abhidhamma there are eighty-nine *cittas* or 'states of mind', each *citta* being a particular configuration of *cetasikas* or 'mental-events' of which there are fifty-two. Thus there is no *citta* apart from *cetasikas*,[46] no state of mind apart from the various factors that make it up. As any configuration of *cetasikas* is made up of affective, conative, and cognitive elements—what I refer to simply as 'affects'—a 'mind' is therefore a particular configuration of these elements, what we might call a 'mind-set'. Just as there is no fixed, unchanging *attan* in Buddhism, neither is there an unchanging substantial 'mind' or any aspect of the mind which remains unchanged. When we talk about *citta-bhāvanā*, therefore, what is implied is the 'cultivation' and 'development' (*bhāvanā*) of certain of these affective elements, not just the 'mind'. Indeed, it would be more fitting to translate *citta-bhāvanā* as 'development of will', understanding 'will' in the Nietzschean sense of a common characteristic of all the affects. And further, as these affects are intrinsically related to the development of 'transformative-insight' (*paññā*; also *vipassanā*) and 'seeing' (*dassana*), the more cognitive aspects of the path, *citta-bhāvanā* is essentially the development of the affective 'power' (*bala*) that enables one 'to see and know things as they really are' (*yathā-bhūta-ñāṇa-dassana*). As Nietzsche also understands each affect as having its own 'perspective' on the world, its own way of interpreting events,[47] we have another link between Nietzsche's will to power and *citta-bhāvanā* in that seeing and understanding are dependent upon and conditioned by the affects. But first, let us

[46] Nārada (1968), 77.

[47] GM iii. 12, and WP 481.

consider the notions of suppressing and cultivating as found in Buddhism.

In Buddhism, both these aspects are found in the sixth 'limb' (*aṅga*) of the Noble Eightfold Path, 'Right Effort' (*sammā-vāyāma*). There are four such 'efforts', two relating to the 'suppression' aspect, and two to the 'cultivating' aspect.

> And, what monks, is 'Right Effort'? Here . . . a monk stirs up energy, exerts himself, rouses his will [*chanda*], vigorously applies his mind and strives to prevent the arising of evil, unskilful states of mind not yet arisen. He stirs up energy . . . and strives to overcome evil unskilful states of mind that have arisen. He stirs up energy . . . and strives to bring into being skilful states of mind that have not yet arisen. He stirs up energy . . . and strives for the stability, the lucidity, for the increase, abundance, development and consummation of skilful states of mind that have arisen. This is called 'Right Effort'. (D-N ii. 312–13)

Elsewhere there is another list of four 'Right Efforts' (*samma-padhānas*), which seem to make a formal list of the four kinds mentioned in the above quote: the 'effort to avoid', (*saṃvara-padhāna*), the 'effort to overcome' (*pahāna-padhāna*), the 'effort to cultivate' (*bhāvanā-padhāna*), and the 'effort to preserve' (*anurakkhaṇa-padhāna*).[48]

The first two efforts are therefore concerned with suppression, and would correspond to Nietzsche's '*first* schooling in spirituality',[49] the 'war against oneself', which is 'self-restraint'.[50] The latter two are concerned with 'nourishment' and 'cultivation' (*bhāvanā*), and would correspond to the sowing and cultivating of Nietzsche's gardener. These four Right Efforts exemplify in a single formulation all that is concerned with self-overcoming in Buddhism: the suppression and final extinction of all unskilful affects; and the cultivation, development, and bringing to perfection of all the skilful affects. Indeed, the *modus operandi* permeating the whole edifice of Buddhist practice and doctrine is found in a single verse in the *Dhammapada*, which epitomizes what Buddhism means by self-overcoming:

[48] A-N ii. 16. The terms *vāyāma* and *padhāna* are more or less synonymous. e.g. the quote above on *sammā-vāyāma* is repeated at A-N ii. 15 as the four *samma-padhānas*. However, there is a slight discrepancy in the fourth stage as the former refers to bringing to perfection skilful states of mind already arisen, whereas the latter only mentions preserving them.

[49] TI viii. 6. [50] BGE 200.

Cease doing all evil;
Cultivate the skilful;
Purify the mind [*citta*];
This is the teaching of the Buddhas. (Dhp. 183)

In order to explore the points of correspondence between Nietzsche's and Buddhism's methods of dealing with unruly drives and the cultivation and nourishment of others, I shall use this division of the four Right Efforts.

First, there is a correspondence between Nietzsche's advice that one 'can avoid opportunities for the gratification of the drive', which can eventually 'make it wither away', and the 'effort to avoid' (*saṃvara-padhāna*) unskilful affects not yet arisen, from arising. In Buddhism, this practice is mainly concerned with the preliminaries to 'meditation' (*jhāna*) practice, and in its most simple form is a matter of staying away from all that might stimulate the unskilful affects. The meditator simply tries to avoid *any* unwanted external stimulus by withdrawing to some secluded spot, for example a forest or a cave. However, this is only effective with five of the six senses, as he still has his 'mind-sense' (*mano-indriya*)—i.e. his own thoughts and affects—to contend with: one takes them with one wherever one goes. At other times, when the practitioner is in the everyday world, the effort is a matter of 'restraint of the [six] sense faculties' (*indriya-saṃvara*), also known as 'guarding the doors of the [six] senses' (*indriyesu gutta-dvāra*), through the practice of constant 'mindfulness' (*sati*) and 'clear-comprehension' (*sampajañña*).[51] For example:

Monks, here a monk, having seen an object with the eye, is not enticed by its general features, nor by its details. Since covetousness and discontent, evil and unskilful states might assail one living with his eye-faculty unrestrained, he sets up restraint of the eye-faculty, guards it, and controls it. [And so on with the other five 'sense faculties'.] (A-N ii. 16–17)

For example, if a heterosexual man was practising chastity, when in the everyday world he would try and avoid unnecessary contact with women he found sexually attractive. And, if chance encounters do occur, then the practitioner is to be very alert to the arising of any erotic thoughts and feelings such an encounter may have upon the mind. The practitioner would also avoid becoming involved with argumentative people and such like in order to lessen

[51] For examples of both practices, see M-N i. 180ff , A-N ii. 16ff, etc. for the former; and D-N i. 63, 70; S-N ii. 218; iv. 103, 112, 119ff., etc. for the latter.

the opportunities for ill-will to arise. By being constantly alert through the practice of 'mindfulness' and 'clear-comprehension', the ground for the arising of unskilful affects is minimized, if not avoided. If this fails, then the practitioner has recourse to the second Right Effort, the 'effort to overcome' (*pahāna-vāyāma*) unskilful states that have arisen.

The second Right Effort, the 'effort to overcome' already-arisen unskilful affects, again bears some comparison with the methods suggested by Nietzsche. The latter, as we saw above, suggests as a remedy, 'the intellectual method of associating its gratification . . . with some very painful thought [such] that . . . the thought of its gratification is itself . . . felt as painful'. The Buddhists suggest something similar: 'if there arise adverse unskilful thoughts associated with desire . . . hatred . . . confusion, then the peril of these thoughts should be scrutinized', so that one understands: 'these thoughts are culpable and will have disagreeable consequences'.[52] Contemplating the consequences of one's actions is therefore seen by both as an effective measure in dealing with some affect that one wants to overcome and banish. Other methods suggested in the same *sutta* are: one can direct one's attention 'to another characteristic . . . associated with what is skilful', in other words, develop the opposite affect; or one can 'bring about forgetfulness (*asati*) and lack of attention (*amanasikāra*) to those unskilful thoughts', in other words, try and forget all about them; or one can 'attend to the thought formation and composition' (*vitakka-saṅkhāra-santhāna*) of these unskilful thoughts, which the commentator understands as questioning oneself: 'What is their cause, what their condition, what the reason for their having arisen?'[53] In other words, the practitioner is invited to investigate their real, contingent, and unsatisfactory nature in order that he might become disillusioned with them, thereby becoming free from their influence. If all else fails the practitioner can simply grit his teeth and

[52] M-N i. 119. An 'evil unskilful thought [*vitakka*]' is not just some passing 'thought', but would include being in the grip of some unskilful affect such as hatred.

[53] Quoted in Conze (1972), 85. (*Vitakka-saṅkhāra-santhāna*) ('thought-formation and composition') is a very difficult term to translate. The example the *sutta* gives is 'Monks, even as it might occur to a man who is walking quickly: "Now, why do I walk quickly? Suppose I were to walk slowly?" It might occur to him as he was walking slowly: "Now why do I walk slowly? Suppose I were to stand?" ". . . I were to sit down? . . . Suppose I were to lie down?" Even so, Monks, that man, having abandoned the very hard posture, might take up the easiest posture itself'. I must confess that the point in this connection evades me. The commentary, however, makes sense.

'with tongue pressed against the palate', wilfully subdue them.[54] He can also simply turn his attention away from any unskilful thoughts that have arisen and concentrate on the breathing process.[55] However, the Buddhists have no methods corresponding to Nietzsche's 'imposing a strict regularity in its gratification', or to 'giving oneself over to wild . . . gratification . . . in order to generate disgust with it', or 'to weaken and depress his *entire* bodily and physical organization' so as to weaken the drive. For the Buddhist, following the law of *kamman* and *kamma-vipāka* or 'action and consequence of action', the consequences of 'giving oneself over to wild . . . gratification' are almost certainly going to strengthen the drive. However, in principle, indulgence could very well lead to disgust, depending upon with which drive the practitioner is trying to generate disgust. For example, if it was craving for sweets and cream cakes, etc., then gorging oneself to the point of sickness might well generate disgust with the drive—at least temporarily. The same could be said of alcohol abuse. But in practice, although such indulgence could work for some who already have a desire to overcome their greed, the majority are more likely to sink further into addiction. But with drives like hatred, the very thought of indulgence would violate the whole spirit of Buddhist practice. The Buddhists, however, also have their 'extreme' methods. For example, to counteract sensual desire (*kāma-chanda*), one can practise the 'meditation on the repulsive' (*asubha-bhāvanā*) and contemplate worm-eaten and bloated corpses in some cremation ground.[56] However, such extreme methods can be counter-productive: some monks, after practising the meditation on the repulsive, became so disgusted with their own bodies that they committed suicide.[57] Other less extreme methods are found elsewhere in the *suttas*. Nietzsche could therefore have learned a few extra methods in dealing with the unruly drives from the Buddhists. And, more importantly, also come across practices such as the four 'applications of mindfulness' (*sati-paṭṭhānas*),[58] which enhance and refine the methods outlined

[54] M-N i. 119–21. [55] S-N v. 321. [56] S-N v. 131. [57] S-N v. 320–2.

[58] For a full account of the practice of these four 'applications of mindfulness', which the Buddha describes as 'This one way to the purification of beings, for the overcoming of grief and lamentation, for the destruction of sorrow and distress, for winning the right path, for realizing *nibbāna*', see the *Mahāsatipaṭṭhāna Sutta* at D-N ii. 290ff. and the *Satipaṭṭhana Sutta* at M-N i. 55ff. Mindfulness is applied to four things: (1) the body; (2) the feelings; (3) the mind (*citta*); (4) mind-objects (*dhammas*).

above by increasing the power of awareness, and the capacity to direct it.

In this way the Buddhist, by having a clear idea of the kind of affects whose arousal he wants to thwart, has recourse to a tradition that has systematically worked out the relations that can exist between various sets of conditions and their corresponding affects. The practitioner, through being alert to the psychological dynamics that exist between himself and the world, has recourse to various methods of dealing with the unskilful affects his environment may stimulate. He is, therefore, in a good position to 'prune' his responses, 'prune' his 'willing'. In Nietzsche's terms, he is attempting to make the first steps in creating a 'rational relationship to the nutritional requirements'[59] of his drives by starving some of their nourishment in order to weaken them. However, one outstanding feature of the Buddhist way of self-overcoming is that all its methods are based upon the practice of 'mindfulness' and 'clear-comprehension': they are the central core of all Buddhist practice. Yet although Nietzsche is often disparaging about 'consciousness',[60] seeing it as an insipid epiphenomenon with little or no bearing on self-overcoming, his methods must surely presuppose its importance: how can one be capable of self-overcoming if there is no clear consciousness of what is going on in the self; if there is no consciousness of the relations that exist between the affects and the world? How could he claim to discern as much as he has without relying upon his own consciousness to discern it? And what about his statement: 'we *whose task is wakefulness itself*'?[61] Surely consciousness has a central part to play here? I shall return to this point later.

In covering these two Right Efforts, we have not been so concerned about 'sublimation' but about 'restraint' and 'suppression' as necessary aspects of creating what Nietzsche calls the 'most fertile ground . . . on which the seeds of good spiritual works' can be sown. But Nietzsche, as we saw, is not too forthcoming about giving us advice as to what is to be developed or the means to it. Nevertheless, there are correspondences. For example, both Buddhism and Nietzsche agree that the sort of affects one has to conquer and 'suppress' are those such as wrath, envy, vengefulness, the lusts, lying, hate, inertia, fanaticism. And that this entails discipline,

[59] D 119. [60] See e.g. GS 354. [61] BGE, Preface.

patience, strength of character, mastery of wrath and revenge, self-control—to use Nietzsche's terms. These are all aspects of the first two Right Efforts. All the above affects Nietzsche wants to be overcome are also considered by the Buddhists to be the kind of unskilful affects that have to be overcome. But what about any correspondence between the kind of affects Nietzsche wishes to cultivate and the skilful affects the Buddhists wish to cultivate? Some of the affects Nietzsche considers worthy of development do indeed have some affinities with the Buddhist's skilful affects. But to create a ground of correspondence around the notion of power—which is Nietzsche's criterion for determining a 'good' affect—I shall examine what it is the Buddhists want to develop, what methods they use, and try to show that it is the sort of model that Nietzsche might have approved of as a means of self-overcoming, and also try to show that what the Buddhists are trying to develop could be talked about in terms of power.

The third and fourth Right Efforts inform us what it is the Buddhists are trying to achieve: 'developing' (*bhāvanā*) skilful affects not yet arisen, and 'preserving' (*anurakkhaṇa*) and bringing to 'perfection' (*pāripūrī*) those already arisen. And all this endeavour is a *means* to a further end, the development of 'transformative insight' (*paññā*). However, when we examine what the texts say about how we are to 'cultivate' (*bhāvanā*) these skilful affects, we are often simply presented with another list—a sublist. For example, if we ask what the texts say about what is to be cultivated under the third of the four Right Efforts, the 'effort to cultivate' (*bhāvanā-padhāna*), we are told: the seven 'limbs of enlightenment' (*sambhojjaṅgas*)—another list. And each of these limbs reveals a further list, for example, the 'four applications of mindfulness'; and each of these four applications is further subdivided. So, rather than play at Chinese boxes and examine each of the boxes in detail, I think a simpler and more methodologically practical approach to the development of the skilful affects is more revealing, and to this end I shall cite the 'cultivation of friendliness' (*mettā-bhāvanā*) practice as found in the *Visuddhimagga*.[62] Here we find a clear example of 'sublimation' proper, i.e. the transference of an affect from one object to another, so as to sublimate it into a higher state. Buddhaghosa's account is rather long and detailed, so I will just

[62] *Mettā* is derived from the term *mitta*, 'friend'. However, as 'friendliness' is a little pale as a translation, I shall simply use the Pāli term. See Vsm., 296ff.

give the salient points. Despite the ubiquitousness of the *anattan* doctrine, the first step of the practice is to 'cultivate' (*bhāvanā*) *mettā* towards one's own self,[63] a step fully endorsed by Nietzsche.[64] To this end the practitioner is encouraged to recollect happy and contented moments in his life and wish that his life will be happy and fulfilling, thereby giving the mind room for such appropriate affects to arise. Then, from that state of healthy self-regard he can call to mind a friend[65] and, on the basis of being in a state of healthy self-regard, a feeling of friendliness towards the friend can arise naturally.

Although Buddhaghosa refers to the feeling one has both for oneself and the friend as *mettā*, this does not seem correct simply because both such feelings can be said to be quite natural to all, in other words not something most people would have to make too much of an effort to develop. There is no inconsistency between having a feeling of friendship towards one person whilst hating another. Also, such affects can involve attachment and, in some contexts, give rise to petty jealousies, etc. Consequently, I would not class them as *mettā* proper. *Mettā*, as a skilful affect, must be distinct from them if it is meant to be more than ordinary friendliness. Yet these more everyday affects are the only conditions out of which *mettā* can spring. Therefore, it seems to me that the real task starts at stage three. Here the practitioner is trying to extend

[63] The point here is that if one does not have a healthy regard for oneself, then the prime condition necessary for developing *mettā* towards others is absent. Buddhaghosa (Vsm. 297) quotes the *Udāna*: 'Since aye so dear the self to others is, | Let the self-lover [*atta-kāma*] harm no other man' (47 and at S-N i. 75). If one 'loves' oneself in the sense of wanting a happy and fulfilling life (narcissism is not what is meant) and reflects that this is what others want too, then the ground for developing a more friendly and less hostile relationship with them can be formed. This is the point.

[64] Nietzsche says: 'Always love your neighbour as yourselves—but first be such as *love themselves*' (Z iii. 5. 3) otherwise: 'Your love of your neighbour is your bad love of yourselves' because 'you . . . do not love yourselves enough' (Z i. 16). Therefore, Nietzsche would agree that the first and necessary step in developing 'love' towards others would be learn to 'love' ourselves.

[65] Buddhaghosa mentions that an appropriate object here is either one's spiritual teacher, an equivalent, or one's preceptor or his equivalent, reflecting the conditions of a monastic life. But obviously, in a non-monastic context, other friends whom one shares 'skilful' experiences with, for example when they have helped one, shared things with one, etc., are adequate substitutes. Buddhaghosa, however, warns against using friends that one has sexual feelings towards or who have died. Reflecting on such friends will more than likely give rise to sexual desire and grief respectively. And when such affects are present, *mettā* is extremely difficult—perhaps even impossible—to develop.

himself, to overcome his natural inclinations by thinking about someone whom he has little or no feeling towards, someone he feels quite indifferent to, what Buddhaghosa calls 'a neutral person'. The underlying assumption here is that if the practitioner's mind is imbued with the feeling of friendliness which has extended beyond his own self to a good friend, that is the ideal condition from which to contemplate some neutral person. In making them the object of his concentrated mind, he can then try and think kind and caring thoughts about them. In this way feelings of kindness may arise towards this neutral person as the practitioner is already in a friendly state of mind. Then, in the fourth stage, he tries to do the same with someone he normally feels hostile towards, an 'enemy'. If the practitioner can come to develop kind and friendly thoughts towards a person he normally hates the sight of, *that* is surely what *mettā* is as distinct from more ordinary feelings of friendliness. He has *overcome* the 'self' that started the practice, which was incapable of such affects towards an enemy. Buddhaghosa also refers to extending *mettā* 'with unspecified pervasion' to all sentient beings throughout the cosmos. As it is a further extension it can be seen as a fifth stage.

What we have here is a kind of self-engendered dialectic. As Nietzsche comments, our affects need nourishment in the form of objects, but the processes by which they come to be nourished are arbitrary. What is nourished is therefore a matter of chance, implying that what we are is mainly the creation of chance. But here, by consciously selecting appropriate objects to present to the mind, one begins to have some say on the kind of affects that will be stimulated. We start from the most natural feeling people have for themselves, which has an objective counterpart as a perspective on the world. It is a world that more or less revolves around 'me and mine'. Its perspective is therefore rather narrow and overtly self-referential and, being such, *excludes* other possibilities and perspectives. Stage two opens the self up and includes another, who, having his own interests and being someone you like, extends the field of interest outside one's own direct interests. This, of course, can be seen as a second-order self-interest, yet it is a different kind of self-interest simply because one has to consider another. That 'having to consider' engenders a different, even though slight, change in perspective: others are part of one's world. But it is, as I've said, the third stage that represents a real shift. The dialectic comes about when one finds oneself in stage two, open to considering others. By focusing one's mind, which is imbued with a degree of friendliness, on to the neutral person, there is the chance of seeing him in a different way from before, and that seeing is accompanied by a 'new' affect,[66] that of feeling kindness towards someone one previously felt completely indifferent to. It is a different affect, although it has, in Wittgensteinian terms, a family resemblance to the former. In a sense, self-interest is still there but, as the 'self' has changed, so too has the interest. Relatively speaking, from the perspective of stage one, it shows a lack of self-interest—at least that's how it would appear to someone at stage one (unless they were a cynic), as the self-interest *they* manifest has, to some degree, been overcome.[67] When the mind is concentrated and more malleable, and the concentration is, in a sense, a focus of *mettā*-like energy, in calling to mind an enemy there is now an opportunity to *see* him less subjectively, in other words not see him from the narrow perspective of what wrongs he has committed against 'me', etc. This new seeing affords the possibility of actually *feeling* differently towards him: with some degree of friendliness and kindness, which in this case is no everyday affect, but *mettā* proper. This is possible because of the condition one is in, because of the kind of 'self' one now is or, better, has *become*. This affect, whatever its strength, is the one I would call true *mettā*, and represents a transformation of one's attitude towards the world: one simply *sees* the

[66] Buddhaghosa refers to 'breaking down barriers' in moving from one stage to the next. We could say that there is a dependent relationship between the state of mind, the affect dominant at the time, and its perspective on the world which, from a greater perspective, is seen as a 'barrier'. It is a barrier in the sense that it delimits one's possible responses to any situation. A mind filled with hate is 'barred' from so many other perspectives, it restricts one's perspective to a too subjective, limited and guarded outlook. In Nietzsche's terms, hate is a sign of weakness, and being such its perspective is limited: 'Beauty is unattainable to all violent wills' (Z ii. 13). Thus, by developing *mettā*, one is, in a manner of speaking, overcoming barriers, overcoming one's previously narrow and overtly self-orientated, limited perspective.

[67] Nietzsche, in a passage on the 'disinterested', notes: 'the great majority of those things which interest and stimulate every higher nature . . . appear altogether "uninteresting" to the average man—if he none the less notices a devotion to these things, he calls it "*désintéressé*" and wonders how it is possible to act "disinterestedly"' (BGE 220). With Nietzsche, therefore, the notion of 'disinterested activity' has its origins in the fact that 'higher natures' have interests beyond the scope of the ordinary person. We might say this is due to their having different 'selves' which, because they 'see' differently, are interested in *other* things—things which others cannot see or respond to.

world differently. And as the self at stage four is a radically changed self from the self at stage one, it would not make too much sense to talk about 'self-interest' at this stage, as from the Buddhist perspective it would bear little relation to what those on stages one and two could *conceive of* as self-interest. This also gives another dimension to the *anattan* doctrine: we have an unfolding series of selves, none of which can be said to be the 'real' self. In Nietzsche's terms, we have a new constellation of forces, a new self whose overall constitution emanates 'love'.

Buddhaghosa relates that if one can develop *mettā* in this way, if a bandit was going to kill one of the four (i.e. yourself, the friend, the neutral, or the enemy), and asked you which of the four you would choose, you would not be able to choose due to the complete impartiality of your mind towards all four. Thus there is no putting others before oneself, which is what some ethical systems would prescribe as, having attained 'such concentration that in this body, together with its consciousness, he has no notion of "I" or "mine", or any tendency to vain conceit',[68] how would one decide? No doubt some decision could be made to resolve such an ethical dilemma, but the point Buddhaghosa is making is that one could not decide on the basis of fear for one's own life, who one likes or dislikes, etc. Perhaps, quite objectively, one might decide that one's life was worth more to the world than some other's. This possibility could not be discounted on Buddhist ethical grounds, as whatever one decided it would not be determined by unskilful factors.

We could say that this process is a straightforward example of what Nietzsche would recognize as *Selbstüberwindung*. Each 'self' at each stage is both 'annulled' and 'preserved', in Hegel's sense of *Aufhebung*, in the following 'self'. What has been annulled are the limitations and narrower perspectives of the lower self, yet the family resemblance of friendliness has been preserved in the higher. A Buddhist, however, would only go as far as saying that in dependence upon the conditions that constitute 'self A', 'self B' comes to be. The notion of something being both annulled and preserved would be seen to fall into the second of the four traditional 'indeterminate points' (*avyākata-vatthus*),[69] or questions

[68] A-N i. 132.

[69] See the *Avyākata-vagga* of A-N iv, and the *Avyākata-saṃyutta* of S-N iv. The questions for which there are no determinate answers are: whether the world is eternal or not; infinite or not, whether the 'life principle' (*jīva*) is identical with the

for which there is no determinate answer, in that 'self A' can be said to both exist and not exist in 'self B', i.e. be both 'annulled' and 'preserved'. To a Buddhist, that would be saying too much. The most one can say is that in dependence upon the conditions that constitute 'self A', 'self B' comes to be. 'Self A' and 'self B' are categories created by the mind which divides experience up for practical purposes. Existence, however, from the Buddhist point of view, is a fluctuating continuum with no gaps between the bits we categorize as 'self A' and 'self B', or as 'cause' and 'effect'. Interestingly enough, this is how Nietzsche sees it:

> Cause and effect: such a duality probably never exists; in truth we are confronted by a continuum out of which we isolate a couple of pieces, ... (GS 112)[70]

Thus what actually happens is, in the limits of analysis, beyond categorical determination.

In this example of Buddhist 'self-overcoming', I have used the *mettā-bhāvanā* practice, but the same can be done with other affects such as 'sympathetic joy' (*muditā*), 'compassion' (*karuṇā*), and 'equanimity' (*upekkhā*),[71] and this principle can be applied to all the affects that Buddhism wishes to develop and nourish. And it will be obvious that the underlying principle behind all these attempts to suppress and develop various affects is *paṭicca-samuppāda*, the doctrine of 'dependent co-arising': all affects come to be when certain conditions are present; if one wishes to eliminate some then the conditions that give rise to them have to be tackled; if one wishes to develop others then they too will only come to be when certain conditions are present.

The fourth 'Right Effort' consists in 'preserving' and bringing to perfection those skilful affects already arisen. With regard to the 'effort to preserve' (*anurakkhaṇa-padhāna*), here the *suttas* advise that one can remain mindful of the 'favourable concentration-mark

body or not, and whether the Tathāgata exists, does not exist, both exists and does not exist, neither exists nor does not exist after death. They can be represented as: (1) A is B; (2) A is not B; (3) A is both B and not B; (4) A is neither B nor not B; (3) would include being 'both annulled and preserved'. The Buddhist 'Middle Way' is to say: 'In dependence upon A, B comes to be. When A ceases, B ceases'. This position claims to maintain continuity, without stating that any 'thing' is either 'annulled' or 'preserved', views which it would see as mistaken.

[70] At WS 11, Nietzsche says that 'all doing and knowing is not a succession of facts and empty spaces but a continuous flux'.

[71] See Vsm., ch. ix.

[*samādhi-nimitta*], [which can be] . . . the idea of a skeleton . . . a worm-eaten corpse, . . . a discoloured corpse . . . a fissured corpse . . . an inflated corpse. This is called "the effort to preserve"'.[72] The concentration mark strictly refers to the object of meditation. However, I think it must extend beyond festering corpses as this practice is usually an antidote to sexual desire, and would therefore seem more appropriate to the second Right Effort. I fail to see the relationship between maintaining and developing a skilful affect, for example *mettā*, and focusing one's mind on decomposing corpses![73] A more natural approach here would be to simply maintain the skilful states by retaining the object in mind that gave rise to them in the first place. With regard to bringing to perfection, as the *mettā-bhāvanā* practice just outlined is ultimately concerned with the perfecting of *mettā*, it would be an example of this level of Right Effort.

Another aspect that has bearing on the above is the importance both Nietzsche and Buddhism give to the basic sensations of pleasure and pain in the process of 'willing'. According to Nietzsche, 'for will to come into being an idea of pleasure and displeasure is needed', and the dynamics of this relationship between sensation and willing 'is actually a mechanism that is so well practised that it all but escapes the observing eye'.[74] However, what is of interest here is the connection between willing being conditional upon and conditioned by the general sensations of pleasure and displeasure. As we saw above, when Buddhists try and develop this Nietzschean 'observing eye', they practice the 'restraint of the sense faculties' accompanied with 'mindfulness' and 'clear-comprehension'. An

[72] A-N ii. 16; D-N iii. 226.

[73] In an interesting incident in the *Vin.* (iii. 67 ff.) some monks, who were 'contemplating upon the impure' (*asubha-bhāvanā*), i.e. contemplating upon decomposing corpses to eliminate sensual lust, actually developed such a loathing for their own bodies that some committed suicide, some agreed to kill each other, and some got the 'sham recluse' Migalaṇḍika to kill them. When the Buddha heard about this incident, he declared such action as entailing 'defeat' (*pārājaka*), for which one is expelled from the *bhikkhu* Sangha or 'community'. However, there is no attempt to deal with the issue as to how such a standard Buddhist practice can lead not to its desired goal, i.e. eliminating sensual lust, but to such self-loathing that one wants to commit suicide. Here, at least, it seems that these monks would have been better advised to do the *mettā-bhāvanā* practice. Also, from what is said elsewhere in the *Vinaya* (iii. 36), the practice of the *asubha-bhāvanā* by some monks had the opposite effect: some had sexual relations with the decomposing corpses, one even with a decapitated head!

[74] GS 127.

aspect of this practice is to try and discern, as they arise, the conditional relations between the consecutive *nidānas* of 'contact' (*phassa*), 'feeling-sensation' (*vedanā*), 'thirst' (*taṇhā*), and 'grasping' (*upādāna*), which are essentially a general analysis of the way the process of 'willing' (*sañcetanā*) comes about. Each *nidāna* is viewed as a collective 'conditional ground' for arising of the following one.[75] If the sensation is pleasant, then because of the general condition of *taṇhā*, there is the tendency to desire the object that is understood to have 'caused' the pleasant sensation, which in turn forms the condition for a grasping-like affect to arise—the will to acquire and appropriate, whose basic 'root' is *rāga* or desire in general; if the sensation is unpleasant, the tendency is for an averting-like affect to arise—the will to aversion whose basic root is *dosa* or antipathy in general.[76] In both cases willing is very much conditioned by the basic sensations of pleasure and pain that arise through contact with objects, both external and internal. Thus what Nietzsche is alluding to above is an aspect of a standard Buddhist practice which, given Nietzsche's disparaging comments about the role of consciousness, ironically enough revolves around a high degree of self-consciousness and purposeful alertness. Surely his 'observing eye' is not a matter of 'instinct' alone?

A further point is that both see a development from this process

[75] The process, up to *vedanā*, is more or less outside of one's present control, being conditioned by the 'effects' (*vipākas*)—direct and indirect—of our past *kamman* or 'action'. As a past 'residue' it forms the ground for present 'willing', but as one can bring other factors to bear, such as one's understanding and awareness, present action need not be completely determined by that ground. To the extent that it is, we set up an habitual 'round', *saṃsāra*, responding in a similar way determined by this ground which is itself the effect of acting in a similar manner in the past. Therefore, the practice of 'guarding the doors of the senses', in Buddhism, plays a crucial role in helping the individual free himself from habitual responses. It is only by becoming aware of how one 'mechanically' responds to situations that one can start the process by which one can become free from such re-activity. This also makes it clear why 'mindfulness' and 'clear-comprehension' are so central to Buddhist practice.

[76] In an interesting encounter between the nun Dhammadinnā and Visākha, her ex-husband, Visākha asks whether the 'latent tendency' (*anusaya*) of *rāga* is to be abandoned in all 'pleasant feelings' (*sukhā vedanā*), whether the latent tendency to 'revulsion' or *paṭigha* is to be abandoned in all 'painful feelings' (*dukkhā vedanā*), and whether the latent tendency to *avijjā* or 'ignorance' is to be abandoned in all 'neutral feelings' (*adukkhamasukhā vedanā*). Dhammadinnā replies that this is not so, and gives an example for each of the three feelings. What follows is not very clear, but the point is that pleasant, unpleasant, and neutral feelings can also lead to skilful actions, as well as unskilful ones (M-N i. 303 ff.).

of willing rooted in the sensations of pleasure and pain (and 'neutral feeling' in the Buddhist case, which is connected to the 'root' of *moha* or 'confusion') to one of conceptualizing about the object, and both consider that much of this conceptualizing is little more than unconscious rationalization. For example, to Nietzsche 'The most delicate sensations of pleasure and displeasure constitute the genuine raw material for all perceiving'[77] which, if there is a 'preponderance of feelings of displeasure over feelings of pleasure [becomes the unacknowledged] *cause* [for example] of a fictitious morality and religion'.[78] In other words, even our religious beliefs and metaphysics are often no more than reactive intellectual reflexes to our basic experience of the world.[79]

In Buddhism, also, it is this raw material of willing that gives rise to 'conceptual proliferation' (*papañca*). In an alternative list of 'dependent co-arising',[80] after 'feeling-sensation' there arises consecutively, 'apperception' (*saññā*), 'initial reasoning' (*vitakka*), 'conceptual proliferation' (*papañca*), and *papañca-saññā-saṇkhā*—the arising of all 'speculative views' (*diṭṭhis*), whether about the weather, people, or the nature of existence, showing the necessary continuity between affective state and intellectualizing.[81] This is probably the reason why, in its final stance on matters conceptual, Buddhism says that the liberated person holds no 'views' (*diṭṭhis*):[82] he sees how views arise conditioned by circumstance, context, quality of emotion, etc., and even though some may be 'useful' (*upāya*) in helping others towards *nirvāṇa*—i.e. those 'right views' (*sammā-diṭṭhis*) that form part of the raft, that are used as a *means*—does not hold on to them or identify with them. Such a person has no *need* of them, simply because they 'see things as they really are'.

[77] P 67. [78] A 15.

[79] Nietzsche's view is summed up in Z i. 3: 'It was suffering and impotence—that created all afterworlds'. For an unfolding of this view and other examples, see *On the Genealogy of Morals.*

[80] M-N i. 111–12.

[81] According to Ñāṇananda (1971: 5), '"*papañca-saññā-saṅkhā*" can mean concepts, reckonings, designations or linguistic conventions characterized by the prolific conceptualising tendency of the mind'.

[82] e.g. at Sn 913 we have the notion that the 'sage [*muni*] is completely released from [all] *diṭṭhis*'. This theme is repeated at Sn 786, 787, 794, 799, 800, 802, and 851. Nietzsche might interpret such a stance as a sign of strength: 'Freedom from convictions of any kind, the *capacity* for an unconstrained view, *pertains* to strength' (A 54). Unfortunately this *sutta* was not included in Coomaraswamy's abridged translation of the *Sutta-Nipāta* read by Nietzsche.

11.3. SELF-OVERCOMING AND POWER

In order to give an account of how this Buddhist version of self-overcoming could be quantified in terms of a gradual development akin to Nietzsche's notion of power, I shall view this process from another perspective. In a rather neglected and progressive account of dependent co-arising,[83] we can glimpse how the Buddhists saw self-overcoming in terms of a dynamic, gradual accumulation of energy and power.

Now with regard to extinction and knowledge [*ñāṇa*] about extinction [of the 'biases' (*āsavas*)][84] I say that they arise in dependence upon a supporting condition [*sa-upanisā*], not the opposite.

And what is that condition [*upanisā*] upon which knowledge about extinction [of the ['biases' (*āsavas*)] comes to be? Liberation [*vimutti*] is the answer. I say that liberation comes to be in dependence upon a supporting condition, not the opposite.

And what is that condition upon which liberation arises? Passionlessness [*virāga*] is the answer. I say that passionlessness comes to be in dependence upon a supporting condition, not the opposite.

And what is that condition upon which passionlessness comes to be? Disenchantment [*nibbidā*] is the answer. I say . . .

And what is that condition upon which disenchantment comes to be? Knowing and seeing things as they really are [*yathā-bhūta-ñāṇa-dassana*] is the answer. I say . . .

And what is that condition upon which knowing and seeing things as they really are comes to be? Meditative concentration [*samādhi*] is the answer. I say . . .

And what is that condition upon which meditative concentration comes to be? Bliss [*sukha*] is the answer. I say . . .

And what is that condition upon which bliss comes to be? Calming [*passaddhi*] is the answer. I say . . .

And what is that condition upon which calming comes to be? Rapture [*pīti*] is the answer. I say . . .

And what is that condition upon which rapture comes to be? Joy [*pāmojja*] is the answer. I say . . .

[83] For full exegesis, see Sangharakshita (1991), 108ff., and (1987), 137ff., and Bodhi (1980).

[84] The *āsavas* or 'biases' being the 'bias' towards 'sensual experience' (*kāma-āsava*), 'the bias of wanting to be something' (*bhava-āsava*), 'the bias towards speculation' (*diṭṭhi-āsava*), and 'the bias towards spiritual ignorance' (*avijjā-āsava*).

And what is that condition upon which joy comes to be? Confidence [*saddhā*] is the answer. I say . . .

And what is that condition upon which confidence comes to be? Unsatisfactoriness [*dukkha*] is the answer. I say . . .

And what is the condition upon which unsatisfactoriness comes to be? Birth [*jāti*] is the answer. I say . . .

And what is the condition upon which birth comes to be? Becoming [*bhava*] is the answer. I say . . .

And what is the condition upon which becoming comes to be? Grasping [*upādāna*] is the answer. I say . . .

And what is the condition upon which grasping comes to be? Thirst [*taṇhā*] is the answer. I say . . .

And what is the condition upon which thirst comes to be? Feeling [*vedanā*] is the answer. I say . . .

. . . feeling with contact [*phassa*] . . .

. . . contact with sixfold sense sphere [*saḷāyatana*] . . .

. . . the sixfold sense sphere with the psycho-physical individual [*nāma-rūpa*] . . .

. . . the psycho-physical individual with consciousness [*viññāṇa*] . . .

. . . consciousness with karmic activities [*saṅkhāras*] . . .

. . . karmic activities with spiritual ignorance [*avijjā*] . . .

Now . . . brethren, karmic activities are in causal association with spiritual ignorance, consciousness is in causal association with karmic activities, the psycho-physical organism with consciousness, the sixfold sense-sphere with the psycho-physical organism, contact with the sixfold sense-sphere, feeling with contact, thirst with feeling, grasping with thirst, becoming with grasping, birth with becoming, *dukkha* with birth, confidence with unsatisfactoriness, joy with confidence, rapture with joy, serenity with rapture, bliss with serenity, meditative concentration with bliss, knowing and seeing things as they really are with concentration, disenchantment with the knowledge and vision into things as they really are, passionlessness with disenchantment, liberation with passionlessness, knowledge of extinction [of the *āsavas*] with liberation. (S-N ii. 30 ff.)

The text then gives a simile of the above in terms of torrential rain coursing down a mountainside, gradually filling up 'hillside clefts and chasms', which overfill and go on to fill up 'tarns . . . lakes . . . little rivers . . . great rivers . . . the sea [and finally] the ocean'.

As Mrs Rhys Davids remarks in a footnote to her translation: 'This series (i.e. from *dukkha* to "knowledge of extinction [of the 'biases']") has never yet won the notice it deserves as a sort of

Causal Law formula *in terms of happiness*'.[85] And, in her *Introduction* she comments: 'How might it not have altered the whole face of Buddhism to the West if that sequence had been made the illustration of the causal law!'[86] Instead, the West was presented only with the sequence of dependent co-arising beginning with spiritual ignorance and culminating in 'old-age, sickness and death'. With the emphasis focusing only on this sequence of dependent co-arising, the Buddhist spiritual path comes to be viewed simply as a path dedicated only to the negation of this sequence of *nidānas*, which misses the whole point in these *nidānas* from spiritual ignorance to old-age, sickness, and death cease to be only as a *consequence* of the development of the *nidānas* from *dukkha* through to 'knowledge of the extinction [of the "biases"]'. If the Buddhist spritual path is understood simply in terms of the unregenerative *nidānas* ceasing, then it is hardly surprising that some will understand *nirvāṇa*, which is the 'end' of this path, to be some kind of 'nothing'. Whereas when *nirvāṇa* is placed at the end of the regenerative sequence of *nidānas*, representing a series of enhanced states of being, one is certainly left with a mysterious and vital 'something' rather than a 'nothing'. As the final *nidāna* reveals, it is only the forms of unregenerative ways of being, represented by the 'biases' (*āsavas*), that cease, that become 'nothing'.

Similar lists of these progressive *nidānas* are also found in the *Aṅguttara* and *Dīgha Nikāyas*,[87] the only difference being that the unregenerate *nidānas* sequence up to and including *dukkha* are not mentioned, and the first regenerate *nidāna*, 'confidence' (*saddhā*), is replaced with alternatives such as the practice of 'skilful conduct' (*kusala sīla*) and 'freedom from remorse' (*avippaṭisāra*),[88] or 'wise consideration', (*yoniso-manasikāra*),[89] with the latter giving rise to 'joy' (*pāmujja*) and so on. Interestingly, all these sequences end with 'liberation through knowing and seeing' (*vimutti-ñāṇa-dassana*) rather than 'knowledge of the extinction [of the "biases"]',[90] implying, perhaps, that the latter is a later addition: as if

[85] In a footnote to her trans. of the above; *The Book of Kindred Sayings* pt ii, 26 n. 1.
[86] Ibid., p. viii. One wonders what Nietzsche might have made of it.
[87] A-N v. 1–6 and 311–17; D-N iii. 288.
[88] A-N v. 1–2.
[89] D-N iii. 288.
[90] Apart from one: D-N iii. 288 ends simply with 'he is liberated' (*vimuccati*).

some redactor felt the need to reassert the language of 'extinction' in relation to the goal. Other accounts, with less *nidānas*, can be found elsewhere in the *Aṅguttara*.[91] A point to note, however, is that although each of these *nidānas* or 'conditional grounds' is grammatically singular, each actually covers a plurality of conditions. As Kalupahana remarks, 'While recognizing several factors that are necessary to produce an effect, it does not select one from a set of jointly sufficient conditions and present it as *the* cause of the effect. In speaking of causation, it recognizes a system whose parts are mutually dependent. . . . Thus although there are several factors, all of them constitute one system or event and therefore are referred to in the singular'.[92] Consequently, while each causal ground or *nidāna* is grammatically singular, it actually refers to a complex of conditions, designated above by the term *upanisā* which, as Kalupahana remarks, is a synonym for terms such as *nidāna* or 'ground', *paccaya* or 'condition', and *hetu* or 'cause'.[93]

Although not mentioned specifically anywhere in these *suttas*, what we have here are two distinct paths of dependent co-arising, two kinds of dynamic unfoldment, an unregenerate form and a regenerate form, a saṃsāric form and a nirvāṇic form[94]—the latter form being an account of a progression towards *bodhi*, representing the Buddhist version of the dialectic of self-overcoming in terms of how a subject's experience unfolds. As the saṃsāric aspect, the *nidānas* from 'spiritual ignorance' (*avijjā*) to 'old-age, sickness and death', is involved in the generation of much of the same—the continuation of similar habits and actions—it is therefore unregenerative and not concerned with self-overcoming.[95] This being so, it is only the nirvāṇic or regenerative development that is of interest here, i.e. the *nidānas* from *dukkha* through to 'knowledge

[91] A-N iii. 19, 200, 360 and iv. 99, 336.

[92] Kalupahana (1975), 59.

[93] Ibid. 57.

[94] See Barua (1944). As he observes (1944: 63), in 'the philosophical position of the Buddha's Causal Genesis [*paṭicca-samuppāda*] both *Saṃsāra* and *Nirvāṇa* may be consistently shown to be included in it, both as possibilities in one and the same reality'. For a further discussion on Barua's point, see Sangharakshita (1987), 138 ff.

[95] An 'unregenerative life' is one in which there is no development of skilful affects. In the Buddhist tradition, which accepts 'rebirth', this means that each life is more or less spent in similar pursuits to the previous one, expressive of the same range of affects and their corresponding 'views', a kind of 'eternal recurrence' of the same. Thus no real change occurs, just the same old habits repeating themselves in different contexts, life after life. This is *saṃsāra*.

of extinction [of the "biases"]'. Nevertheless, as in the example of *taṇhā*, it is quite clear that the regenerative aspect comes to be in dependence upon the unregenerative aspect in that *dukkha*, which is the link between the two aspects, arises in dependence upon experiences represented by the unregenerative *nidānas*: *dukkha* could not arise without the unregenerative *nidānas*.

The link between the saṃsāric and the nirvāṇic aspects of 'dependent co-origination' is therefore *dukkha*, the first Noble Truth, which I would understand here as meaning that, in relation to the saṃsāric process, there is a response of gradual dissatisfaction and disillusionment with it. The old forms and aims of life which *were* seen as worthwhile—what were thought of as forming a meaningful life—no longer satisfy. Why this dissatisfaction should arise is never stated. Perhaps a Buddhist reply would be that that is just the way things are; it is just a fact of existence—the 'given' as Nietzsche might call it—that as mundane life cannot fully satisfy us we will naturally 'thirst' for more. If we thirst for more (even though when we look for that 'more' it is usually within the mundane that we look!), then there is the potential of becoming more— providing that a 'becoming more' is a possibility, which it clearly is with both Buddhism and Nietzsche. This can give rise to a tension between the actual and the potential which manifests as a feeling of dissatisfaction with the present state of affairs, i.e. *dukkha* in the form of disillusionment arises. Thus *dukkha* is the transitional stage between the saṃsāric and the nirvāṇic aspects. As a traditional example of this state of affairs we have the 'Four Sights'.[96] The first three sights—an old man, a sick man, and a corpse—represent the saṃsāric aspect, the unregenerative life that when seen as unfulfilling and deficient can give rise to disillusionment (*dukkha*). This state then provides the necessary tension for the possibility of an Hegelian-like dialectic to emerge: the present state, the actual, which is now felt as inadequate (*dukkha*), combined with the fact that we still thirst for more than worldly life can offer, can result in our 'seeing' the actual as *dukkha*. This state of *dukkha*, a mixture of the actual and the potential, allows one to stand in a looser relationship to one's usual life-forms, and also becomes the necessary condition for being open to and capable of responding to new possibilities. This is where the 'fourth sight' comes in. Because one

[96] D-N ii. 21–30.

is now open to new possibilities, when such a possibility presents itself one is *able* to see it and respond to it.[97] Prior to this, one may not have even noticed these possibilities, but *dukkha* in the form of disenchantment affords the condition for the emergence of a new way of looking at life, for a new perspective to emerge—a kind of 'epistemic shift'—and, therefore, a *new response* to emerge. In the tradition, the fourth sight was a member of the alternative *religieux*, a 'wandering mendicant' (*samaṇa*), which I would take as a symbol for a new form of life, the *brahmacariya* or 'life in pursuit of excellence'. The Buddha responded by leaving home and becoming a wandering mendicant in pursuit of truth. Thus a degree of the nirvāṇic potential unfolds, becomes actual, and the dialectic of self-overcoming, represented by the regenerative *nidānas*, begins. In terms of Nietzsche's will to power, one could speculate that the dissatisfaction is felt due to the fact that the expression of the forms of one's life, which are now well established, have become inadequate as expressions of life's overall *nisus*, which is to overcome its actual and established expressions and go on to new, more fulfilling expressions. Perhaps this dissatisfaction leaves one open to new possibilities, and then one can get the 'the scent of a kind of *pleasure* we have not known before', which gives rise to a 'new *desire*'.[98] In the above list of regenerative *nidānas*, the new desire that arises as a response to *dukkha* is *saddhā*, usually translated as 'faith', but which, partly following Guenther, I translate as 'confidence', the confidence to pursue the path whose goal is Enlightenment.[99]

Yet, although *dukkha* is a necessary condition for the arising of such 'confidence', I would not count it as sufficient. As we saw in the above four sights, *dukkha* on its own was not sufficient—a fourth sight was necessary for the Buddha to actually leave home,

[97] Of course, life may not offer any such possibilities. One may have to create one's own from what exists, otherwise one might just become a nihilist.

[98] D 110.

[99] Guenther translates *saddhā* as 'confidence-trust' (1975: 38) and 'confidence-respect' (1959: 62), so as to distinguish it from any misunderstanding that might arise by translating it as 'faith'. *Saddhā* has nothing to do with 'mere belief or blind faith' and comprises all the conceptions we express by 'confidence', 'certitude', 'reverence', 'respect' (1959: 61). Quoting from the *Aṭṭhasālanī*, he adds that 'confidence-respect has the nature of paving the way' (1959: 63). As the *Abhidharmasamuccaya* puts it, 'What is confidence-trust? It is a deep conviction, lucidity, and longing for those things which are real, have value, and are possible' (Guenther 1975: 38).

become a wandering mendicant, and pursue his quest. *Dukkha*, on its own, may simply lead to either despair, or carrying on within the old but now unsatisfactory forms of life without gaining what satisfaction one previously gained from them, or it may even lead the more thoughtful to nihilism. Another factor, therefore, is necessary for *saddhā* to arise: after all, what is it one has 'confidence' in? In the fourth sight it was an alternative way of life in the form of a wandering mendicant that sparked the Buddha off on his spiritual quest. To me this indicates that *dukkha* alone is not enough, it is a necessary condition but not a sufficient one: another condition is necessary for *saddhā* to arise, and I think this also shows us what *saddhā* actually is: it is an energetic and heart-felt response that arises in dependence upon *seeing* an alternative to one's old way of life now characterized as *dukkha*.[100] This is how I would interpret *saddhā* in this context, the confidence and energy to pursue the *brahmacariya* whose goal is 'liberation' (*vimutti*). In Nietzsche's terms, the wandering mendicant would provide, as it were, 'the scent of a kind of *pleasure* we have not known before', and *saddhā* would correspond to the 'new *desire*'. And, switching to the Buddhist language of desire, the movement from the unregenerative to the regenerative *nidānas* would correspond to the shift from unregenerate *taṇhā* to *dhamma-chanda* or the 'desire' for that which is ultimately worthy of pursuing, i.e., the Dhamma. Therefore we could add that *saddhā* also includes the *chanda*, the 'desire' or 'will' to pursue the *brahmacariya.*

As a consequence of pursuing the *brahmacariya*—which, according to some of the alternative nirvāṇic *nidāna* lists, begins with the practice of *sīla*, or 'virtuous conduct'—there arises quite naturally, as a consequence, 'joy' (*pāmojja*). At this juncture, we begin to enter certain states of consciousness normally associated with meditation practice: a concentrated mind filled with joy eventually gives rise to—or we could say, is overcome by—'rapture' (*pīti*). According to Buddhaghosa, *pīti* or 'rapture' refreshes the body and mind by pervading them with energy which thrills and elates. He lists five levels of *pīti*: 'slight' (*khuddikā*), which can raise the hairs on the body; 'momentary' (*khaṇikā*), which is compared to flashes of lightning; 'oscillating' (*okkantikā*), which is compared to waves

[100] In GS, Preface, 3, Nietzsche says that 'Only great pain is the ultimate liberator of the spirit'; for 'great pain' read *dukkha*.

breaking on the seashore; 'transporting' (*ubbegā*), which it is claimed can actually lift the body off the ground; and 'all-pervading' (*pharaṇā*), where 'the whole body is completely pervaded, like a filled bladder, like a rock cavern invaded by a huge inundation'.[101] These descriptions are obviously concerned with the release, in various stages, of emotional and psychic energy. When it all subsides by being absorbed and integrated, i.e. through one *becoming* a new and energized being—a more powerful being—through a process which forms the following stage, called 'calming' (*passaddhi*),[102] one can go on to experience a deeply felt 'bliss' (*sukha*). Remaining concentrated and absorbed in *sukha* can then give rise to a state of fully developed 'meditative concentration' (*samādhi*). This latter stage represents a mind that is 'concentrated, purified and cleansed, unblemished, free from impurities, malleable, workable, established and having gained imperturbability' can now be directed 'to the knowledge of the destruction of the biases [*āsavas*]'or, in more positive language, to 'liberation through knowing and seeing' (*vimutti-ñāṇa-dassana*).[103] In other words, this whole process of *citta-bhāvanā* can be seen as a means to achieving a state of being *capable* of 'knowing and seeing things as they really are' (*yathā-bhūta-ñāṇa-dassana*), the *nidāna* that arises out of *samādhi*. The stages following on from this represent the movement from the initial 'transformative-insight' (*paññā*) to the full accomplishment of *bodhi* or, 'liberation through knowing and seeing'.[104]

[101] Vsm., 143 ff.

[102] This 'calming' is said to be twofold, of the 'body' (*kāya*) and the 'mind' (*citta*). However, as Guenther (1959: 54) points out, it would be wrong to 'translate [these] by bodily and mental relaxation' as 'the Buddhist term *kāya* . . . [does] not so much denote the physical body but an integrated organization and function pattern. *Kāya* comprises the function patterns of feeling [*vedanā*], sensation [*saññā*], and motivation [*saṅkhāras*]', which, along with *citta*, reflect the calming-down of the whole psychic organization of the individual into a new psychic configuration. We could say, a new 'self' or using, Nietzschean terms, into a new organization of 'power'.

[103] D-N i. 84. For a parallel account traversing the *jhānas*, see sections prior to this from D-N i. 73 onwards.

[104] The unfolding of the *nidānas* from 'seeing and knowing things as they really are' onwards, could be viewed as the operation of the *dhamma-niyama* or 'Reality order' (see 7.1). After all, it is through 'knowing and seeing' that karmic activity is destroyed in the sense that actions arising out of 'transformative insight' do not create karmic consequences. This would imply that the individual was free from the operations of the *kamma-niyama* in regard to his present actions, i.e. his present actions do not create consequences under the law of *kamman*. This need not necessarily imply that his present actions have no consequences whatever, but only

This account of the Buddhist version of self-overcoming reveals what can be described as a progressive unfoldment of energy and 'power'. It involves the unfolding of new configurations of energy and power each of which, in agreement with what Stack said earlier in relation to Nietzsche's self-overcoming, can be viewed as the unfolding of a series of new 'selves'. Therefore the Buddhist way, rather than being a relatively healthy but limp expression of life combined with the wish to eventually extinguish life altogether, which is how Nietzsche understands it, seems more concerned with the enhancement and generation of fuller expressions of life, even though those expressions in their higher aspects may be said to take us beyond what we in the West understand as 'human'. Rather than running away from life because it is deemed to be *dukkha*, what unfolds as a response to *dukkha* is a life-enhancing unfoldment of ameliorated states beginning with 'confidence' (*saddhā*). Consequently, one could say that the Buddhist response to *dukkha* is in principle in full agreement with Nietzsche, when he says:

> Creation—that is the great redemption from suffering, and life's easement. (Z ii. 2)

Given the above, Buddhism would also, in principle, agree with Nietzsche when he says:

> What is good?—All that heightens the feeling of power, the will to power, power itself in man.
> What is bad?—All that proceeds from weakness.
> What is happiness?—The feeling that power *increases*—that a resistance is overcome. (A 2)

Or, at least, Buddhism can be said to attach a sense to this talk in terms of its notion of *citta-bhāvanā* as I have just described it.

The above regenerative unfoldment of increasingly energized, self-determined, and concentrated states of being is certainly what Buddhism regards as 'the good', and it no doubt 'heightens the feeling of power' in the sense that resistance is being overcome and energy is being released, leaving one with a greater sense of mastery over one's life. And, as 'the feeling of power increases' and the various resistances and barriers at each stage are overcome, this

that whatever those consequences might be—if, indeed, there are any consequences—they will not bear 'fruit' (*phala*) within the range of *saṃsāra*. Again, to me, this makes more sense of the *dhamma-niyama* than 10-month pregnancies.

overcoming certainly results in various degrees of happiness. And all this, from the Buddhist perspective, is 'natural'.[105] Nothing supernatural is involved, no outside agency or 'grace' is involved, just the natural order of life. When Nietzsche asks whether we know what we are at liberty to do, the Buddhist would say 'yes', and with regard to his notion of self-overcoming could have given him more than a few hints, methods, and practices as to how to go about it.

[105] In an alternative account of the regenerative *nidānas*, the fact that each *nidāna* emerges 'naturally' from the preceding one when it is fully developed, is indicated by the expression *esā dhammatā*, 'this happens naturally'. For an account of this term in this context, see Rahula (1974).

12

'Learning to *See*' and 'Seeing and Knowing Things as they Really Are'

12.1. NIETZSCHE'S CONSCIOUSNESS AND THE BUDDHIST *VIÑÑĀṆA*

Earlier, I drew attention to a possible impasse in any comparative study between the Buddhist way and that envisaged by Nietzsche, in that whereas 'mindfulness' (*sati*) and 'clear-comprehension' (*sampajañña*) are at the heart of the Buddhist version of 'self-overcoming', Nietzsche's comments about 'consciousness' (*Bewußtsein*)[1] are usually disparaging, judging it to be some superficial, untrustworthy, and insipid epiphenomenon that, being 'in the main *superfluous*',[2] might be thought to have no role to play in his notion of self-overcoming:

> whatever becomes conscious *becomes* by the same token shallow, thin, relatively stupid, general, sign, herd signal; all becoming conscious involves a great and thorough corruption, falsification, reduction to superficialities, and generalization. Ultimately, the growth of consciousness becomes a danger; and anyone who lives among the most conscious Europeans even knows that it is a disease. (GS 354)

One outcome of this growth of consciousness is that we become '*absurdly rational* . . . [making] a tyrant out of *reason*, as Socrates did', in order to 'counter the dark desires by producing a permanent *daylight*—the daylight of reason. One must be prudent, clear, bright at any cost: every yielding to the instincts, to the unconscious, leads *downwards*'.[3] Yet, he also says that it is 'through lack of self-observation' that the passions are 'allowed . . . to develop into . . . monsters', rather than 'joys',[4] implying that self-

[1] Nietzsche doesn't distinguish between consciousness and self-consciousness. As his notion of consciousness is peculiar to humans, I suggest that it is self-consciousness that Nietzsche has in mind.

[2] GS 354. [3] TI ii. 10. [4] WS 37.

observation is essential to any method of self-overcoming. He also says that 'All unspirituality, all vulgarity, is due to the incapacity to resist a stimulus—one *has* to react, one obeys every impulse'. One has, therefore, to learn '*not* to react immediately to a stimulus, but to have the restraining, stock-taking instincts in one's control'. We have to learn 'to *see*—habituating the eye to repose, to patience . . . to defer judgement . . . [to] become slow', and this 'Learning to *see*' is Nietzsche's '*first* preliminary schooling in spirituality'.[5] As he comments elsewhere, the chief '*task is wakefulness itself*'.[6] The question here, therefore, is if one has to practise self-observation, exercise restraint with regard to our unruly instincts and passions, learn to see what is actually happening, within and without, thereby becoming more 'awake', how is this possible without consciousness and awareness playing, as they do in the Buddhist *citta-bhāvanā*, an essential role? The way out of this apparent dilemma is to step back and ask why Nietzsche has such a low opinion of consciousness.

In the *Will to Power*, Nietzsche gives us a list of the 'Tremendous blunders' that have been made with regard to consciousness, the first being 'the absurd overestimation of consciousness, the transformation of it into a unity, an entity: "spirit", "soul", something that feels, thinks, wills'. Consciousness has also been misunderstood as the 'cause' and source of our actions, the source of the 'good', the faculty through which we attain to 'knowledge' and have access to 'the "real world" as a spiritual world'.[7] 'Formerly one saw in man's consciousness, in his "spirit", the proof of his higher origin, his divinity'.[8] One therefore 'thinks that it constitutes the *kernel* of man; what is abiding, eternal, ultimate, and most original in him. One takes consciousness for a determinate magnitude. One denies its growth and its intermittences'.[9] To counteract this 'absurd overestimation of consciousness', Nietzsche turns this view upside-down and posits the 'body' as the '*kernel* of man'. In *Zarathustra*, in the section 'Of the Despisers of the Body', we find Nietzsche's more balanced view:

> I wish to speak to the despisers of the body. Let them not learn differently nor teach differently, but only bid farewell to their own bodies—and become so dumb.

[5] TI viii. 6. [6] BGE, Preface. [7] WP 529. See also TI vi. 2; viii. 3 and 4.
[8] A 14. [9] GS 11.

'I am body and soul'—so speaks the child. And why should one not speak like children?

But the awakened [*Erwachte*], the enlightened [*Wissende*] man says: I am body entirely, and nothing beside; and the soul is only a word for something in the body.

The body is a great intelligence, a multiplicity with one sense, a war and a peace, and a herd and a herdsman.

Your little intelligence, my brother, which you call 'spirit' [*Geist*], is also an instrument of your body, a little instrument and a toy of your great intelligence.

You say 'I' and you are proud of this word. But greater than this—although you will not believe in it—is your body and its great intelligence, which does not say 'I' but performs 'I'.

What the sense feels, what the spirit perceives, is never an end in itself. But the sense and spirit would like to persuade you that they are the end of all things: they are as vain as that.

Sense and spirit are instruments and toys: behind them still lies the Self. The Self seeks with the eyes of sense, it listens too with the ears of the spirit.

The Self is always listening and seeking: it compares, subdues, conquers, destroys. It rules and is also the Ego's ruler.

Behind your thoughts and feelings, my brother, stands a mighty commander, an unknown sage—he is called Self. He lives in your body, he is your body.

There is more reason in your body than in your best wisdom. And who knows for what purpose your body requires precisely your best wisdom? (Z i. 4)

The 'Self' (*Das Selbst*) here is not, of course, some metaphysical 'self' or Nietzsche's version of the Upaniṣadic *ātman*, but his poetic metaphor for the will to power. The 'body' is a term for the whole nexus of waxing and waning forces, each of which bears the stamp of the will to power. However, in this instance, Nietzsche does not throw out consciousness completely: there is a role for consciousness[10] as an 'instrument', through which the Self can 'see' and thereby 'perform that act which it most desires to perform: to create beyond itself . . . [which] is its whole ardour'.[11] As he says elsewhere:

In relation to the vastness and multiplicity of collaboration and mutual opposition encountered in the life of every organism, the *conscious* world of feelings, intentions, and valuations is a small section. We have no right

[10] Here as 'sense' (*Sinn*), 'spirit' (*Geist*), and 'Ego' (*Ich*).

[11] Z i. 4.

whatever to posit this piece of consciousness as the aim and wherefore of this total phenomenon of life: becoming conscious is obviously only one more means towards the unfolding and extension of the power of life. . . .
The fundamental mistake is simply that, instead of understanding consciousness as a tool and particular aspect of the total life, we posit it as the standard and the condition of life that is of supreme value: it is the erroneous perspective of a *parte ad totum* [from a part to the whole]. (WP 707)

Linking consciousness to the will to power, he says

that *not* 'increase in consciousness' is the aim, but enhancement of power—and in this enhancement the utility of consciousness is included. (WP 711)

Consciousness, therefore, has to be relegated from its absurdly overestimated place in life and, rather than being understood as the spiritual essence of man, is best understood as simply a part of the whole. Nevertheless, it is quite clear that Nietzsche does consider it as an integral aspect to the enhancement of life. Just like any other phenomenon, consciousness has evolved *naturally*: it is simply 'the last and latest development of the organic and hence also the most unfinished and unstrong'.[12] Speculating on the origins of consciousness, Nietzsche surmises that '*consciousness has developed only under the pressure of the need for communication*'. Man, 'as the most endangered animal . . . *needed* help and protection, he needed his peers, he had to learn to express his distress and to make himself understood; and for this he needed "consciousness" first of all, he needed to "know" himself what distressed him . . . how he felt . . . what he thought'.[13] Consciousness is therefore the means by which we can come to know ourselves by becoming an object to ourselves in self-conscious. And although 'It is not the directing agent, . . . [it is] an organ of the directing agent'.[14]

Given this more rounded view of Nietzsche's opinions on consciousness, notwithstanding his disparaging rhetoric against its ridiculous overestimation by previous thinkers, what emerges is a notion of consciousness as an 'instrument' and 'tool', which, although being as yet 'unfinished and unstrong', can be a 'means towards the unfolding and extension of the power of life'. There-

[12] GS 11.
[13] GS 354. This is all very reminiscent of Herder. See Herder, trans. Barnard (1969).
[14] WP 524.

fore, if we are to develop 'self-observation' and the 'observing eye', take up the 'task [which] is wakefulness itself' and learn 'to *see*', all of which we have seen are essential aspects in Nietzsche's notion of self-overcoming, then consciousness has its role to play as these undertakings would be impossible without it.[15] In other words, such activities are only available to self-conscious beings.

This overestimation of consciousness, however, has been at a cost, in that the part the affects play in our seeing and knowing has been grossly underestimated:

> There is *only* a perspective seeing, *only* a perspective 'knowing'; and the *more* affects we allow to speak about one thing, the *more* eyes, different eyes, we can use to observe one thing, the more complete will be our 'concept' of this thing, our 'objectivity'. But to eliminate the will altogether, to suspend each and every affect, supposing we were capable of this—what would that mean but to *castrate* the intellect? (GM iii. 12)

This is Nietzsche's attack on the notion of the kind of 'pure objectivity' that is supposed to be available either to some 'pure, will-less, painless, timeless knowing subject', or to 'pure reason', or to 'contemplation without interest (which is a nonsensical absurdity)' or, we could add, to a 'pure will-less consciousness'. Such notions are absurd to Nietzsche because they 'demand that we should think of an eye that is completely unthinkable, an eye turned in no particular direction, in which the active and interpreting forces, through which alone seeing becomes seeing *something*, are supposed to be lacking'.[16] Those who attempt to become such pure, will-less subjects are characterized by Nietzsche as attempting to become like 'thinking frogs . . . objectifying and registering mechanisms with their innards removed',[17] in pursuit of some '"pure will-less knowledge" [that] is merely scepticism and will-paralysis dressed up'.[18] But we cannot sever our thinking, knowing, and seeing from our affective constitution.[19] This would be like cutting our

[15] See Wilcox (1974: 172–9). He remarks that the 'theme of the utility of consciousness is important in Nietzsche's notes; and *it is inconsistent with his claim that consciousness has no effects*. Nothing that is impotent can have utility' (174). He concludes: 'Consciousness may be a sign of trouble; but if so, it also can be a way out of trouble . . . [as] a means, and perhaps a most valuable means' (179). Sasso (1977) also concurs with this view.

[16] GM iii. 12.

[17] GS, Preface for the Second Edition, 3.

[18] BGE 208.

[19] See BGE 19 and 187.

heads off in order to see what the world is like in itself, unconditioned by our phenomenal being.[20]

Our seeing and knowing are always perspectival, are invariably conditioned by and reflect our affective disposition. They are, therefore, always relative and can never become purely objective or absolute. But this is not to retreat into mere subjectivism. Nietzsche's notion of perspectivism is merely preparing 'the intellect for its future "objectivity"', which involves the discipline of employing 'a *variety* of perspectives and affective interpretations in the service of knowledge',[21] a discipline that obviously requires consciousness as a means. The more perspectives we have at our disposal, the more facets we are conscious of, the more 'objective' will be our understanding. In other words, we can have a meta-perspective on the first-order perspectives, which although not independent of all perspectives, includes a knowledge of the affective conditions that give rise to these first-order perspectives. Therefore, although the notion of pure objectivity in the sense employed above is now debunked, all is not mere crude subjectivism and naïve relativism—we are still left with the possibility of degrees of objectivity, as some interpretations will be more objective than others, more 'true' and valuable for human culture as a whole. It is the kind of subject we are, which in Nietzsche's language translates as the nexus of affects that we are, that conditions and determines the limits of our ability to see and understand, our capacity to be objective, and, as 'A greater power implies a different consciousness',[22] determines the quality of our consciousness. Therefore, it is not just a question of the number of affects we can bring to bear on any event, of even greater importance are the kind of affects: their measure of quality and 'power'. If quality did not matter then 'hate' and 'resentment' would have as much right to their interpretation of an event as 'love'. And if it were simply the case that the number of affective perspectives, when taken together, constituted a greater capacity for objectivity, then if there were more affects coloured by hatred, resentment, aversion, jealousy, etc. than the more benevolent affects, the former could be said to offer a greater degree objectivity. But this is not Nietzsche's view. This would be a form of naïve relativism, i.e. the kind of relativism that has its roots in Plato's *Theaetetus*, where Protagoras is reported to

[20] HAH 9. [21] GM iii. 12. [22] WP 564.

have said 'that any given thing "is to me as it appears to me, and is to you such as it appears to you" ',[23] implying, at least to Socrates, that what is right or wrong, good or bad, beautiful or ugly, higher or lower, is simply a matter of how the individual perceives them, regardless of who the individual is. Thus, whether some action can be said to be good or bad, whether some view is right or wrong, etc. may be no more than judgements based upon a passing whim, or some irrational prejudice, etc.—in other words, a kind of ethical, aesthetical, and philosophical solipsism. But this is not Nietzsche's view. As Nietzsche himself says, 'Growth in wisdom can be measured precisely by decline in bile',[24] implying that if one wants to become wise, then certain affects, such as resentment, wrath, vengefulness, hatred, and the various 'lusts', must be overcome. If one is stuck in such states of mind, other more enriching perspectives are thereby excluded. Therefore, it is only certain other bileless affects that form the necessary conditions for becoming wise, for seeing more objectively. The person full of bile, regardless of what they think and feel about their own status in this regard, cannot, in truth, be adjudged wise. As we saw in Part I, 'passive nihilism' is a '*Weltanschauung* expressive of the psychological condition of the "decline and recession of the power of the spirit". Life and the world now *appear* as if they were worthless and meaningless *because* they are seen through the dull eyes of spiritual weariness'. That the world may appear to some as worthless and meaningless is not simply an alternative view of the world with the same claim to objectivity and truth as that which would be seen through the 'bright eyes of spiritual strength'. Here it is quite clear that Nietzsche considers such an interpretation of the world as simply wrong, as it is a view that is the objective correlative of a will become sick. He who sees the truth that the whole of existence is a flux of becoming and that there is no 'Being', sees the world more truly.[25] Even in the realm of aesthetics, where the notion of 'beauty in itself' is now dismissed,[26] Nietzsche still considers that 'Beauty is unattainable to all violent wills'.[27] As he puts it in the *Twilight of the Idols*, 'Every error, of whatever kind, is a consequence of degeneration of instinct, degeneration of will'.[28] Therefore, whether in the world of ethics, epistemology, or aesthetics, the capacity for judging whether something is 'good', 'true', or 'beautiful' is

[23] *Theaetetus*, 152. [24] WS 348. [25] TI iii. 2.
[26] TI ix. 19. [27] Z ii. 13. [28] TI vi. 2.

determined by the affective constitution of the subject, the rank and quality of his will to power. As there is a hierarchy of affects, so there is also a hierarchy of judgements in these matters,[29] even though there can be no more absolutes, and any judgement or view is always open to the possibility of being superseded. Not only that, but as there are no more absolutes, there is the possibility that there may be different perspectives that can be said to be equally true.

We can therefore see that 'Learning to *see*' and correct 'self-observation', as essential aspects of 'self-overcoming', are inextricably linked to our affective constitution, and that although consciousness has been relegated from its previously esteemed position to that of being just an aspect of the whole which is man, it nevertheless has a necessary and essential role to play. But what kind of role would it play in Nietzsche's scheme?

Apart from saying that consciousness can be an 'instrument', a 'tool', and a 'means towards the unfolding and extension of the will to power', Nietzsche does not give much away concerning what its role would be. However, he does give a general hint:

> Consciousness—beginning quite externally, as co-ordination and becoming conscious of 'impressions'—at first at the furthest distance from the biological centre of the individual; but a process that deepens and intensifies itself, and continually draws nearer to that centre. (WP 504)

Although consciousness in itself cannot be said to have any purpose of its own,[30] the interaction and struggles of our 'under-wills', which go on unconsciously, do eventually 'rise to our consciousness' as 'impressions'.[31] Everything we become conscious of is therefore a 'terminal phenomenon, an end',[32] and an oversimplification of something which is 'tremendously complex'[33] and unknown to us. Nevertheless, consciousness is our only means of 'self-observation', the only way we can attain some objectivity as to what we actually are as a whole, a whole that is continually shifting and changing. Indeed, self-observation is a mode of consciousness. Going back to Nietzsche's gardener analogy, it is our only means of

[29] WP 462. As Nietzsche suggests here 'In place of "epistemology", a perspective theory of affects (to which belong a hierarchy of the affects; the affects transfigured; their superior order, their "spirituality".')
[30] WP 526.
[31] GS 333 and WP 490. [32] WP 478. [33] WP 489.

getting to know what in us needs nourishing, pruning, weeding, and planting. As he says, we are 'our experiments and guinea pigs',[34] and the 'gardening' is going to be, to some degree, a matter of trial and error. Therefore, consciousness is the starting-point of 'a process that deepens and intensifies itself'. In other words, through self-overcoming we have to make that which we know in consciousness into instinct, in the sense that what we do instinctually springs from the depths of what we have become. For example, if we become conscious that we are rather mean-spirited and that our meanness is something that must be overcome, and we eventually overcome our meanness and become a more generous person, then our generous activity, in Nietzsche's terms, will then be instinctual as it expresses what we authentically are. In contrast to this Nietzsche deprecates the kind of moral activity that is overly self-conscious, that expresses not what we actually are but how we think we should be, i.e. acting out of the consciousness that we ought to behave like this. The latter, being merely conscious, is superficial and inauthentic in comparison, and can even be disingenuous. Nevertheless, as a starting-point, it may be a means of becoming more generous: in order to restrain our meanness and cultivate generosity, we must begin this process of self-overcoming by consciously restraining our more instinctual meanness, and consciously try to become more generous. In this way the process of self-overcoming can move from consciousness to instinct, become 'a process that deepens and intensifies itself'. When Nietzsche judges instinct to be superior to consciousness, he is not affirming our animal nature as against our human nature, but emphasizing that for actions to be truly 'good' they must express what we actually and authentically are. This is what he means when he says that 'All perfect acts are unconscious',[35] and that 'Genius resides in instinct; goodness likewise. One acts perfectly only when one acts instinctively'.[36] However, even after overcoming one's unregenerate character and becoming what Nietzsche calls a '*sovereign individual*', one who is 'liberated from the morality of custom, autonomous and supramoral', such a person still possesses consciousness, but a different order of consciousness. He now has

> a proud consciousness, quivering in every muscle, of *what* has at length been achieved and become flesh in him, a consciousness of his own power

[34] GS 319. [35] WP 289. [36] WP 440.

and freedom, a sensation of mankind come to completion. . . . The proud awareness of the extraordinary privilege of *responsibility*, the consciousness of this rare freedom, this power over oneself and over fate, has in his case penetrated to the profoundest depths and become instinct, the dominating instinct. (GM ii. 2)

And as he says elsewhere:

Might all quantities not be signs of qualities? A greater power implies a different consciousness, feeling, desiring, a different perspective; growth itself is a desire to be more. (WP 564)

We could, therefore, relating these views about consciousness to his notion of self-overcoming, talk of degrees of self-overcoming in terms of degrees of becoming conscious, as it is quite clear that one could not become either a 'sovereign individual', or become aware of one's 'extraordinary privilege of *responsibility*', or become 'a greater power', without a corresponding change in consciousness. There is, therefore, a consciousness aspect corresponding to each level of self-overcoming, which clearly implies that consciousness is an integral part of self-overcoming. Consciousness may be only an aspect of the whole individual and could be said to be, in itself, neutral. Yet it is what one is conscious of that reveals the level—or lack of it—of one's 'self-overcoming'. It is only consciousness that can give one the necessary perspective on oneself without which self-overcoming would be an impossible task. Otherwise, it would all be a matter of pure chance. Nature may occasionally have its 'lucky hits', but the real task is 'to replace that "obscure impulse" with conscious willing',[37] and to that end consciousness has an essential role to play. As D. H. Lawrence, a writer who was influenced by Nietzsche, puts it:

The aim is *not* mental consciousness, We want *effectual* human beings, not conscious ones. The final aim is not to *know*, but to be. There never was a more risky motto than that: *Know thyself.* You've got to know yourself as far as possible. But not just for the sake of knowing. You've got to know yourself so that you can at least *be* yourself. 'Be yourself' is the last motto.[38]

But how does all this compare with the Buddhist notion of consciousness and 'seeing and knowing things as they really are'?

[37] SE 6. [38] Lawrence (1971), 68.

Although the term *viññāṇa* or 'consciousness'[39] is used on its own in the Pāli *suttas*, this is really an abstraction as it is quite clear from various *suttas* that there are only kinds of *viññāṇa*, each being differentiated and named according to the conditions that give rise to it, there being no *viññāṇa per se*. For example:

And what, monks, is *viññāṇa*?

There are six kinds of *viññāṇa*: eye-consciousness, ear-consciousness, nose-consciousness, tongue-consciousness, tactile-consciousness, and mind-consciousness [*mano-viññāṇa*]. This, monks, is what is called *viññāṇa*. (S iii. 62)

Apart from conditions, there is no arising of *viññāṇa*. . . . It is because, monks, appropriate conditions arise that *viññāṇa* is known by this or that name. If *viññāṇa* arises because of the eye and material forms, it is known as eye-consciousness . . . if it arises because of mind [*manas*] and mental objects [*dhammas*], it is known as mind-consciousness. (M-N i. 259)

However, from what is said elsewhere, it is clear that *mano-viññāṇa* or 'mind-consciousness' is of a different order than the other sense-based consciousnesses. For example, mind-consciousness can become 'detached' (*nissaṭṭha*) from the other sense-consciousnesses, and enter other levels of consciousness represented by the *jhānas* or levels of 'meditative absorption',[40] giving it a kind of existence independent of the sense consciousnesses. Elsewhere, it is said to be the common 'resort' (*paṭisaraṇa*) of the five sense-consciousnesses, as it alone 'experiences each of the pastures and realms [of the other five sense consciousnesses]',[41] making it a '*sensus communis*'.[42] The *sutta* then goes on to add that 'mindfulness' (*sati*) is the 'resort of mind-consciousness', *vimutti* or 'liberation' is the 'resort of mindfulness', and *nibbāna* is the 'resort of liberation', signifying a hierarchy of resorts. As *paṭisaraṇa* means 'shelter, help, protection, or refuge', I would understand this

[39] At M-N i. 292, it is said that that *viññāṇa* is called *viññāṇa* because 'it discriminates [*vijānāti*]'. e.g. 'it discriminates pleasure and pain, and that which is neither pleasure nor pain'. Therefore a fuller translation would be 'discriminating consciousness'. However, for the sake of brevity, I shall use the term 'consciousness'. For a modern and thoughtful account of *viññāṇa*, placing it in its contemporary Indian context, see Ross Reat (1990).

[40] M-N i. 293.

[41] S-N v. 218. See also M-N i. 295.

[42] Mrs Rhys Davids, quoted in PED under 'Mano & Mana(s)'. See also Ross Reat (1990), 317.

passage to imply that the senses are to be guarded or protected by means of their common resort, which is mind-consciousness, which in its turn can only be protected by resorting to the practice of mindfulness. In other words, it is referring to the common practice of 'guarding the doors of the senses' through the practice of mindfulness, whose spiritual aim is a process that eventually leads to 'liberation' (*vimutti*) and finally *nirvāṇa*.[43] As we have already seen, this process is what is termed *citta-bhāvanā*. Therefore, given that 'which we call "thought" (*citta*), that we call "mind" (*manas*), that we call "consciousness" (*viññāṇa*)',[44] we could talk about the 'development of consciousness' (*viññāṇa-bhāvanā*) or the 'development of mind' (*mano-bhāvanā*), as well as *citta-bhāvanā*. I will look at the implications of this later. To return to Nietzsche, I would suggest that it is this *mano-viññāṇa* that Nietzsche would have recognized as 'consciousness'. Hereafter, when I refer to 'consciousness', it is *mano-viññāṇa* that I have in mind, and, on the whole, this is how I interpret all references in the *suttas* where *viññāṇa* is mentioned on its own.

Buddhist thinkers were also, at times, disparaging about consciousness, and for reasons similar to those of Nietzsche. For example, we saw above that Nietzsche's main attack on consciousness is not an attack on consciousness itself, but the view that 'it constitutes the *kernel* of man; what is abiding, eternal, ultimate . . . One denies its growth and intermittences'.[45] As we saw earlier in the *Brahmajāla Sutta*, one of the views (*diṭṭhis*) held by some *samaṇas* and *brāhmaṇas* is that

> Whatever is called eye or ear or nose or tongue or body, that is impermanent, unstable, non-eternal, liable to change. But what is called *citta* or *manas* or *viññāṇa*, that is a 'Self' [*attan*] that is permanent, stable, eternal, not subject to change, the same for ever and ever. (D-N i. 21)

The Buddha rejects this view as 'merely [the product of] the experience [*vedayita*] of those who do not know and see, [the product of] the worry and vacillation of those immersed in thirst'. Another

[43] The term *paṭisaraṇa* obviously has different connotations at each stage. Whereas the process from *sati* to *nibbāṇa* is concerned with the central spiritual act of Buddhism, that of 'Going for Refuge [*saraṇa*] to the Buddha, his Dhamma or "teaching", and his Saṅgha or "spiritual community"', the relationship between the sense *viññāṇas* and the *mano-viññāṇa* is not of the same order. This is simply a pun on the term 'refuge' or [*paṭi-*]*saraṇa*.

[44] S-N ii. 94. [45] GS 11.

example, which I have already used in an earlier context, is that of the monk Sāti, who understood the Buddha to have taught what is in fact an Upaniṣadic view, that 'just this one and the same consciousness runs on [unchanged] and is reborn again and again'.[46] The Buddha admonishes him, calling him a 'foolish man', as such a view can only lead to disappointment and suffering. Elsewhere, consciousness is said to be so capricious and fickle that it would be 'better . . . if the common worldling approached this body . . . as the Self rather than the mind [*citta*]', as the body at least persists for a whole lifetime, whereas 'that which we call *viññāṇa* . . . *manas* . . . *citta*, that arises as one thing, ceases as another, both by night and by day'.[47] Nietzsche would, therefore, agree with Buddhism that to understand consciousness, as many of the Buddha's contemporary *religieux* did, amounts to an 'absurd overestimation' because they understood consciousness as being some kind of 'eternally enduring substance', in this case the *ātman*.

Nevertheless, although Buddhism completely rejects the view that consciousness (or *citta* or *manas*) is some sort of eternal and unchanging essence in man, it does often talk of the spiritual life in terms of the development of consciousness. It also talks of the higher spiritual levels as accessible only to certain configurations of consciousness, as well as in terms of consciousness, for example the attainment of the 'sphere of infinite consciousness',[48] and also speaks of the goal in terms of a consciousness, i.e. as consciousness which 'is without attribute (*anidassana*), boundless (*ananta*), all luminous (*sabbata pabhā*),'[49] as well as in terms of an 'unsupported consciousness' (*apatiṭṭhita viññāṇa*), a consciousness that is unsupported by any of the saṃsāric affects.[50] This is certainly not the kind of language Nietzsche would ever use to characterize the process of self-overcoming. Yet, as I suggested above in relation to Nietzsche's notion of the sovereign individual, one could talk of degrees of self-overcoming in terms of degrees of becoming conscious, since what one is conscious of is an integral aspect of self-overcoming. Consciousness, not being some static, unchanging 'thing' separate from the affects, is a feature of the whole process of

[46] M-N i. 256 ff. [47] S-N ii. 94.

[48] *Viññāṇa-anañca-āyatana*, the second of the four *arūpa-jhānas* or 'formless meditative absorptions'. See e.g. D-N ii. 69.

[49] D-N i. 223 and M-N i. 329.

[50] S-N iii. 53–4 and D-N iii. 105. See also Harvey (1995).

self-overcoming. As different configurations of affects, or 'selves', emerge, so too will different forms of consciousness.

With Buddhism the tendency is the other way round: it tends to use the language of consciousness or mind as that in which development and transformation occurs. But as I pointed out above in the case of *citta-bhāvanā*, although Buddhism uses the language of mind and consciousness, the development of both is as much a development of the affects, and even the 'will', as it is a development of consciousness: both are aspects of one and the same process. Indeed, from what has been said about *citta-bhāvanā*, if one had to make a distinction between the affective and the cognitive, then the affective would form the primary condition from which the cognitive could be said to be formed. In other words, the form of consciousness would be determined by the affects. As we saw earlier, the *saṅkhāras* or 'affective forces' are so called 'Because they compose (*abhisaṅkharonti*) a compound (*saṅkhata*)', one of which is 'aggregate of consciousness [*viññāṇa-khandha*]'.[51] This reminds us of Nietzsche's statement that it is the affects that are the 'active and interpreting forces', not consciousness itself.[52] Therefore, when we read, for example, the well-known opening verses of the *Dhammapada*

> Mind [*manas*] precedes all mental states [*dhammas*], and is their chief; they are all mind-made. If one speaks or acts with a wicked mind, then suffering follows one just as the wheel follows the hooves of the ox.
>
> Mind precedes all mental states, and is their chief; they are all mind-made. If one speaks or acts with a pure mind, then happiness follows one just like one's shadow. (Dhp. 1–2)

we have to remember that what makes a mind (*manas*) either 'wicked' (*paduṭṭha*) or 'pure' (*pasanna*) is the *saṅkhāras* or 'affective forces' that make it up. It is action springing from these that determines whether the consequences will be either happiness or suffering, because they determine how one cognizes and interprets any situation, and therefore whether one acts skilfully or unskilfully. Therefore, although Buddhism uses the language of mind and consciousness in its account of self-overcoming, it is the *saṅkhāras* that are, to use Nietzsche's language, the active and interpreting forces in this process: they form *the* affective and determining forces in what constitutes a mind. The main difference, here, be-

[51] S-N iii. 86. [52] GM iii. 12.

tween Buddhism and Nietzsche is, therefore, a semantic one, as both agree that it is, to use Nietzsche's language, the active and interpreting forces or, in Buddhist terms, the *saṅkhāras*, that are the primary and formative forces in their respective versions of self-overcoming.

12.2. SELF-OBSERVATION AND 'CLEAR-COMPREHENSION'

Nietzsche says that the '*task is wakefulness itself*', and that to this end the practices of self-observation and 'Learning to *see*' would be necessary foundations. He also gives us his reasons why these forms of awareness are necessary to his proposed path of self-overcoming:

> Learning to *see*—habituating the eye to repose, to patience, to letting things come to it; learning to defer judgement, to investigate and comprehend the individual case in all its aspects. This is the *first* preliminary schooling in spirituality: *not* to react immediately to a stimulus, but to have the restraining, stock-taking instincts in one's control. Learning to *see*, as I understand it, is almost what is called in unphilosophical language, 'strong will-power': the essence of it is precisely *not* to 'will', the *ability* to defer decision. All unspirituality, all vulgarity, is due to the incapacity to resist a stimulus—one *has* to react, one obeys every impulse. (TI viii. 6)

> Through a neglect of the *small* facts, through lack of self-observation . . . it is you [dismal philosophical blindworms] yourselves who first allowed the passions to develop into such monsters that you are overcome by fear at the word 'passion'! It was up to you, and it is up to us, to *take from* the passions their terrible character and thus prevent their becoming devastating torrents. (WS 37)

What Nietzsche elsewhere calls his 'immediate urgent task',[53] is the task of applying self-observation as a means developing a measured and sustained critical awareness of what is actually happening within and without, as well as being a means of restraining and overcoming the unruly passions, such as 'wrath . . . choler . . . revengefulness . . . lusts',[54] in order to 'prevent their becoming devastating torrents'. It is only then that one can '*sow* the seeds of good spiritual works in the soil of the subdued passions'.[55]

[53] WS 53. [54] WS 65. [55] WS 53.

The Buddhist *suttas*, for similar immediate ends to Nietzsche, give us detailed accounts as to how one may go about practising these forms of self-awareness, all of which are summed up in the compound term *sati-sampajañña*, 'mindfulness and clear comprehension'. Although 'mindfulness' is often mentioned on its own, I think it is quite clear that 'clear comprehension' is always conjoined with it.[56] In distinguishing the two, Nyanaponika suggests: 'The term "Clear Comprehension" should be understood to mean that to the *clarity* of bare mindfulness is added the full *comprehension* of purpose and of actuality'.[57] 'Clear comprehension' can therefore be understood as that which maintains continuity of purpose, keeps the reason why the practitioner is practising mindfulness before him through maintaining awareness of the spiritual framework within which he practises. We could therefore say that it provides both the motivational and intellectual support for the practice of mindfulness. After all, if the practitioner forgot why he was practising mindfulness, he would have become 'unmindful' (*asati*) of and distracted from his reason for practising in the first place, which is certainly not 'Right Mindfulness' (*sammā-sati*).

Two *suttas* devoted to the development of mindfulness and clear comprehention are the *Mahāsatipaṭṭhāna Sutta* and the *Satipaṭṭhāna Sutta*.[58] The 'applications of mindfulness' (*satipaṭṭhāna*) of these titles refers to the four exercises of mindfulness in relation to the 'body' (*kāya*), 'feelings' (*vedanā*), 'mind' (*citta*), and 'mental objects' (*dhammas*). For example, with regard to the body, the practitioner has to be constantly aware of all the body's movements and postures: whether he is walking, standing, sitting, lying down, 'he knows that he is walking . . .', etc.; whether he is 'going forward or back . . . looking forward or back . . . bending or stretching . . . eating, drinking, chewing and savouring . . . passing excrement or urine . . . falling asleep or waking up, in speaking, or in staying silent, he is clearly aware [*sampajāna*] of what he is doing'. Here is also included the *ānāpānasati* or 'mindfulness of breathing' meditation practice, where the practitioner, 'having gone into the forest, or to the root of a tree, or to a secluded place, sits down cross-legged, holding his

[56] See Nyanaponika (1962), 28 ff. [57] Ibid. 46.

[58] D-N ii. 290 f. and M-N i. 55 f. respectively. Nyanaponika's book is essentially a commentary on these two *suttas*.

body erect, having established mindfulness before him', concentrates his attention on the respiratory process. It is through such practices that the practitioner can attain the *jhānas* or levels of 'meditative absorption', which culminate in the state of *samādhi*, the necessary condition for the arising of 'transformative insight' (*paññā*). Secondly, the practitioner has to be aware of his feelings, whether they are 'pleasant . . . painful . . . indifferent . . . pleasantly sensual [*sāmisa*] . . . pleasantly non-sensual [*nirāmisa*] . . . painfully sensual . . . painfully non-sensual . . . neither painfully nor pleasantly sensual . . . neither painfully nor pleasantly non-sensual'. Thirdly, he has to be aware whether his mind is 'lustful . . . free from lust . . . hateful . . . free from hate . . . deluded . . . free from delusion . . . slothful . . . distracted . . . developed . . . undeveloped', etc. Finally, with regard to 'mental objects', if any of the five 'hindrances' (*nīvaraṇas*) of 'sensual desire', 'ill-will', 'sloth and torpor', 'worry and anxiety', or 'irrational doubt', arise in him, 'he knows how unarisen sensual desire comes to arise . . . how the abandonment of sensual desire comes about . . . how the non-arising of the abandonment of sensual desire comes about, and he knows how the non-arising of the abandoned sensual desire in the future will come to be'. The same formula is repeated with the other four 'hindrances'. And although not specifically mentioned here, all the above would have to be imbued with what was covered previously under the four 'Right Efforts'. Indeed, I would surmise that this is what clear comprehention signifies. In this way, the Buddhist practitioner does not 'neglect the *small* facts, through lack of self-observation', and by practising in this way he learns how '*not* to react immediately to a stimulus, but to have the restraining, stock-taking instincts under . . . control'. And it is through such practices that the practitioner comes to see for himself that all phenomena, whether physical, emotional, volitional, or spiritual, are impermanent, subject to change, without any unchanging essence. This would be the Buddhist version of 'Learning to *see*'.

In Buddhism, mindfulness and clear comprehension are the foundation of practice:

> There is monks, this one way to the purification of beings, for the overcoming of sorrow and distress, . . . for the gaining of the right path, for the realization of *nibbāna*—that is to say the four applications of mindfulness. (D-N ii. 315)

And, as the eighth-century Indian poet and philosopher Śāntideva puts it:

Of those desirous to guard the mind, this salutation is made by me: 'Guard with full diligence both mindfulness and clear comprehension'.

As a man agitated by disease is unfit for any activity, so too a mind lacking mindfulness and clear-comprehension.

When a mind lacks clear comprehension, what is learned through reflection and instruction will not be retained, like water in a jar full of holes.[59]

Although these verses were written some thirteen centuries or so after the Buddha, and Śāntideva lived in the famous Buddhist university of Nālandā in North India and belonged to a highly developed school of Mahāyāna Buddhism known as the Madhyamaka, they could easily have been taken from an early Pāli *sutta*.

12.3. SELF-OVERCOMING AS A PATH FROM CONSCIOUSNESS TO 'INSTINCT'

There is also a parallel in Buddhism to Nietzsche's idea that self-overcoming involves a movement from consciousness to instinct, a movement from being conscious of what affects have to be developed and nourished, to actually developing them to such an extent that one fully and naturally embodies them in action.

With reference to *paññā* or 'understanding', Buddhists recognize three levels: *suta-mayā paññā* or 'understanding by way of what is heard'; *cinta-mayā paññā* or 'understanding by way of reflection'; and *bhāvanā-mayā paññā* or 'understanding by way of development'.[60] The first two are relatively straightforward: 'understanding

[59] Bca, ch. 5, verses 23–5 (author's trans.).

[60] These are only mentioned once in the *suttas*—simply as a list at D-N iii. 219. They are listed in the Abhidhamma work, the *Vibhaṅgha* or 'Book of Analysis', and by Buddhaghosa in his *Visuddhimagga*, neither of which is very illuminating, especially the former. All it has to say regarding *bhāvanā-mayā paññā*, is: 'All the understanding of one who has attained [an attainment] is understanding by means of development' (325). Buddhaghosa has: 'Understanding that has reached absorption [*jhāna*], having been somehow produced by [meditative] development, is that consisting in development' (Vsm. 439). They are also mentioned in Vasubandhu's *Abhidharmakośabhāṣam*. In the Pāli texts, *cintā-mayā paññā* is listed first, with *suta-mayā paññā* second. I've followed the order of *Abhidharmakośabhāṣam*: as they are said to be levels of *paññā*, this order makes more sense.

by way of what is heard' is understanding gained by what one has 'heard' (*suta*) or, in a literate society, what one has read. The context here, is, of course, the Buddha's teaching. 'Understanding by way of reflection' is understanding that gains depth by 'reflecting and thinking' (*cintā*) on what one has heard and relating it to actual experience. Understanding now begins to become one's own, being produced by one's own reflections on experience and not so dependent upon the received tradition. *Bhāvanā-mayā paññā* or 'understanding by way of development' is understanding that comes by way of 'development' (*bhāvanā*) and the attainment of 'meditative concentration' (*samādhi*), the *nidāna* from which 'seeing and knowing things as they really are' (*yathā-bhūta-ñāṇa-dassana*) arises. This level corresponds to *paññā* in the sense of 'transformative insight'.

The first level is therefore relatively superficial. The practitioner understands conceptually, for example, the truth that all things are impermanent, or, with regard to practice, what needs to be restrained, what is to be overcome, what is to be developed. But when he tries to act on this level of understanding, he would realize that there are deeper aspects of his being that are not in the least affected by this understanding. The practitioner can be conscious of what has to be done, and give intellectual assent to it, but be far from being able to fully and naturally embody it in action: there is much that needs to be overcome and developed before understanding even begins to naturally inform action. Conscious application of practices such as the four Right Efforts form the necessary conditions from which the second level, 'understanding by way of thinking and reflecting', arises. This level signifies a deepening of understanding based on some degree of practice and experience. The practitioner brings together conceptual understanding of, for example, the concepts that all things are impermanent (*anicca*) and insubstantial (*anattan*), with his experience of these concepts in life, especially in regard to those things he is deeply attached to. In other words, the practitioner's understanding begins to affect him existentially, and as a consequence his behaviour and action quite naturally begin to become more informed by understanding. Understanding is no longer merely conceptual. At this level, understanding signifies an affective shift in how the practioner sees and understands himself and the world: 'knowing' is now based to some extent on experience and reflection, and action begins to embody understanding, or, in Nietzsche's language, understanding becomes more 'instinctual'.

The third level, 'understanding by way of development', constitutes *paññā* in the sense of transformative insight. It arises out of the development of 'meditative concentration' (*samādhi*), as found in the previously mentioned list of regenerative *nidānas*. There we saw that this state of *samādhi* represents a state of being that is 'concentrated, purified and cleansed, unblemished, free from impurities, malleable, workable, established, and having gained imperturbability, [can now be] directed and inclined towards knowing and seeing'.[61] The practitioner's unregenerate nature has been, at least temporally, transformed and overcome, and is now capable of 'knowing and seeing things as they really are', of developing *paññā* as transformative insight. As with Nietzsche, what we see and understand is conditional upon our affective disposition. In Buddhism, for understanding to be truly transformative, in the sense that we can never again be as we were before, such insight can only arise out of an affective disposition signified here by *samādhi*. *Samādhi* arises in the regenerative *nidānas* as the culmination of a dynamic unfoldment of energy. From a state of 'joy' (*pāmojja*) the practitioner traverses various stages of 'rapture' (*pīti*), leading to a potent state of blissful and imperturbable calm. With a mind so composed, he can contemplate, for example, that all phenomena are impermanent, are without any enduring essence, offer no permanent security, and because his affective disposition has been so transformed, he is now capable of seeing fully just what the implications of these concepts are. As a consequence, he is said to 'enter the [nirvānized] stream' (*sotāpatti*), destroying at least three of the ten 'fetters' (*saṃyojanas*) that bound him to *saṃsāra*.[62] Although the *suttas* just present us with bare statements here, by looking at the three fetters that are said to be broken, we can get some idea of the kind of implications breaking them has for the individual.

The first fetter of *sakkāya-diṭṭhi*, literally 'true-body-view', or

[61] D-N i. 84.

[62] It is by breaking the first three fetters that one becomes a 'stream-entrant' (*sotāpanna*). Although still effected by the more refined unregenerative affects, represented by the other seven fetters, one is said to be guaranteed full enlightenment within seven more rebirths, each of which is said to be within the 'better' areas of *saṃsāra*. It is as if one has *seen* too much, such that, from this point on, understanding will naturally inform action more and more, and will naturally become more insinctual until it is fully instinctual.

'true-substance-view', is concerned with the kind of *diṭṭhis* relating to the Upaniṣadic *ātman* and other kindred *diṭṭhis* that were the subject of much heated debate among the Buddha's contemporaries. By breaking this fetter, the Buddhist practitioner can be said to have transcended any reliance upon concepts, dogmas, or doctrines, even those of Buddhism itself: we must remember that after having used the 'raft' of the Buddha's doctrines and practices to attain this state, the practitioner is to leave the raft behind, let alone what the Buddhists saw as the *miccha-diṭṭhis* or 'wrong-views' of the other *religieux*. One is therefore free from being fettered by any beliefs or views. Taking the third fetter next, it is similar to the first except that it refers to 'being attached to rites and rules' (*sīlabbataparāmāsa*) as ends in themselves. By overcoming this fetter, the practitioner is no longer dependent on the external supports of the Buddhist liturgy (*vata*), or even the ethical precepts (*sīla*), in order to sustain his skilful activity and understanding. The reason being that through attaining the kind of 'insight' (*paññā*) that comes through 'development' (*bhāvanā*), he has *become* such an individual, an *ariya*, who is now capable of resorting to his own depth of experience as support and guidance for action. There is now no effective dichotomy between what the practitioner thinks he should do in order to act skilfully, and what he wants to do. His actions quite naturally express what he has become—a being whose affective constitution revolves around skilful affects such as *mettā* and 'compassion', supported by 'knowing and seeing' (*ñāṇa-dassana*). Therefore, when he acts generously or compassionately, these acts spring naturally from what he now is, express his 'knowing and seeing'. These qualities, from being consciously directed and concept-dependent in the earlier stages of practice have now become, in Nietzsche's language, instinctual. The breaking of the third fetter, 'doubt' or 'uncertainty' (*vicikicchā*), represents, we can say, the confidence of action based upon the fact that one now knows and sees for oneself.

Using these models of the three levels of *paññā* and the three fetters, we can say that the Buddhist path of self-overcoming can also be understood as a movement which, beginning in consciousness, 'deepens and intensifies itself' until it finally becomes instinctual. Or, in Lawrence's terms, we have come to know ourselves so that we can be ourselves.

Many forms of Buddhist practice can therefore be understood as offering an intensive and practical model that parallels Nietzsche's statements about the necessary conditions for self-overcoming. But although we have a parallel between Nietzsche's 'self-observation' and 'Learning to *see*' and these Buddhist practices, it is an imbalanced one: for the Buddhist the aim is not simply a question of 'Learning to *see*', but of 'knowing and seeing things as they really are'. The natural question that follows, therefore, is just what does Buddhism tell us about knowing and seeing things as they really are?

12.4. SEEING AND KNOWING THINGS AS THEY REALLY ARE

If we turn to the *suttas* for an answer, we have to conclude 'not very much'. This is not so surprising, however, as Buddhism is very wary about the human tendency, evident in the *suttas* among the various *samaṇas* and *brāhmaṇas*, to become embroiled in arguments and disputes about the various 'views' (*diṭṭhis*) expounded by this or that teacher or school of thought.[63] The impression the *suttas* give is that the Buddha simply refused to become involved in any metaphysical disputes and, to counter this human tendency, emphasized the practical aspect of the *brahmacariya*—the way to become such as can 'see things as they really are', i.e. the way of *citta-bhāvanā*. We must remember that as the Buddha's teaching was mainly directed at his fellow *samaṇas* and *brāhmaṇas*, who had left home and gone forth on some spiritual quest, he would not so much have had to convince them that there was a goal, than that his was the way to achieve it. What the *suttas* do say, therefore, from a philosophical point of view, is a form of intellectual minimalism: that the whole of saṃsāric existence unfolds in accordance with the principle of 'dependent co-arising', and is characterized by three 'marks' (*lakkhaṇas*): *anicca* or 'impermanence', *dukkha* or 'unsatisfactoriness' and *anattan* or 'insubstantiality'.[64] Some have found this a little confounding. Mrs Rhys Davids remarks:

[63] See esp. the *Aṭṭhaka-vagga* of the *Sutta-Nipāta*.

[64] Remembering that nirvāṇic existence can also be said to unfold according to this principle of *paṭicca-samuppāda*, and is still characterized by one of the three *lakkhaṇas*, *anattan*.

> Buddhists concentrated their attention not on a cause or mover of the order of things physical and moral, but on the order itself. They held that this order was one of constant universal change, organically conceived, *i.e.*, as growth and decay, and conceived as proceeding by cause and effect. Things become, as the sequels of certain assignable other things having become.
>
> That may all be true, we say, and intellectually noteworthy, but it leaves us cold and morally indifferent. The Buddhists may have seen, in what seemed to many the mere mechanism of a soulless universe, an eternal orderly procedure, but we do not see how they could draw thence any motive making for righteousness, let alone piety and devotion.[65]

It confounds Rhys Davids as Buddhism obviously does have a highly esteemed moral tradition and has 'commend[ed] itself, at first and subsequently, to the intelligence of the thoughtful, as well as to the hearts of the million'.[66] Although understanding the principle of dependent co-arising may not at first seem much, this is probably because its existential implications are not fully understood and appreciated. When Ānanda extols the principle of dependent co-arising to the Buddha, saying: 'It is wonderful, lord, it is marvellous how profound this dependent co-arising is, and how deep it appears. And yet it appears to me as clear as clear!' The Buddha responds:

> Do not say this, Ānanda, do not say this! This dependent co-arising is profound and appears profound. It is through not understanding, not penetrating this doctrine that this generation has become like a tangled ball of string, and covered with a blight, tangled like course grass, unable to pass beyond states of woe, the woeful destiny, ruin and *saṃsāra*. (S-N ii. 92)

Ānanda thinks he fully understands the doctrine, but the Buddha, who does know it, thinks otherwise. We can assume that Ānanda's understanding is merely conceptual, on the level of *suta-mayā paññā*: he understands the concepts but he does not fully know it in the Buddhist sense of 'knowing and seeing' (*ñāṇa-dassana*). Whether one fully comprehends dependent co-arising in the Buddhist sense of *ñāṇa-dassana* or not depends upon the extent to which one is *affected* by this understanding. If it leads 'naturally' (*dhammatā*) to the next *nidāna*, to becoming radically

[65] Rhys Davids (1912), 111. [66] Ibid. 113.

'disenchanted' and 'disillusioned' (*nibbidā*) with saṃsāric life—of never again becoming caught up in *saṃsāra* through activity grounded on non-regenerative affects—then one understands it in the sense of *ñāṇa-dassana*. If not, then, from the Buddhist perspective, one has not really understood it even though one might give intellectual assent to the doctrinal formulation. And the reason one has not understood it in the sense of *ñāṇa-dassana* is that one has not 'overcome' one's unregenerative nature, one has not developed one's being to the level of 'psychic integration' represented by *samādhi*, which is the necessary condition for 'knowing and seeing things as they really are'. Without *samādhi* there is no *ñāṇa-dassana*; and without *ñāṇa-dassana* there is no real disenchantment—no real 'disillusionment' (*nibiddā*)—with the forms of life viewed by the Buddhists as unregenerative. Therefore, there can be no 'freedom' and 'liberation' (*vimutti*), no *nirvāṇa*, no truly effective 'self-overcoming'.[67]

Philosophically, this intellectual minimalism may be seen by some as rather inadequate and even frustrating. Yet we must remember that the Buddha's Dhamma is about creating a spiritual path in the form of *practical* methods to aid *citta-bhāvanā*. As I've mentioned above, the Buddha was acutely perceptive of the human tendency, evidenced among his contemporaries, to argue and dispute about the *diṭṭhis* of the various religious teachers—which the Buddha adjudged a complete waste of time from the spiritual point of view, and actively discouraged such interests among his own disciples—we can at least understand the reasoning behind it. The whole spiritual enterprise has one aim: to become such as can see things as they really are. An episode from the *suttas*, called the 'Siṃsapā Forest', makes the Buddha's position quite clear:

What do you think, monks? Which are the more numerous, just this handful of *siṃsapā* leaves I have here, or those in the forest overhead?

Very few in number, sir, are the leaves in the handful gathered up by the Exalted One: much more in number are those in the forest overhead.

Just so, monks, much more in number are those things that I have realized, but have not revealed; very few are those things I have revealed. And why, monks, have I not revealed them? Because they are not con-

[67] There would be no 'truly effective self-overcoming' as, from the Buddhist perspective, all that one develops up to and including 'meditative concentration' (*samādhi*) can be lost: one can fall away from the path into unregenerative forms of life.

cerned with spiritual prosperity, they are not constituents of the life of excellence [*brahmacariya*], they do not conduce to disentanglement, to dispassion, to cessation, to tranquillity, to knowing, to perfect enlightenment, to *nibbāna*. This is why I have not revealed them. (S-N v. 438)

So there is little doubt that the reason the Buddha decided only to proffer a few leaves is that, from the Dharmic aspect, this was all he considered practically necessary in order to attain the goal of *nirvāṇa*. Perhaps this was an indirect encouragement for those inclined to philosophical speculation: if they would only get down to some practical *citta-bhāvanā* and thereby become capable of entering the 'Siṃsapā Forest' themselves, only then will their intellectual appetite be fully appeased. However, a modern philosopher might think that a few more philosophical 'leaves' might have been more of an encouragement than a danger, at least for some.

13

Epilogue

In assessing Nietzsche's views on Buddhism, I have given an account of how Nietzsche's notion of nihilism is linked to his understanding of Buddhism. He saw a direct historical parallel between certain cultural developments of his own time and the India of the Buddha's age. This historical parallel rested on an emerging nihilism with the consequent loss of belief in the accepted and dominant *Weltanschauung*. The Buddha's teaching was interpreted by Nietzsche as a response to the nihilism of his own time, and that response, rather than being an insightful answer to nihilism, was merely a particular form of nihilism—'passive nihilism'. The Buddha failed to understand that nihilism was a particular cultural phase that could be overcome, and therefore accepted its *Weltanschauung* of a meaningless and purposeless universe as an ultimate statement upon life. Instead, he created what Nietzsche considered a noble and humane teaching—the Dhamma—as a means of helping his contemporaries overcome the psychological despair they felt at having their purpose in life undermined by nihilism. As a result of following the Buddha's teaching, they could become such as could face up to this cold, meaningless universe and their own annihilation at death with cheerfulness and equanimity. Passing his eye over his cultured contemporaries, Nietzsche foresaw that as their old world-view was gradually being undermined by the emergence of nihilism, particularly by the new sciences, they would see in the message of Buddhism a means of dealing with their growing existential *Angst*. But to Nietzsche, such a prospect offered only a cultural catastrophe: he saw that the acceptance of Buddhism could become a very real threat to the future of Europe, even though he admired many of its qualities, especially when contrasted with Christianity. However, after examining whether Buddhism could be said to be nihilistic—in that it understands the universe as being without any meaning or purpose and that its goal, *nirvāṇa*, simply helps the individual to cheerfully accept their complete annihilation at death, which is how Nietzsche understood it—my conclusion is that Buddhism is far from being a nihilistic religion.

I then presented what I see as the affinities that exist between Nietzsche's answer to nihilism, which turns on his key notions of 'will to power' and its individualization as 'self-overcoming', and the Buddhist notions of *taṇhā* and *citta-bhāvanā* respectively. The will to power, derived from his reading of the early Greeks and given a scientific underpinning by Boscovitch's dynamic theory of 'matter', becomes Nietzsche's replacement for 'God'. In this theory, all phenomena, from the atomic through to the elements that constitute a human being, are characterized by a *nisus* to overcome all resistance, what Nietzsche terms 'will to power'. Within the individual, this will to power, if employed intelligently, manifests as 'self-overcoming'. And it is through this notion of self-overcoming that Nietzsche sought to forge a new spiritual path which culminates in a new kind of being, an *Übermensch*.

Through examining the Buddhist notion of *taṇhā*, using the model of *Erōs* as found in Plato's *Symposium* as well as the Buddhist texts, I have tried to show that *taṇhā*, which, traditionally, is nearly always presented as a hindrance to the spiritual path, can be understood as simply the basic condition of being in the world, a condition of incompleteness, of existential insecurity. It is from this basic condition that all mankind's strivings, whether for material or spiritual ends, can be said to spring. In this sense, it has affinities with Nietzsche's will to power as the most 'primitive form of affect'. And just as Nietzsche's will to power can be channelled to spiritual ends through self-overcoming, when the objects of *taṇhā* are of a spiritual nature, *taṇhā* can be said to become *dhamma-chanda* or 'striving after the Dhamma', whose expression is the path of *citta-bhāvanā*. On the basis of this comparison, my conclusion is that, ironically enough, it is something akin to the Buddhist notion of *citta-bhāvanā* that Nietzsche was aiming at. And, as the Buddhist notion has been thoroughly worked out as a *practical* method, there is much that Nietzsche could have learned and borrowed from the Buddhists that would have helped him in his quest for a practical answer to nihilism. *Citta-bhāvanā*, like Nietzsche's 'self-overcoming', is rooted in man's natural psychological make-up. By skilfully channelling certain deep rooted tendencies, man can venture on a path of continual self-overcoming that eventually culminates in a new kind of being: a Buddha. Perhaps, by borrowing much from the Buddhists, Nietzsche could have found a practical way of creating his as yet hypothetical *Übermensch*. Indeed, if Nietzsche had lived in an age where Buddhism was better understood, he might even have considered the Buddha to be such an *Übermensch*.

BIBLIOGRAPHY

PRIMARY TEXTS

A. Nietzsche

Werke: *Kritische Gesamtausgabe*, ed. G. Colli and M. Montinari, 30 vols. (Berlin, 1967–78).

The Birth of Tragedy, trans. W. Kaufmann, in *Basic Writings of Nietzsche* (New York, 1968).

Untimely Meditations, trans. R. J. Hollingdale (Cambridge, 1983).
1. 'David Strauss, the Confessor and Writer';
2. 'On the Use and Disadvantages of History for Life';
3. 'Schopenhauer as Educator';
4. 'Richard Wagner in Bayreuth'.

Human, All Too Human, trans. R. J. Hollingdale (Cambridge, 1986).
1. 'Human, All Too Human';
2. 'Assorted Opinions and Maxims';
3. 'The Wanderer and his Shadow'.

Daybreak, trans. R. J. Hollingdale (Cambridge, 1982).

The Gay Science, trans. W. Kaufmann (New York, 1974).

Thus Spoke Zarathustra, trans. R. J. Hollingdale (Harmondsworth, 1961).

Beyond Good and Evil, trans. R. J. Hollingdale (Harmondsworth, 1973).

On the Genealogy of Morals, trans. W. Kaufmann, in *Basic Writings of Nietzsche* (New York, 1968).

The Case of Wagner, trans. W. Kaufmann, in *Basic Writings of Nietzsche* (New York, 1968).

Twilight of the Idols, trans. R. J. Hollingdale (Harmondsworth, 1968).

The Antichrist, trans. R. J. Hollingdale (Harmondsworth, 1968)

Ecce Homo, trans. R. J. Hollingdale (Harmondsworth, 1979).

Nietzsche Contra Wagner, trans. W. Kaufmann, in *The Portable Nietzsche* (New York, 1954).

The Will to Power, trans. W. Kaufmann and R. J. Hollingdale (New York, 1968).

Homer's Contest, trans. M. A. Mügge, vol. ii, of *The Complete Works of Friedrich Nietzsche*, ed. O. Levy (Edinburgh, 1911), partly trans. Kaufmann in *The Portable Nietzsche* (New York, 1954).

The Greek State, trans. M. A. Mügge, vol. ii, of *The Complete Works of Friedrich Nietzsche*, ed. O. Levy (Edinburgh, 1911).

Philosophy in the Tragic Age of the Greeks, trans. M. Cowan (Indianapolis, 1962).

On the Pathos of Truth, trans. D. Breazeale, in *Philosophy and Truth* (Sussex, 1979).

On Truth and Lies in the Nonmoral Sense, trans. D. Breazeale in *Philosophy and Truth* (Sussex, 1979).

The Philosopher, trans. D. Breazeale in *Philosophy and Truth* (Sussex, 1979).

The Struggle between Science and Wisdom, trans. D. Breazeale in *Philosophy and Truth* (Sussex, 1979).

We Classicists, trans. W. Arrowsmith in *Unmodern Observations*, ed. W. Arrowsmith (New Haven, 1990).

The Portable Nietzsche, trans. W. Kaufmann (New York, 1968).

Basic Writings of Nietzsche, trans. and ed. W. Kaufmann (New York, 1968).

Selected Letters of F. Nietzsche, ed. and trans. C. Middleton (Chicago, 1969).

B. Buddhism

Dīgha-Nikāya: ed. T. W. Rhys Davids and J. E. Carpenter, 3 vols. (London, 1889–1910); *Dialogues of the Buddha*, 3 vols., trans. T. W. and C. A. F. Rhys Davids (London, 1889–1921); *Thus have I Heard*, trans. M. Walshe (London, 1987).

Majjhima-Nikāya: ed. V. Trenckner and R. Chalmers, 3 vols. (London, 1888–1902); *Middle Length Sayings*, 3 vols., trans. I. B. Horner (London, 1954–9); *The Middle Length Discourses of the Buddha*, trans. Bhikkhu Ñāṇamoli and Bhikkhu Bodhi (Boston, 1995).

Saṃyutta-Nikāya: ed. L. Feer, 5 vols. (London, 1884–98); *The Book of Kindred Sayings*, 5 vols. trans. C. A. F. Rhys Davids and F. L. Woodword (London, 1917–30).

Aṅguttara-Nikāya: ed. R. Morris and E. Hardy, 5 vols. (London, 1885–1900); *The Book of Gradual Sayings*, 5 vols., trans. F. L. Woodword and E. M. Hare (London, 1932–6).

Vinayapiṭaka: ed. H. Oldenberg, 5 vols. (London, 1879–83); *The Book of Discipline*, 6 vols., trans. I. B. Horner (London, 1938–66).

Dhammapada: ed. Ven. S. Sumangala (London, 1914); trans. Ven. Buddharakkhita (Bangalore, 1966).

Itivuttaka: ed. E. Windisch (London, 1889); *As it was Said*, trans. F. L. Woodword in *Minor Anthologies*, ii (London, 1948).

Udāna: ed. P. Steinthal (London, 1885); *Verses of Uplift*, trans. F. L. Woodword in *Minor Anthologies*, ii (London, 1948); *The Udāna: Inspired Utterances of the Buddha*, trans. J. D. Ireland (Kandy, 1990).

Suttanipāta: ed. D. Anderson and H. Smith (London, 1913); *The Rhinoceros Horn*, trans. K. R. Norman (London, 1985).

Milindapañha: ed. V. Trenckner (London, 1880); *The Questions of King Milinda*, 2 pts., trans. T. W. Rhys Davids (Oxford, 1890–4).
Kathāvatthu: ed. A. C. Taylor (London, 1887); *Points of Controversy*, trans. S. Z. Aung and C. A. F. Rhys Davids (London, 1915).
Dhammasaṅgaṇī: ed. Max Müller (London, 1885); *Buddhist Psychological Ethics*, trans. C. A. F. Rhys Davids (3rd edn., London, 1974).
Vibhaṅga: ed. C. A. F. Rhys Davids (London, 1904); *The Book of Analysis*, trans. Ven. U. Thillila (London, 1969).
Nettippakaraṇa: ed. E. Hardy (London, 1902); *The Guide*, trans. Ven. Ñāṇamoli (London, 1962).
Aṭṭhasālinī of Buddhaghosa: ed. E. Müller, 2 vols. (London, 1897); *The Expositor*, trans. Pe Maung Tin (London, 1920–1).
Visuddhimagga of Buddhaghosa: ed. C. A. F. Rhys Davids, 2 vols. (London, 1920–1); *The Path of Purification*, trans. Bhikkhu Ñyāṇamoli, 2 vols. (Berkeley and Los Angeles, 1976).
Abhidhammattha-Saṅgaha: ed. T. W. Rhys Davids, *Journal of the Pali Text Society* (1884); *Compendium of Philosophy*, trans. S. Z. Aung, rev. and ed. by C. A. F. Rhys Davids (London, 1910).
Abhidharmakośabhāṣyam of Vasubandhu. *See* PRUDEN (1988–90).
Bodhicaryāvatāra of Śāntideva: ed. P. L. Vaidya. Buddhist Sansktit Texts, 12 (Darbhanga, India, 1960); trans. K. Crosby and A. Skilton (Oxford, 1996).
Pali–English Dictionary eds. T. W. Rhys Davids and W. Stede (London, 1979).
A Sanskrit–English Dictionary ed. Sir M. Monier-Williams (Oxford, 1899).

C. Other

Darwin, C. (1975), *On the Origin of Species* (facsimile reprint of the 1st edn. of 1859, Harvard).
Edwards, P. (1967) (ed. in chief), *The Encyclopedia of Philosophy*, 8 vols. (New York).
Hegel, G. W. F. (1953), *Reason in History*, trans. R. S. Hartmann (New York).
Herder, J. G. (1969), *J. G. Herder on Social and Political Culture*, trans. and ed. F. M. Barnard (Cambridge).
Hesiod (1973), *Theogeny* and *Works and Days*, trans. D. Wender (with Theognis' *Elegies*) (Harmondsworth).
Hume, D. (1978) (2nd edn.), *A Treatise of Human Nature* (Oxford).
Kant, E. (1933), *Critique of Pure Reason*, trans. N. K. Smith (2nd impression with corrections) (London).
——(1971), *Kant's Political Writings*, ed. H. Reiss, trans. H. B. Nesbit (Cambridge).
O'Flaherty, W. D. (1981), trans. *The Rig Veda: an Anthology* (Harmondsworth).

Olivelle, P. (1996), trans. *Upaniṣads* (Oxford).
Plato (1969), *Phaedo* trans. H. Tredennick in *The Last Days of Socrates* (Harmondsworth).
——(1973), *Phaedrus and Letters VII and VIII*, trans. W. Hamilton (Harmondsworth).
——(1975) (2nd edn.), *The Republic*, trans. D. Lee (Harmondsworth).
——(1951), *The Symposium*, trans. W. Hamilton (Harmondsworth).
——(1935), *Theaetetus*, trans. F. M. Cornford in *Plato's Theory of Knowledge* (London).
Schopenhauer, A. (1969), *The World as Will and Representation* 2 vols., trans. E. F. J. Payne (New York).
——(1974), *Parerga and Paralipomena*, 2 vols., trans. E. F. J. Payne (Oxford).
Zaehner, R. C. (1969), trans. and comm., *The Bhagavad-Gītā* (Oxford).

SECONDARY SOURCES

Alderman, H. (1980), 'Origin and Telos', *Research in Phenomenology*, 10: 192–207.
Allison, D. B. (1985) (ed.), *The New Nietzsche*, (Cambridge, Mass.).
Anderson, T. (1975), 'Anatta: a Reply to R. Taylor', *Philosophy, East and West*, 25: 187–93.
——(1990), 'Kalupahana on Nirvana', *Philosophy East and West*, 40: 221–34.
Ansell-Pearson, K. J. (1987), 'Nietzsche's Overcoming of Kant and Metaphysics: From Tragedy to Nihilism', *Nietzsche Studien*, 16: 310–39.
Aronson, H. B. (1979), 'The Relationship of the Karmic to the Nirvanic in Theravada Buddhism', *Journal of Religious Ethics*, 7: 28–36.
Aschenbrenner, K. (1971), 'Nietzsche's Triumph over Nihilism', *Ratio* 13: 103–18.
Aschheim, S. E. (1988), 'After the Death of God: Varieties of Nietzschean Religion', *Nietzsche Studien* 17: 218–49.
Balasooriya, S. (1980) (with A. Bareau, R. Gombrich, S. Gunasingha, U. Mallawarachchi, E. Perry, ed. comm.), *Buddhist Studies in Honour of Walpola Rahula* (London).
Bapat, P. V. (1958), 'Sramana or Non-Brahmanical Sects', in *Cultural Heritage of India*, i (2nd edn., Calcutta), 389–99.
Barbour, I. G. (1966), *Issues in Science and Religion* (New York).
Barby T. (1989) (ed. with B. Egyed and B. Jones), *Nietzsche and the Rhetoric of Nihilism* (Ottawa).
Baringay, S. S. (1985), 'The Concepts of Dukkha, Trishna and Vaira as found in the Dhammapada', *Indian Philosophical Quarterly*, 12: 221–37.

Barrack, C. M. (1974), 'Nietzsche's Dionysus and Apollo', *Nietzsche Studien*, 3: 115–29.

Barua, B. M. (1921), *A History of Pre-Buddhistic Indian Philosophy* (Calcutta).

——(1944), 'Buddhism as a Personal Religion', *Maha Bodhi*, 52: 54–68.

——(1958), 'Some Aspects of Early Buddhism', in *Cultural Heritage of India*, i (2nd edn., Calcutta), 442–55.

——(1974) (2nd edn.), *Prolegomena to a History of Buddhist Philosophy* (Delhi).

Basham, A. L. (1966), 'The Rise of Buddhism in its Historical Context', *Asian Studies*, 4/3: 395–411.

——(1982) (2nd edn.), *History and Doctrines of the Ajīvakas* (Delhi).

——(1989), *The Sacred Cow* (Boston).

Bastow, D. (1969), 'Buddhist Ethics', *Religious Studies*, 5: 195–206.

——(1988), 'An Example of Self-Change: the Buddhist Path', *Religious Studies*, 24: 157–72.

Bearn, G. C. F. (1986), 'Nietzsche, Feyerabend, and the Voices of Relativism', *Metaphilosophy*, 17: 135–52.

Bechert, H. (1980) (ed.), *The Language of the Earliest Buddhist Tradition* (Gottingen).

Bergmann, F. (1988), 'Nietzsche's Critique of Morality', in Solomon (1988), 29–45.

Bodhi, Bhikkhu (1980), *Transcendental Dependent Arising* (Kandy).

Bohm, D. (1984) (2nd edn.), *Causality and Chance in Modern Physics* (London).

Booth, D. (1985), 'Nietzsche on "the Self as Multiplicity"', *Man and World*, 18: 121–46.

Breazeale, D. (1975), 'The Hegel–Nietzsche Problem', *Nietzsche Studien*, 4: 146–64.

——(1979), *Philosophy and Truth* (Sussex).

——(1983*a*), 'Aground on the Ground of Values', *Analecta Husserliana*, 15: 335–49.

——(1983*b*), 'The Meaning of the Earth', in Goicoechea (1983), 113–41.

Brockington, J. L. (1981), *The Sacred Thread* (Edinburgh).

Brogan, W. A. (1984), 'The Battle Between Art and Truth', *Philosophy Today*, 28: 349–57.

Brown, R. S. G. (1983), 'Does the "True World" Not Remain a Fable?', in Goicoechea (1983), 98–111.

Carella, M. J. (1976), 'Heisenberg's Concept of Matter as Potency', *Diogenes*, 96: 25–37.

Carus, P. (1913), 'Deussen's Recollections of Nietzsche', *Open Court*, 27: 616–19.

Chadwick, H. (1986), *Augustine* (Oxford).
Chakravarti, U. (1987), *The Social Dimensions of Early Buddhism* (Delhi).
Chandhuri, H. (1952), 'The Concept of Brahman in Hindu Philosophy', *Philosophy East and West*, 2: 47–66.
Chandra, P. (1971), 'Was Early Buddhism Influenced by the Upanisads?', *Philosophy East and West*, 21: 317–24.
Chatalian, G. (1983), 'Early Buddhism and the Nature of Philosophy', *Journal of Indian Philosophy*, 11: 167–222.
Chatterjee, H. (1956), 'A Critical Study of the Buddhism Conception of Nirvana', *Journal of the Bihar Research Society*, 2: 492–7.
Chowdhury, R. P. (1955), 'An Interpretation of the Annata Doctrine of Buddhism', *Indian Historical Quarterly*, 31: 52–67.
Clark, M. (1983), 'Nietzsche's Doctrine of the Will to Power', *Nietzsche Studien*, 12: 458–68.
——(1990), *Nietzsche on Truth and Philosophy* (Cambridge).
Collingwood, R. G. (1946), *The Idea of History* (Oxford).
Collins, S. (1982), *Selfless Persons* (Cambridge).
——(1985), 'Buddhism in Recent British Philosophy and Theology', *Religious Studies*, 21: 475–93.
Conway, D. W. (1992), 'Heidegger, Nietzsche and the Origins of Nihilism', *Journal of Nietzsche Studies*, 3: 11–43.
Conze, E. (1962), *Buddhist Thought in India* (London).
——(1972), *Buddhist Meditation* (London).
Coomaraswamy, Sir Muthu (1874), *Dialogues and Discourses of Gotama Buddha* (London).
Copleston, F. (1980), 'Schopenhauer and Nietzsche', in Fox (1980), 215–25.
Cousins, L. (1974) (ed. with A. Kunst and K. R. Norman), *Buddhist Studies in Honour of I. B. Horner* (Dordrecht).
Coward, H. (1977) (ed. with K. Sivaraman), *Revelation in Indian Thought* (Emeryville, Calif.).
Crawford, C. (1988), *The Beginnings of Nietzsche's Theory of Language* (Berlin).
Cruise, H. (1983), 'Early Buddhism: Some Recent Misconceptions', *Philosophy East and West*, 32: 149–66.
Dannhauser, J. (1974), *Nietzsche's View of Socrates* (Ithaca, NY).
De Jong, J. W. (1972), Review of Welbon's 'The Buddhist Nirvana and its Western Interpreters', *Journal in Indian Philosophy*, 1: 396–403.
——(1987) (2nd revised and enlarged edn.), *A Brief History of Buddhist Studies in Europe and America* (Delhi).
Deleuze, G. (1983), trans. H. Tomlinson, *Nietzsche and Philosophy* (London).

Desmond, A. (1991) (with J. Moore), *Darwin* (London).
Deussen, P. (1906), *The Philosophy of the Upanishads*, trans. Rev. A. S. Geden (Edinburgh).
——(1909), *Elements of Metaphysics*, trans. C. M. Duff (London).
——(1912), *The System of Vedânta*, trans. C. Johnston (Chicago).
Dharmasiri, G. (2nd edn., n.d.), *A Buddhist Critique of the Christian Concept of God* (Singapore).
Doore, G. (1979), 'The Radically Empiricist Interpretation of Early Buddhist Nirvana', *Religious Studies*, 15: 55–64.
Dumoulin, H. (1981), 'Buddhism and 19th Century German Philosophy', trans. J. M. Chang, *Journal of the History of Ideas*, 42: 457–70.
Dutt, S. (1962), *Buddhist Monks and Monasteries of India* (London).
——(1978), *The Buddha and Five After-Centuries* (Calcutta).
——(1984) (2nd edn.), *Early Buddhist Monachism* (Delhi).
Elder, J. (1970) (ed.), *Chapters on Indian Civilisation*, i (Dubugue).
Elman, B. A. (1983), 'Nietzsche and Buddhism', *Journal of the History of Ideas*, 44: 671–86.
Flew, A. (1967), *Evolutionary Ethics* (London).
——(1983) (ed.), *A Dictionary of Philosophy* (London).
——(1984), *Darwinian Evolution* (London).
Fouillée, A. (1901), 'Nietzsche and Darwinism', *International Monthly*, 2: 134–65.
Fox, M. (1980) (ed.), *Schopenhauer: His Philosophical Achievement* (Sussex).
Frauwallner, E. (1956), 'On the Historical Data We Possess on the Person and Doctrine of the Buddha', *East and West*, 7: 309–12.
——(1973), *History of Indian Philosophy*, 2 vols. (Delhi).
Frazer, A. M. (1975), 'A European Buddhism', *Philosophy East and West*, 25: 145–60.
Freeman, D. A. (1988), 'Nietzsche: Will to Power as a Foundation of a Theory of Knowledge', *International Studies in Philosophy*, 20: 3–14.
Friedman, M. (1966), 'The Father of Atheistic Existentialism', *Journal of Existentialism*, 6: 269–77.
Geiger, W. (1968) (2nd edn.), trans. B. Ghosh, *Pali Literature and Language* (Delhi).
Gerber, R. (1968), 'Nietzsche: Reason as Power for Humanism', *Philosophy Today*, 12: 75–93.
Gillespie, N. C. (1979), *Charles Darwin and the Problem of Creation* (Chicago).
Goicoechea, D. (1983) (ed.), *The Great Year of Zarathustra* (New York).
Golomb, J. (1986), 'Nietzsche's Phenomenology of Power', *Nietzsche Studien*, 15: 289–305.
——(1989), *Nietzsche's Enticing Psychology of Power* (Ames, Ia.).

Gonda, J. (1950), *Notes on Brahman* (Utrecht).
——(1975), *Selected Studies*, iv (Leiden).
Goudsblom, J. (1980), *Nihilism and Culture* (Oxford).
Govinda, L . A. (1969), *The Psychological Attitude of Early Buddhist Philosophy* (London).
Griffiths P. J. (1982), 'Notes Towards a Critique of Buddhist Karmic Theory', *Religious Studies*, 18: 277–91.
Guenther, H. V. (1959), *Philosophy and Psychology in the Abhidharma* (Delhi).
——(1975), *Mind in Buddhist Psychology* (Emeryville, Calif.).
Gupta, R. (1977), 'Schopenhauer and Indian Thought', *East and West*, NS, 8: 163–86.
Hare, W. L. (1916), 'Nietzsche's Critique of Buddhism', *The Buddhist Review* (London), 21–35.
Harrison, P. H. (1987), 'Buddhism: A Religion of Revelation After All?', *Numen*, 34: 256–64.
Harvey, P. (1983–4), 'Developing a Self Without Boundaries', *Buddhist Studies Review*, 1: 115–26.
——(1989), 'Consciousness Mysticism in the Discourses of the Buddha', in Werner (1989), 82–102.
——(1990), *An Introduction to Buddhism* (Cambridge).
——(1995), *The Selfless Mind: Personality, Consciousness and Nirvana in Early Buddhism* (Richmond).
Hayman, R. (1980), *Nietzsche: A Critical Life* (Oxford).
Heine, S. (1981), 'Dionysus Against the Buddha: Nietzsche's "Yes" and the Buddha's "No"', in Katz (1981), 244–66.
Heller, E. (1988), *The Importance of Nietzsche* (Chicago).
Heller, P. (1980) (ed.), *Studies on Nietzsche* (Bonn).
Herman, A. L. (1989), 'Religions as Failed Theodicies: Atheism in Hinduism and Buddhism', in Perrett (1989), 35–60.
——(1979), 'The Solution to the Paradox of Desire in Buddhism', *Philosophy East and West*, 29: 91–4.
Hinman, L. M. (1977), 'Nihilism and Alienation in Marx and Nietzsche', *Philosophy Today*, 21: 90–100.
Hiriyanna, M. (1949), *Essentials of Indian Philosophy* (London).
Hoffman, F. J. (1987), *Rationality and Mind in Early Buddhism* (Delhi).
——(1991), 'Towards a Philosophy of Buddhist Religion', *Asian Philosophy*, 1: 21–7.
Holbrook, P. E. (1988), 'Metaphor and the Will to Power', *International Studies in Philosophy*, 20: 19–28.
Hollingdale, R. J. (1965), *Nietzsche: The Man and His Philosophy* (Baton Rouge, La.).
——(1973), *Nietzsche* (London).
Hopkins, J. H. (1971), *The Hindu Religious Tradition* (Mass.).

Hoy, D. C. (1986), 'Nietzsche, Hume and the Genealogical Method', in Yovel (1986), 20–38.

Hunt, L. H. (1991), *Nietzsche and the Origin of Virtue* (London).

Inada, K. K. (1969), 'Some Basic Misconceptions of Buddhism', *International Philosophical Quarterly*, 9: 101–19.

Janaway, C. (1989), *Self and World in Schopenhauer's Philosophy* (Oxford).

Jayasuriya W. F. (1963), *The Psychology and Philosophy of Buddhism* (Colombo).

Jayatilleke, K. N. (1963), *Early Buddhist Theory of Knowledge* (Delhi).

——(1968), 'The Buddhist Doctrine of Karma', *Maha Bodhi*, 76: 314–20.

——(1970), 'Ethical Theory of Buddhism', *Maha Bodhi*, 78: 192–7.

Johansson, R. E. A. (1965), 'Citta, Mano, Viññana: A Psycho-Semantic Investigation', *University of Ceylon Review*, 23: 165–215.

——(1969), *The Psychology of Nirvana* (London).

——(1979), *The Dynamic Conception of Early Buddhism* (Oxford).

——(1981), *Pali Buddhist Texts* (London).

Joshi, L. M. (1968), 'The Mind and the Mere Mind in Buddhism', *Maha Bodhi*, 76: 130–5.

——(1977), *Studies in the Buddhistic Culture of India* (Delhi).

——(1980), 'The Meaning of Nirvana', in Narain (1980), 189–95.

——(1983), *Discerning the Buddha* (New Delhi).

Kalansuria, A. D. P. (1989), 'The Dhamma and the Notion of "Perception": A Conceptual Technique Made Explicit', *Indian Philosophical Quarterly*, 16: 291–302.

Kalupahana, D. J. (1975), *Causality: The Central Philosophy of Buddhism* (Honolulu).

——(1976), *Buddhist Philosophy* (Honolulu).

——(1987), *The Principles of Buddhist Psychology* (Honolulu).

——(1988), 'The Buddhist Conceptions of "Subject" and "Object" and their Moral Implications', *Philosophy East and West*, 38: 280–306.

——(1989), 'The Concepts of Self and Freedom in Buddhism', in Perrett (1989).

Kapstein, M. (1988), 'Indra's Search for the Self and the Beginnings of Philosophical Perplexity in India', *Religious Studies*, 24: 239–56.

Katz, N. (1981) (ed.), *Buddhist and Western Philosophy* (New Delhi).

Kaufmann, W. (1960), 'How Nietzsche Revolutionised Ethics', in id., *Shakespeare to Existentialism* (New York), 207–17.

——(1974), *Nietzsche: Philosopher, Psychologist, Antichrist* (Princeton).

Keown, D. (1992), *The Nature of Buddhist Ethics* (London).

Kishan, B. V. (1972), 'Schopenhauer and Buddhism', *Schopenhauer Jahrbuch*, 53: 185–90.

Kloetzli, R. (1983), *Buddhist Cosmology* (Delhi).

Knipe, D. M. (1975), *In the Image of Fire: Vedic Experiences of Heat* (Delhi).
Kockelmans, J. J. (1983), 'The Challenge of Nietzsche's "God is Dead"', in Goicoechea (1983), 63–80.
Krishna, D. (1983), 'The Upanishads: What are They?', *Journal of the Indian Council of Research*, 1: 71–82.
Lamotte, E. (1974), 'Passions and Impregnations of the Passions in Buddhism', in Cousins (1974), 91–104.
——(1988), *History of Indian Buddhism*, trans. S. Webb-Boin (Louvain).
Larson, G. J. (1987) (ed.), *Samkhya: A Dualist Tradition in Indian Philosophy* (Princeton).
Lawrence, D. H. (1971), *Fantasia of the Unconscious and Psychoanalysis and the Unconscious* (Harmondsworth).
Lingis, A. (1978), 'The Last Form of the Will to Power', *Philosophy Today*, 22: 93–205.
Lloyd-Jones, H. (1976), 'Nietzsche and the Study of the Ancient World', in J. C. O'Flaherty (ed.) (1976), 1–15.
Lopez. D. S. (1988) (ed.), *Buddhist Hermeneutics* (Honolulu).
Loy, D. (1983), 'The Difference Between Samsara and Nirvana', *Philosophy East and West*, 33: 355–65.
Luft, E. von der (1984), 'Sources of Nietzsche's "God is Dead!" and its Meaning for Heidegger', *Journal of the History of Philosophy*, 45: 263–76.
McDermott, J. P. (1984), 'Scripture as the Word of the Buddha', *Numen*, 31: 22–39.
——(1980), 'Karma and Rebirth in Early Buddhism', in W. D. O'Flaherty (1980), 165–92.
Madanayake, B. (1985), *Is there Consciousness in Nibbana?*, in Warder (1985), 18–25.
Magnus, B. (1978), *Nietzsche's Existential Imperative* (Bloomington, Ind.).
——(1980), 'Nietzsche's Mitigated Scepticism', *Nietzsche Studien*, 9: 260–7.
——(1983*a*), 'Overman: An Attitude or an Ideal?', in Goicoechea (1983), 142–65.
——(1983*b*), 'Perfectibility and Attitude in Nietzsche's Übermensch', *Review of Metaphysics*, 36: 633–59.
——(1986*a*), 'Nietzsche and the Project of Bringing Philosophy to an End', in Yovel (1986), 39–57.
——(1986*b*), 'Nietzsche's Philosophy in 1988: The Will to Power and the Übermensch', *Journal of the History of Philosophy*, 24: 79–98.
——(1989), 'Nietzsche and Post Modern Criticism', *Nietzsche Studien*, 18: 301–16.
Masefield, P. (1979), 'The Nibbana-Parinibbana Controversy', *Religion*, 9: 215–30.

Mathews, B. (1975), 'Notes on the Concept of Will in Early Buddhism', *Sri Lanka Journal of Humanities*, 1: 152–60.
Matilal, B. K. (1980), 'The Enigma of Buddhism', *Journal of Dharma*, 2: 302–6.
——(1985), *Logic, Language and Reality* (Delhi).
Mazlish, B. (1968), 'Freud and Nietzsche', *Psychoanalytic Review*, 55: 360–75.
Melling, D. J. (1987), *Understanding Plato* (Oxford).
Mercer, J. (1915), 'Nietzsche's Darwinism', *Nineteenth Century*, 77: 421–31.
Miller, J. (1985), *The Vision of Cosmic Order in the Vedas* (London).
Mistry, F. (1981), *Nietzsche and Buddhism* (Berlin).
Mitchell, D. W. (1974), 'An Early View of Man in Indian Buddhism: The Sarvastivadin Concept of the Self', *International Philosophical Quarterly*, 14: 189–99.
Mittelman, W. (1980), 'The Relation Between Nietzsche's Theory of the Will to Power and his Earlier Conception of Power', *Nietzsche Studien*', 9: 122–41.
Moles, A. (1990), *Nietzsche's Philosophy of Nature and Cosmology* (New York).
Mostert, P. (1979), 'Nietzsche's Reception of Darwinism', *Bijdragen Tot de Dierkonde*, 49: 235–46.
Müller, M. (1873), *Introduction to the Science of Religion* (London).
——(1881), *Selected Essays on Language, Mythology and Religion*, ii (London).
——(1889) *Natural Religion* (London).
Nakamura, H. (1955),'Upanisadic Tradition and the Early School of Vedanta as Noticed in Buddhist Scripture', *Harvard Journal of Asiatic Studies*, 18: 74–104.
——(1977), 'The Problem of Self in Buddhist Philosophy', in Coward, (1977), 99–118.
——(1980), *Buddhist Studies* (Tokyo).
Ñāṇajivako, Bhikkhu (1977), 'The Philosophy of Disgust: Buddho and Nietzsche, *Schopenhauer Jahrbuch*, 58: 112–32.
Ñāṇananda, Bhikkhu (1971), *Concept and Reality in Early Buddhist Thought* (Kandy).
Nārada, Mahā Thera (1968), *A Manual of Abhidhamma* (Kandy).
Narain, A. K. (1978) (ed.), *Studies in Pali Buddhism* (New Delhi).
——(1980) (ed.), *Studies in the History of Buddhism* (Delhi).
Nehamas, A. (1985), *Nietzsche: Life as Literature* (Cambridge, Mass).
——(1986), 'Will to Knowledge, Will to Ignorance and Will to Power in *Beyond Good and Evil*', in Yovel (1986), 90–108.
Njarakunnel, G. (1981), 'Religion Beyond Religions in Nietzsche', *Journal of Dharma*, 5: 399–405.

Norman, K. R. (1981), 'A Note on Atta in the Alagaddupama-Sutta', *Studies in Indian Philosophy* (Ahmedabad), 19–29.

——(1983), *Pali Literature* (Wiesbaden).

Nyanaponika, T. (1962), *The Heart of Buddhist Meditation* (London).

——(1965) (2nd ed.), *Abhidhamma Studies* (Kandy).

Nyanatiloka (1976), *Buddhistisches Wörterbuch* (Konstanz).

Obeyesekere, G. (1980), 'The Rebirth Eschatology and its Transformations: A Contribution to the Sociology of Buddhism', in W. D. O'Flaherty (1980), 137–64.

O'Flaherty, J. C. (1976) (ed.), *Studies in Nietzsche and the Classical World* (Chapel Hill, NC).

O'Flaherty, W. D. (1980) (ed.), *Karma and Rebirth in Classical Indian Traditions* (Berkeley and Los Angeles).

Oldenberg, H. (1882), trans. W. Hoey, *The Buddha: His Life, His Doctrine, His Order* (London).

Pande, G. C. (1983) (3rd edn.), *Studies in the Origin of Buddhism* (Delhi).

Parsons, K. P. (1973), 'Nietzsche and Moral Change', in Solomon (1973*a*), 169–93.

Peerboom, R. P. (1989), 'Buddhist Process Ethics', *Indian Philosophical Quarterly*, 16: 247–68.

Perrett, R. W. (1987), 'Egoism, Altruism and Intentionalism in Buddhist Ethics', *Journal of Indian Philosophy*, 15: 71–85.

——(1989) (ed.), *Indian Philosophy of Religion* (Dordrecht).

Poole, R. (1990), 'Nietzsche: The Subject of Morality', *Radical Philosophy*, 54: 2–7.

Potter, K. H. (1964), 'The Naturalistic Principle of Karma', *Philosophy East and West*, 14: 39–50.

Prebish, C. S. (1975) (ed.), *Buddhism: a Modern Perspective* (University Park, Pa.).

Premasiri, P. D. (1972), *The Philosophy of the Atthakavagga* (Kandy).

——(1976), 'Interpretation of two Principle Ethical Terms in Early Buddhism', *Sri Lanka Journal of the Humanities*, 1: 63–74.

Pruden, L. M. (1988–90), *Abhidharmakośabhāṣyam* of Vasubandhu, trans. in 4 vols., being a trans. of Poussin's French trans. with reference to the Sanskrit text and with additional notes (Berkeley and Los Angeles).

Pye, M. (1979), *The Buddha* (London).

Rachels, J. (1991), *Created From Animals* (Oxford).

Radhakrishnan, S. (1953) (ed. and trans.), *The Principle Upanisads* (London), includes complete Sanskrit texts of the 18 Upaniṣads translated.

Rahula, W. (1974), 'Wrong Notions of *Dhammatā (Dharmatā)*', in Cousins (1974), 181–91.

Reichenbach, R. (1988), 'The Law of Karma and the Principle of Causation', *Philosophy East and West*, 38: 399–410.
Reynolds, F. E. (1979), 'Buddhist Ethics: A Biographical Sketch', *Religious Studies Review*, 5: 40–8.
Rhys Davids, C. A. F. (1912), *Buddhism* (London).
——(1924), *Buddhist Psychology* (London).
——(1925), 'Will in Early Buddhist Scriptures', *Indian Historical Quarterly*, 1: 443–56.
——(1936), *The Birth of Indian Psychology and its Development* (London).
——(1938), *What was the Original Gospel in 'Buddhism'?* (London).
——(1939), 'A Dynamic Conception of Man', *Indian Culture*, 6: 235–9.
——(1939–40), 'The Will in Buddhism', *Hibbert Journal*, 38: 251–60.
Robinson, R. H. (1969), 'Early Buddhist Theory of Knowledge', *Philosophy East and West*, 19: 69–81.
——(1972), 'Some Buddhist and Hindu Concepts of Intellect-will', *Philosophy East and West*, 22: 299–307.
Rollmann, H. (1978), 'Deussen, Nietzsche, and Vedanta', *Journal of the History of Ideas*, 39: 125–32.
Rosen, S. (1989), 'Remarks on Nietzsche's "Platonism"', in Barby (1989), 145–63.
——(1980), 'Nietzsche's Image of Chaos', *International Philosophical Quarterly*, 20: 3–23.
Ross Reat, N. (1990), *Origins of Indian Psychology* (Berkeley and Los Angeles).
Rudolph, A. W. (1969), 'Nietzsche's Buddhism: An Aspect of the Doctrine of Nihilism', *ITA Humanidades*, 5: 33–43.
Rupp, G. (1971), 'The Relationship Between Nirvana and Samsara: An Essay on the Evolution of Buddhist Ethics', *Philosophy East and West*, 21: 55–67.
Sander, L. G. (1987) (ed.), *Conversations With Nietzsche* (New York).
Sangharakshita (1987) (6th edn.), *A Survey of Buddhism* (London).
——(1991), *The Three Jewels* (Glasgow).
——(1994), *Who is the Buddha* (Glasgow).
Sasso, J. (1977), *The Role of Consciousness in the Thought of Nietzsche* (Washington).
Schacht, R. (1973), *Hegel and After* (London).
——(1983), *Nietzsche* (London).
Scheler, M. (1973), 'Ressentiment', in Solomon (1973*a*), 244–57.
Schlechta, K. (1972), 'The Hidden Beginnings of the Nietzschean Philosophy', *Malahat Review*, 139–44.
Schmithausen, L. (1976), 'On the Problem of the Relation of Spiritual Practice and Philosophical Theory in Buddhism', *German Scholars on India*, ii (Delhi).

Schmitt, R. (1961), 'Nietzsche's Psychological Theory', *Journal of Existential Psychiatry*, 2: 71–92.

Schrift, A. D. (1985), 'Language, Metaphor, Rhetoric: Nietzsche's Deconstruction of Epistemology', *Journal of the History of Philosophy*, 23: 371–95.

Schumann, H. W. (1989), *The Historical Buddha*, trans. M. O'C. Walsh (Harmondsworth).

Schutte, O. (1984), *Beyond Nihilism* (Chicago).

Sedlar, J. W. (1982), *India in the Mind of Germany* (Washington).

Siderits, M. (1979), 'A Note on the Early Buddhist Theory of Truth', *Philosophy East and West*, 29: 491–9.

Silva, P. de (1973), *Buddhist and Freudian Psychology* (Colombo).

——(1979), *An Introduction to Buddhist Psychology* (London).

Simmel, G. (1986), trans. H. Loiskandl, D. Weinstein, and M. Weinstein, *Schopenhauer and Nietzsche* (Amherst).

Small, R. (1982), 'Nietzsche's God', *Philosophy Today*, 26: 41–53.

Smart, N. (1981), 'Problems of the Application of Western Terminology to Theravāda Buddhism, with Special Reference to the Relationship between the Buddha and the Gods', in Katz (1981), 444–9.

Smith, C. U. P. (1987), 'Clever Beasts Who Invented Knowledge: Nietzsche's Evolutionary Biology of Knowledge', *Biology and Philosophy*, 2: 65–91.

Soll, I. (1986), 'The Hopelessness of Hedonism and the Will to Power', *International Studies in Philosophy*, 18: 97–112.

Solomon, R. C. (1973*a*) (ed.), *Nietzsche: A Collection of Critical Essays* (New York).

——(1973*b*), 'Nietzsche, Nihilism and Morality', in Solomon (1973*a*), 201–25.

——(1985), 'A More Severe Morality', *Journal of the British Society for Phenomenology*, 16: 250–67.

——(1987), *From Hegel to Existentialism* (New York).

——(1988) (ed. with K. M. Higgins), *Reading Nietzsche* (Oxford).

Southwold, M. (1978), 'Buddhism and the Definition of Religion', *Man*, 13: 362–79.

Sprung, G. M. C. (1983), 'Nietzsche's Interest in and Knowledge of Indian Thought', in Goicoechea (1983), 166–80.

Stack, G. (1981*a*), 'Nietzsche and Perspectival Interpretation', *Philosophy Today*, 25: 221–41.

——(1981*b*), 'Nietzsche and Boscovitch's Natural Philosophy', *Pacific Philosophical Quarterly*, 62: 69–87.

——(1982*a*), 'Nietzsche's Myth of the Will to Power', *Dialogus*, 17: 37–49.

——(1982*b*), 'Nietzsche's Influence on Pragmatic Humanism', *Journal of the History of Philosophy*, 20: 369–406.

——(1982*c*), 'Nietzsche's Analysis of Causality', *Idealistic Studies*, 12: 260–75.
——(1983*a*), *Lange and Nietzsche* (Berlin).
——(1983*b*), 'Nietzsche as Structuralist', *Philosophy Today*, 27: 35–51.
——(1984), 'Eternal Recurrence Again', *Philosophy Today*, 28: 242–64.
——(1989*a*), 'Emerson's Influence on Nietzsche's Concept of Will to Power', *Modern Schoolman*, 66: 175–95.
——(1989*b*), 'From Lange to Nietzsche', *International Studies in Philosophy*, 21: 113–24.
——(1991), 'Nietzsche's Antinomianism', *Nietzsche Studien*, 20: 109–33.
Stambaugh, J. (1972), 'Thoughts on Pity and Revenge', *Nietzsche Studien*, 1: 27–35.
——(1989), 'Thoughts on the Innocence of Becoming', *Nietzsche Studien*, 14: 164–78.
Stephens, A. (1986), 'Nietzsche: The Resurrection of Parts', *Thesis Eleven*, 13: 94–108.
Stout, J. (1978), 'Buddhism Beyond Morality: A Note on Two Senses of Transcendence', *Journal of Religious Ethics*, 6: 319–25.
Strong, T. (1989), 'The Deconstruction of the Tradition: Nietzsche and the Greeks', in Barby (1989), 55–69.
Suzuki, D. T. (1957), *Mysticism: Christian and Buddhist* (New York).
Takakusu, J. (1956) (3rd edn.), *The Essentials of Buddhist Philosophy* (Honolulu).
Taylor, C. (1975), *Hegel* (Cambridge).
——(1988), 'Nietzsche's Schopenhauerianism', *Nietzsche Studien*, 17: 45–73.
Tejera, V. (1987), *Nietzsche and Greek Thought* (Dordrecht).
Thatcher, D. S. (1982), 'Nietzsche, Bagehot, and the Morality of Custom', *Victorian Newsletter*, 62: 7–13.
——(1983), 'Nietzsche's Debt to Lubbock', *Journal of the History of Ideas*, 44: 293–309.
Tuck, A. P. (1990), *Comparative Philosophy and the Philosophy of Scholarship* (New York).
Upadhyaya, K. N. (1968), 'The Impact of Early Buddhism on Hindu Thought', *Philosophy East and West*, 18: 163–73.
Vaihinger, H. (1924), *The Philosophy of 'As If'* (New York).
Varma, V. D. (1963), 'The Origins and Sociology of the Early Buddhist Philosophy of Moral Determinism', *Philosophy East and West*, 13: 25–47.
Vattimo G. (1989), 'Nihilism: Reactive and Active', in Barby (1989), 15–21.
Verdu, A. (1985), *Early Buddhist Philosophy* (Delhi).
Wagle, N. K. (1985), 'The Gods in Early Buddhism in Relation to Human

Society: An Aspect of their Function, Hierarchy, and Rank as Depicted in the Nikāya Texts of the Pali Canon', in Warder (1985), 57–80.
Walters, K. S. (1982), 'The Ontological Basis of Nietzsche's Perspectivism', *Dialogue* (Phi Sigma Tau periodical), 24: 35–46.
Warder, A. K. (1980) (2nd edn.), *Indian Buddhism* (Delhi).
——(1984) (2nd edn.), *Introduction to Pali* (London).
——(1985) (ed.), *New Paths in Buddhist Research* (Durham, NC).
Warren, H. C. (1962), *Buddhism in Translations* (New York).
Warren, M. (1984), 'Nietzsche's Concept of Ideology', *Theory and Society*, 13: 541–65.
Welbon, G. R. (1968), *The Buddhist Nirvana and its Western Interpreters* (Chicago).
Werner, K. (1989) (ed.), *The Yogi and the Mystic* (Richmond).
Westphal, K. R. (1984), 'Was Nietzsche a Cognitivist?', *Religious Studies*, 22: 343–63.
White, A. (1987), 'Nietzschean Nihilism: A Typology', *International Studies in Philosophy*, 19: 29–44.
Wijayaratna, M. (1990), *Buddhist Monastic Life*, trans. C. Grangier and S. Collins (Cambridge).
Wijesekera, O. H. De A. (1964), 'The Concept of Viññana in Theravada Buddhism', *Journal of the American Oriental Society*, 84: 254–9.
Wilcox, J. T. (1974), *Truth and Value in Nietzsche* (Washington).
——(1983*a*), 'Zarathustra's Yes', in Goicoechea (1983), 20–32.
——(1983*b*), 'Nietzsche's Epistemology', *International Studies in Philosophy*, 15: 67–77.
Williams, D. M. (1976), 'The *Paṭiccasamuppāda*: A Developed Formula', *Religious Studies*, 14: 35–56.
Williams, P. (1981), 'On Abhidhamma Ontology', *Journal of Indian Philosophy*, 9: 227–57.
——(1989), *Mahayana Buddhism* (London).
Yovel, Y. (1986) (ed.), *Nietzsche as Affirmative Thinker* (Dordrecht).

GLOSSARY OF KEY BUDDHIST TERMS

Abhidhamma	see under *sutta*.
akusala	'unskilful', 'unwholesome'. The Buddhist term for what is unethical. Technically, any action informed with either 'greed', 'hatred', or 'confusion'.
anātman	see *anattan*.
anattan (Skt., *anātman*)	the doctrine that there is no autonomous, eternal, and unchanging 'Self', essence, or substance to be found anywhere, either subjectively or objectively, on any level of existence, including *nirvāṇa*.
ariya (Skt., *ārya*)	an Āryan or 'Noble One', which in Buddhism refers only to an individual who has attained a deep enough spiritual insight into the nature of reality such that future spiritual progress becomes irreversible.
āsavas	'biases'; these are deeply rooted dispositions towards 'sensuality', 'being', 'speculation', and 'spiritual ignorance'. By overcoming these one attains *nirvāṇa*.
ātman	see *attan*.
attan (Skt., *ātman*)	the term for 'self', which in the pre-Buddhist Upaniṣads becomes the 'Self', the essential and eternal 'soul' of man.
avijjā	'spiritual ignorance'.
bhava	'being' or 'becoming'.
bhāvanā	'cultivation', 'development', literally 'bringing into being'. A term often translated as 'meditation'.
bodhi	literally, the state of being 'awake', which in Buddhism represents the state of 'Supreme Enlightenment' or 'Supreme Awakening'. The term Buddha or 'Awakened One' is derived from the same grammatical root.
Brahmā	a class of *deva*. Also a name for the chief of the Brahmās, also called Mahā Brahmā or 'Great Brahmā'.

brahmacariya	a term for the Buddhist spiritual life, the 'life of excellence'.
brahman	the impersonal absolute of the Upaniṣads.
Brāhman	Anglicization of *brāhmaṇa*. Sometimes Brahman or Brahmin.
brāhmaṇa	a member of the Brāhmanical priestly caste.
chanda	'impulse', 'intention', 'resolution', 'desire', 'will'.
citta	a rich term that can mean 'thought', 'mind', 'affect', 'will', depending upon context.
citta-bhāvanā	'mind-cultivation': the cultivation and bringing into being of skilful states and ways of being.
deva	a divine being; one of the 'gods'.
Dhamma	the Teaching of the Buddha, or the reality pointed to by this Teaching.
dhamma	a term that can refer to any phenomenon, whether a mental state, an object of perception, an ethical rule, or whatever.
diṭṭhi	'view' or 'speculative view'. These can be 'wrong' (*micchā*) or 'right' (*sammā*). The later form part of the Buddhist path.
dukkha	'suffering', 'dissatisfaction'. As a Noble Truth it represents the way all forms of saṃsāric existence, including those of a heavenly nature, appear to an *ariya*, i.e. 'unsatisfactory'.
kamman (Skt., *karman*)	'action' which is either ethically skilful or unskilful or neutral.
kamma-vipāka	the 'effect of action', which, depending on whether the action was either skilful or unskilful, will tend to be either pleasant or unpleasant respectively.
khandhas	the five 'aggregates' or 'collections' that constitute a human being: *rūpa* or 'form', *vedanā* or 'feeling-sensation', *saññā* or 'apperception', *saṅkhāras* or 'karmic forces and their effects', and *viññāna* or 'discriminative consciousness'.
mettā	'friendliness', 'amity', 'good-will', taken to a high degree of development.
nibbāna	the Pāli term for *nirvāṇa*.
nidāna	'ground', 'foundation', 'source'. As a technical term, denotes the particular aspects that constitute the process of 'dependent co-arising' (see *paṭicca-samuppāda*), sometimes referred to as

	a 'link'. Different versions of 'dependent co-arising' have different numbers of *nidānas*.
nirvāṇa	the *summum bonum* of Buddhism, the term *nirvāṇa* breaks down into the prefix *nir-* (*niḥ-*), meaning 'out; away' when prefixed to a verb, and the √*va*, meaning 'to blow' and so *nirvāṇa*, which is derived from the verb *nirvāti* meaning 'is blown out or extinguished', quite literally means 'blown out' or 'extinction'. As *nirvāti* also means 'is refreshed', *nirvāṇa* also implies 'health', 'become cool' (as when recovering from a fever), 'calmed', 'refreshed'.
paññā	'insight', 'understanding'. There are levels of *paññā*, from ordinary conceptual 'understanding' through to the kind of 'insight' that makes one an *ariya*. In this work, apart from the one reference to the three kinds of *paññā*, it is *paññā* in the later sense that is used throughout, which I translate as 'transformative insight' so as to distinguish it from its mundane counterparts.
paṭicca-samuppāda	'dependent co-arising' or 'conditioned co-production', what many regard as the central teaching of Buddhism. Simply stated, this doctrine teaches that all things whatsoever come to be in dependence upon other conditions. This being so, nothing can be said to possess an eternal and essential nature. Therefore nothing has to be as it is, and radical transformation becomes possible. This transformation is represented by a series of *nidānas* starting, for example, in 'confidence' (*saddhā*) and ending in 'liberation through knowing and seeing' or 'knowledge of the destruction of the *āsavas*'.
Ṛg-Veda	see under Veda(s).
rūpa	'form', can be defined as the objective constituent in any perceptual situation, including one's own body. One of the five *khandhas*.
samādhi	'meditative concentration'.
samaṇa	a 'wanderer' or 'recluse'. The *samaṇas* made up the non-orthodox *religieux* at the time of the Buddha, all of whom had 'gone forth from home into the homeless life'. They were united in that they rejected the spiritual authority of

	the Veda(s) and the orthodox *brāhmaṇas*. They tended to form groups (*gaṇas*) around some particular leader. The Buddha was such a *samaṇa*.
sampajañña	'clear comprehension', usually together with *sati*.
saṃsāra	literally, 'to wander through', *saṃsāra* represents the wandering, life after life, through various forms of existence, each of which is determined by the skilfulness or unskilfulness of one's *kamman*. *Saṃsāra* comprises all the various forms of unenlightened existence.
saṅkhāra	a difficult term to translate, a *saṅkhāra* can be both an active 'karmic force' such as 'love' or 'hate' as well as the trace 'disposition' left over, as it were, as a consequence of the expression of that 'karmic force'. *Saṅkhāras* as 'karmic forces' therefore create *saṅkhāras* as 'dispositions', which, if they are expressed, become *saṅkhāras* as 'karmic forces' and so on in a chain of action and reaction. The Buddhist spiritual path can be said to represent the way to break free from this process of habitual action and reaction through skilful action.
saññā	'apperception', the process by which any new perception is recognized and assimilated in terms of the old. One of the five *khandhas*.
sassatavāda	'doctrine of eternalism'.
sati	'mindfulness', 'recollectedness'.
sīla	'behaviour', which in Buddhism becomes the term for 'ethical behaviour' or 'moral practice'. There are various lists of *sīlas* or 'ethical rules' or 'guidelines'.
sutta	a *sutta* is a 'dialogue' or 'discourse', usually by the Buddha, on various topics concerned with the practice of the Buddhist spiritual life. They are of varying length, and include myth, stories, similes, poetry. These *suttas* are collected together into five *Nikāyas* or 'collections' forming the *Sutta-Piṭaka* or 'Basket of Discourses', which together with the *Vinaya-Piṭaka* or 'Basket of Discipline' and *Abhidhamma-Piṭaka* or 'Basket of Further Teachings', form the Theravāda Canon.

taṇhā	'thirst', understood by this author as the general condition we find ourselves in in the world. As such, it is the ground from which the various attempts, both skilful and unskilful, to find security, happiness, self-esteem, and meaning arise.
Tathāgata	an epithet of the Buddha.
ucchedavāda	'doctrine of annihilationism'.
Veda(s)	The four Veda(s) form the textual backbone of Brāhmanism. The oldest, the *Ṛg-Veda*, is said to have been composed between 1500 and 900 BCE, and is a collection of hymns to various gods chanted at sacrifices. The Buddhist texts refer to only three Veda(s).
vedanā	'feeling-sensation', either pleasant, unpleasant, or neutral. One of the five *khandhas*.
Vinaya	see under *sutta*.
viññāṇa	'consciousness', sometimes 'discriminative consciousness' as it is defined as 'that which discriminates'. One of the five *khandhas*.

INDEX